**TEACHER'S EDITION
GRADE 5**

Dr. Cathy Collins Block
*Professor of Education
Texas Christian University
and Member, Board of Directors
International Reading Association (2002–2005)*

Dr. John N. Mangieri
*Director
Institute for Literacy Enhancement*

SCHOLASTIC

New York ❋ Toronto ❋ London ❋ Auckland ❋ Sydney
Mexico City ❋ New Delhi ❋ Hong Kong ❋ Buenos Aires

Scholastic Inc. grants teachers permission to photocopy the reproducibles in this book for classroom use only. No other part of this publication may be reproduced in whole or in part, or stored in a retrieval system, or transmitted in any form or by any means, electronic, mechanical, photocopying, recording, or otherwise, without written permission of the publisher. For information regarding permission, write to Scholastic Inc., 557 Broadway, New York NY 10012.

ISBN: 0-439-64058-X

Cover design by James Sarfati
Interior design by Solas
Interior Illustrations by Mike Moran and Teresa Southwell

Copyright © 2004 by Scholastic Inc. All rights reserved. Printed in the U.S.A.

TABLE OF CONTENTS

**Research Base for *Powerful Vocabulary*
for Reading Success** 5
How to Use the Program 11

CHAPTER 1

Context Clues 19
   Lesson 1:   Nouns to Know 20
   Lesson 2:   Verbs to Know 27
   Lesson 3:   More Verbs to Know 34
   Lesson 4:   Adjectives to Know 41
   Lesson 5:   More Adjectives to Know 48
   Lesson 6:   Adverbs to Know 55
   Lesson 7:   Multiple-Meaning Words to Know 62
   Lesson 8:   Synonyms to Know 69
   Lesson 9:   Antonyms to Know 76
   Lesson 10: Putting It Together 83

CHAPTER 2

Words and Their Parts 91
   Lesson 11: Words With Prefixes (*bi-, multi-, oct-/octa-/octo-, tri-*) . . . 92
   Lesson 12: Words With Suffixes (*-an/-ian, -er/-or, -ee, -ist*) 99
   Lesson 13: Words With Roots (*cur/curs, micro, mort, scope*) 106
   Lesson 14: Compound Words With *Brain, Head, Heart,* and *Foot* . . 113
   Lesson 15: Word Families (*name, nomen/nomin, onym*) 120
   Lesson 16: Word Families (*graph*) 127

TABLE OF CONTENTS

CHAPTER 3

Content Words **135**
    Lesson 17: Words About Problem Solving **136**
    Lesson 18: Words About the Circulatory System **143**
    Lesson 19: Words About the Water Cycle **150**
    Lesson 20: Words About Great Leaders **157**
    Lesson 21: Words About Research **164**
    Lesson 22: Test-Taking Words **171**

CHAPTER 4

Words and Their Histories **179**
    Lesson 23: Words From Other Languages **180**
    Lesson 24: Homophones **187**
    Lesson 25: Easily Confused Words **194**
    Lesson 26: Idioms and Other Common Expressions **201**

Definitions **208**
Sample Sentences **217**
Blackline Masters of Transparencies **223**
Graphic Organizers **226**
Flashcards for Blackline Masters **233**
Transparencies .... **inside backcover**

Research Base for *Powerful Vocabulary for Reading Success*

A lack of vocabulary is a key component underlying school failure for many students, especially children who are economically challenged.

(Biemiller, 2001; Biemiller & Slonium, 2001; Hart & Risley, 1995; Hirsch, 2001).

As a classroom teacher, one of the many challenges you are likely to face is how to help your students master the vocabulary strategies they need to be successful readers. *Powerful Vocabulary for Reading Success* gives you the latest research-based instructional strategies to help you significantly improve your students' vocabulary abilities. In addition, the program is flexible to better meet the diverse learning needs of all your students.

EDUCATIONAL RESEARCH FINDINGS

Powerful Vocabulary for Reading Success addresses the following findings, or understandings, about how students learn vocabulary:

1. All English words are not of equal importance.

High-Frequency Words

Research shows that students should be taught words that they will encounter often in print (NICHD, 2000). The National Reading Panel (NRP, 2000) reports that the more thoroughly students learn high-frequency vocabulary, the better able they will be at comprehending text that contains these or similar words. Students who are taught high-frequency words retain their meanings better than students who are not taught them (Baumann, Kame'enui & Ash, 2003; Biemiller & Slomin, 2001). In addition, students' mastery of these basic English words is reinforced by many exposures to them as they repeatedly reread and work with these words in print.

Powerful Vocabulary for Reading Success provides you with the tools you need to teach *high-frequency words*—the *important* words that are necessary for literacy success. It includes vocabulary words selected from many of the most widely referenced English word lists, including the Harris-Jacobson, Francis Kucera, Dolch, Hirsch Core Vocabulary, McRel Basic Words, and Fry Basic Words of the English Language. In addition, it includes the most widely used terms on norm-referenced standardized reading and content-area achievement tests, as well as state-based competency accountability measures.

Important Words That Transfer In *Powerful Vocabulary for Reading Success*, students learn important words that represent major aspects of the English language (e.g., high-frequency words, words with special word parts, words that sound alike), and they have many effective learning opportunities with words that transfer to a wide array of similar words in our language. Since the words are characteristic of a core set of word families, the learning of one word creates a key to unlocking the meaning of several dozen other new words. This means that when you teach the words in this program, you help students learn not only these particular words but many other words as well.

2. **Students retain newly taught words when they understand their meaning.**

Rich, Effective Instruction in Word Meaning In order for most students to understand a word's meaning, they must experience rich, effective instruction around the word. (Beck, McKeown, & Kucan, 2002; Block, 2004). When you teach *Powerful Vocabulary for Reading Success,* you are giving your students this instructional support. You go beyond asking your students to merely say and memorize important words by teaching students the meaning of these words through a series of targeted, varied, and research-based learning opportunities.

Multiple Exposures to Words and Meanings The lessons in *Powerful Vocabulary for Reading Success* teach word meanings incrementally and repeatedly. Research demonstrates that when students first encounter a new word, they recognize its appearance letter by letter. Repeated exposures increase the size of the visual unit they recognize, so that they can understand many words with the same letter or meaning-based patterns automatically (Samuels, 2003). In every lesson of *Powerful Vocabulary for Reading Success*, you provide your students with a range of ten to fifteen research-based, highly effective vocabulary-building learning experiences for each word (and the family of words it represents).

Reach Grade-Level Expectations
Research shows that without the rich instruction that this program provides, many students would not reach grade-level reading expectations (Mangieri, 1972; Ordonez, Carbot and Snow, 2002; Scott and Nagy, 1997).

For example, as early as age four, the typical student in an impoverished environment has been exposed to thirteen million fewer vocabulary words than the typical child in a working class family, and thirty million fewer total words than the typical child in a professional family (Hart & Risley, 2003). This creates an alarming situation. Because students learn more new words through directed vocabulary instruction than when left alone to learn (Carver, 1994, 1995; Nagy & Herman, 1987), without the type of focused instruction presented in this program, most kindergartners would take twelve years of reading words daily and learning at least seven new vocabulary words every day to reach the level of reading vocabulary that most children of affluent parents possess by fourth grade (Block, Rodgers & Johnson, 2004).

3. **Word learning principles and vocabulary building strategies should be taught together.**

Synergy of Principles and Strategies
Powerful Vocabulary for Reading Success teaches word learning principles (called "word learning

tips" in the student book) and **vocabulary building strategies** together in every lesson. As a result, most students increase their vocabulary more rapidly than when they learn only either one word learning principle or one vocabulary building strategy a week (Block & Mangieri, 1995/6). This enhanced instructional method has been proven to also develop students' word consciousness (Block & Mangieri, 1996; 2003; Block, 2004)—their ability to think about words and use them in meaningful contexts. Students at all levels quickly gain the ability to use their word knowledge to learn new words beyond the program.

Vocabulary Linked to Common Themes Word consciousness develops even more deeply when vocabulary words are tied to a common theme. For this reason, lessons in *Powerful Vocabulary for Reading Success* relate to high-interest themes and topics with words that students experience daily in content area and language arts classes. As a result, when students confront an unknown word, the deep understanding of word learning principles, vocabulary building strategies, and word consciousness that has been created by this program enables them to independently begin the thinking processes necessary to unlock the meaning of it and other theme-based words not included in this program.

More Strategies Than Any Other Program Research shows that expert readers know and use more reading strategies than less able readers (Block & Mangieri, 2003; Pressley & Afflerbach, 1995). Because of this, *Powerful Vocabulary for Reading Success* teaches more strategies than other vocabulary programs.

4. Words should be taught in context.

Vocabulary and Comprehension Skills Built Simultaneously Every lesson teaches words in context so that vocabulary and comprehension are built simultaneously. This increases reading comprehension as well as students' positive attitudes toward reading (Block & Mangieri, in preparation). The more motivated students feel to learn words, the more words they will learn. As they learn more words, their reading abilities advance to higher levels. As you teach *Powerful Vocabulary for Reading Success,* you are supporting a continuous, upward spiral of reading power that leads to greater, continued reading success and pleasure.

Wide Array of Reading Experiences *Powerful Vocabulary for Reading Success* includes a vast array of interesting contexts in which students learn words. These wide reading experiences, the teaching of core generalizable words, and the development of a broad-based expansive word consciousness combine as powerful forces that enable you to bring reading success to even the most vocabulary-challenged readers.

Both Definitional and Contextual Information Research findings have consistently shown that vocabulary instruction is most effective when learners receive both definitional and contextual information (Stahl, 1998). Because of this convincing data, *Powerful Vocabulary for Reading Success* includes both types of instruction in every lesson of this program.

EVIDENCE-BASED RESEARCH FINDINGS

Numerous Research Studies *Powerful Vocabulary for Reading Success* is the result of numerous research studies. Its lessons were field-tested extensively with diverse student populations and the lessons address the shortcomings of many instructional programs. We know that although some students acquire vocabulary on their own, many other children do not. As a result, they do not learn important words. For this latter group of students, a negative cycle occurs. These students lack the ability to understand words, which keeps them from reading independently. Consequently, they are unable to acquire new words or to practice and refine their vocabulary building abilities in literacy situations. As a result, these students frequently fall behind their peers in overall reading ability and develop a negative attitude toward reading.

Assurance of Success *Powerful Vocabulary for Reading Success* helps you address this negatively spiraling condition. The authors developed the program after careful analysis of best practices and evidence-based research findings. They paid particular attention to actions that produce students' acquisition of important vocabulary words; their retention of these words; and the strategies that can help them to understand additional words containing similar patterns, uses, sounds, spellings, or histories. As a result, the program teaches vocabulary directly and in motivational contexts, providing assurance of success because its content is not only interesting but also important.

On page 9, you will find some of the research used in the program's development. Because the research in this area is vast, we present only the key investigations. The data from each study was studied carefully so that it could inform this program's instructional design.

Research Findings

Words and Word Lists

Varied types of vocabulary words must be taught for an instructional program to be highly effective. Scott (2004); Baumann, Ware & Edwards (2004); Baumann (2002); Ordonez, Carlo, & Snow (2002).

Words must be taught in many different ways. Scott (2004); Ordonez, Carlo, & Snow (2002); Schwanenflugel, Stahl & McFalls (1997); Mangieri (1972).

Relevant words should be selected and learned deeply through reading. Lehman & Schraw (2002); Blessman & Myszczak (2001); Block (2001); Dole, Sloan & Trathen, (1995).

Concrete referent words are learned more rapidly than non-picturable nouns. Ordonez, Carlo & Snow (2002); Scott & Nagy (1997); Mangieri (1972).

No more than ten words per week should be taught below grade 3, and no more than 15 in grades 4–6. Blachowicz & Fisher (2000); Senecal (1997); Senecal & Cornell (1993).

Strategies

Breadth of vocabulary increases when words are taught in context. Ordonez, Carlo & Snow (2002); Scott & Nagy (1997); Mangieri (1972).

Repeated readings of passages increases vocabulary. Blachowicz & Fisher (2002); Senecal (1997).

Transfer of words to automatic use will not occur if generalizable core words are not taught in vocabulary program. NICHD (2000); Rinaldi, Sells, & McLaughlin (1997).

Using different learning modalities in vocabulary program has a positive effect on students' ability to identify unknown words independently. Heller, Sturner, Funk & Feezor (1993); Stump, Lovitt, Fisher, Kemp, Moore & Schroeder (1992).

Instruction

Listening to orally presented passages or reading vocabulary in context builds independent vocabulary abilities most rapidly. Block & Stanley (in press); Stahl, Richek & Vandevier, (1991).

Students learn more words when placed in smaller groups or pairs; especially poorer readers. Nagy, Berninger, Abbott, Vaughn & Vermeulen (2003); O'Conner, Notari-Sverson & Vadasy (2002).

Flashcards, when used judiciously and as a varied teaching aid, significantly increase students' vocabulary and reading comprehension. Barry (2002); Nicholson (1998); Taka (1997); Tan & Nicholson (1997); Gorman (1993); Carr (1985); McCullough (1955).

Students taught morphology learn more words. Baumann, et al. (2002); Yopp & Yopp (2000); Mangieri (1972).

Effective instruction provides both the definitions and explanation of words in a conceptualized manner. Brabham & Lynch-Brown; (2002); Bauman & Kameenui (1991); Brabham & Villuame (2002).

Working in pairs has a positive effect of learning. Brabham & Lynch-Brown, (2002); Bauman & Kameenui (1991); Brabham & Villuame (2002).

Use of meaning-based images and mnemonic devices increases vocabulary acquisition. Graham (2000); NRP (2000); Levin, Levin, Glasman & Nordwall (1992).

Vocabulary instruction should build students' inference abilities. Graham (2000); NRP (2000); Levin, Levin, Glasman & Nordwall (1992).

Vocabulary can be developed through group-assisted reading. NICHD (2000); Eldredge (1990).

Direct instruction should be given; and word meanings should be derived from context activities. NRP (2000); Tomeson & Aarnoutse (1998); Block (1993).

Altering the presentation of vocabulary definitions is highly effective in increasing transfer. Scott & Nagy (1997); Block (1993).

Reciprocal peer-tutoring is effective for vocabulary development. Malone & McLaughlin (1997); Block (1993).

Vocabulary instruction should be delivered for 10–20 minutes daily. Levin, Levin, Glasman & Nordwall (1992); Mangieri (1972).

BIBLIOGRAPHY

Research Base of *Powerful Vocabulary for Reading Success*

Barry, A. (2002). Reading strategies teachers say they use. *Journal of Adolescent & Adult Literacy, 46*(2), 132–141.

Baumann, J. F. (2002). Teaching morphemic and contextual analysis to fifth–grade students. *Reading Research Quarterly, 37*(1), 150–176.

Baumann, J.F., Kame'enui, E.J., & Ash, G. (2003). Research on vocabulary instruction: Voltaire redux. In J. Flood, D. Lapp, J. R. Squire, & J. Jensen (Eds.). *Handbook of research on teaching the English Language Arts* (2nd ed.). Mahwah, NJ: Lawrence Erlbaum, pp 752–785.

Baumann, J., & Kameenui, E. (1991). Research on Vocabulary Instruction: Ode to Voltaire. In J. Flood, J. Jensen, D. Lapp, and J. Squire (eds.). *Handbook on Teaching the English Language Arts*, 604–632. New York: Macmillan.

Baumann, J. F., Ware, D., & Edwards, E. C. (2004, December). Teaching vocabulary in fifth grade: A year-long formative experiment. Paper presented at the Annual Meeting of the National Reading Conference.

Biemiller, A. (2001, Spring). Teaching reading and language to the disadvantaged—What we have learned from field research. *Harvard Educational Review, 47*, 518–543.

Biemiller, A., & Slonim, M. (2001). Estimating root word vocabulary growth in normative and advantaged populations: Evidence for a common sequence of vocabulary acquisition. *Journal of Educational Psychology, 93*(3), 498–520.

Blachowicz, C.L.Z and P. Fisher. (2000). Vocabulary instruction. In M.L. Kamil, P.B. Mosenthal, P.D. Pearson, and R. Barr (Eds.). *Handbook of Reading Research, Vol. III*. Matwah, NJ: Lawrence Erlbaum Associates, pp. 504–523.

Blachowicz, C. & Fisher, P. (2002). *Teaching Vocabulary in All Classrooms. Second Edition* Upper Saddle River, NJ: Merrill Prentice Hall.

Blessman, J. & Myszczak, B. (2001). Mathematics, vocabulary and its effect on student comprehension. IL: St. Xavier University Master of Arts Action Research Project and Skylight Professional Development Filed-based Masters Program.

Block, C. C. (1993). Effective strategy instruction in a literature approach. *Elementary School Journal, 92*, 131–139.

Block, C. C. (2001). Effects of Exemplary Literacy Instruction on students' literacy achievement. *National Reading Conference Yearbook, 48*, 391–416.

Block, C. C. & Stanley, C. (in press). Effects of audio-tape supported instruction on students' vocabulary and comprehension instruction. *Journal of Literacy Behavior*.

Block, C. C. (2003). *Teaching Comprehension: The Comprehension Process Approach*. Boston, MA: Allyn & Bacon.

Block, C. C., Rodgers, L. & Johnson, R. (2004). *Teaching Comprehension in Kindergarten through Grade 3: Building Success for All Students*. New York, NY: Guilford Press.

Block, C. C., & Mangieri, J. N. (2003). *Exemplary Literacy Teachers: Literacy Success in Grades K–5*. New York, NY: Guilford Press.

Brabham, E.G. & Lynch-Brown, C. (2002). Effects of teachers' reading aloud styles on vocabulary acquisition & comprehension of students in the early elementary grades. *Journal of Educational Psychology, 94* (3), 465–473.

Brabham, E.G. & S.K. Villuame. (2002). Vocabulary instruction: Concerns and visions. *The Reading Teacher, 56*(3), 264–268.

Bromley, K. (2002). *Stretching Students' Vocabulary*. New York, NY: Scholastic, Inc.

Carr, E. (1985). The vocabulary overview guide: A metacognitive strategy to improve vocabulary comprehension and retention. *Journal of Reading, 21*, 684–689.

Community Consolidated School District 15, *Vocabulary for Increased Achievement, Grade 3*. (2000). Bar Mills, NE: Bonny Eagles DAD #6 Central Administration Building.

Cudd, E. T., & Roberts, L. L. (1993/1994). A scaffolding technique to develop sentence sense and vocabulary. *The Reading Teacher, 47*(4), 167–172.

Dole, J.A., Sloan, C., & Trathen, W. (1995). Teaching vocabulary within the context of literature. *Journal of Reading, 38*(6), 452–460.

Donley, K. M. (2001). Using Corpus Tools to Highlight Academic Vocabulary in SCLT. *TESOL Journal (10)*, 2–3, p. 7–11.

Foil, C. R. & Alber., S. (2002). Fun and Effective Ways To Build Your Students' Vocabulary. *Intervention in School and Clinic* (37), 3, p. 131–139, 2002.

Glowacki, D., C. Lanucha, & Pietrus, D. (2001). *Improving Vocabulary Acquisition through Direct and Indirect Teaching*. New York, NY: Scholastic, Inc.

Gorman, M. (1993). Footprints on the class-room wall. *The Reading Teacher, 47*(2), 98.

Hall, A. K. (1995). Sentencing: The psycho-linguistic guessing game. *The Reading Teacher, 49*(1), 23–25.

Harmon, J. M. and W. B. Hedrick. (2001). Zooming In and Zooming Out for Better Vocabulary Learning. *Middle School Journal* (32), 5, p. 22–29.

Hart, B., & Risley, T. R. (1995). *Meaningful differences in the everyday experiences of young American children*. Baltimore: Paul H. Brookes.

Hayward, C. C. (1998). Monitoring spelling development. *The Reading Teacher, 51* (5), 278–283.

Henry, M. K., & Redding, N. C. (1990). *Tutor 2*. Los Gatos, CA: Lex Press.

Holden, W. R. (1999). Learning to learn: 15 vocabulary Acquisition Activities. Tips and Hints. *Modern English Teacher (8)*, 2, p. 42–47.

HuffBenkoski, K. A., & Greenwood, S. C. (1995). The use of word analogy instruction with developing readers. *The Reading Teacher, 48*(5), 161–165.

IRA Literacy Study Groups. (2002). *Vocabulary: Discussion and Related Journal Articles*. Newark, DE: International Reading Association.

Kotrla, M. (1997). What's literacy? *The Reading Teacher, 50*(8), 403–406.

Lapp, D., Block, C. C., Cooper, E., Flood, J., Tinajero, J. & Roser, N. *Teaching all children to read: Strategies for developing literacy in urban settings*. New York, NY: Guilford Press.

Mangieri, J. N. (1972). Difficulty of Learning Basic Sight Words. Unpublished Dissertation. Pittsburgh, PA: University of Pittsburgh.

McCullough, C. (1955). Flash cards—The opiate of the reading program? *Elementary English, 32*, 372–381.

Mohr, Carole and S. L. Nist. (2002). *Building Vocabulary Skills*. West Berlin, NJ: Townsend Press, Inc.

Nagy, W.E. (1998). *Teaching vocabulary to improve reading comprehension*. Urbana, IL & Newark, DE: National council of Teachers of English and International Reading Association.

Nicholson, T. (1998). The flashcard strikes back. *The Reading Teacher, 52*(92), 117–9.

Nilsen, A. P. & Nilsen, D. L. (2002). Lessons in the teaching of vocabulary from September 11 and Harry Potter. *Journal of Adolescent & Adult Literacy, 46*(3), 254–260.

Nist, S. L., & Mohr, C. (2002). *Building Vocabulary Skills, Third Edition*. West Berlin, NJ: Townsend.

Palmer, B. C., & Brooks, M. A. (2004). Reading until the cows come home: Figurative language and reading comprehension. *Journal of Adolescent & Adult Literacy, 47*(6), pp.370–377.

Poliakof, A. R. (Ed.) (2001). *Reading: Phonemic Awareness, Vocabulary Acquisition, Teaching and Intervention*. Washington, DC: Council for Basic Education.

Rasinski, T. V., Padak, N. D., Church, B. W., Fawcett, G., Hendershot, J., Henry, J. M., Moss, B. G., Peck, J. K., Pryor, E., & Roskos, K. A. (Eds.). (2000). *Teaching word Recognition, Spelling and Vocabulary: Strategies form The Reading Teacher*. Newark, DE: International Reading Association.

Robb, L. (1999). *Easy Mini-Lessons for Building Vocabulary*. NY: Scholastic.

Rosenblaum, C. (2001). A word map for middle school: A tool for effective vocabulary instruction. *Journal of Adolescent & Adult Literacy, 45*(1), 44–50.

Ryder, R. J., & Graves, M. F. (1994). Vocabulary instruction presented prior to reading in two basal readers. *The Elementary School Journal, 95*, 139–153.

Stahl, S. A. (1998). Four questions about vocabulary. In C. R. Hynd (Ed.), *Learning from text across conceptual domains* (pp. 73–94). Mahwah, NJ: Erlbaum.

Stahl, S. & B. Kapinus. (2001). *Word Power: What Every Educator Needs To Know about Teaching Vocabulary*. Washington DC: NEA Success in Reading Series.

Taka, M. L. (1997). *Word game bingo and adult literacy students. Sight word acquisition and reading comprehension*. Unpublished master's thesis, The University of Auckland, Auckland, New Zealand.

Tan, A. & Nicholson, T. (1997). Flashcards revisited. Training poor readers to read words faster improves their comprehension of text. *Journal of Educational Psychology, 89*, 276–288.

Towell, J. (1997/1998). Fun with vocabulary. *The Reading Teacher, 51*(4), 199–2204.

Watts, S. M. (1995). Vocabulary instruction during reading lessons in six classrooms. *Journal of Reading Behavior, 27*, 399–424.

Wood, E. M. (1998). Into the curriculum: Reading and language arts/art: Using Amelia Bedelia Books to teach figurative and literacy meanings. *School Library Media Activities Monthly, 5*(2), 11–14.

Wood, J. (2001). Can software Support Children's Vocabulary development? *Language Learning and Technology, 5*(1), 166–201.

Yopp, R.H. & Yopp, H.K. (2003). Ten Important Words: Identifying the Big Ideas in Informational Text. *Journal of Content Area Reading. 2*(1), 7–13.

Sources for Words Used in The Program

Dolch, E. (1936). Dolch basic sight words. Des Moines, IO: University of Iowa.

Francis, W.N. & Kucera, H. 1982. *Frequency Analysis of English Usage: Lexicon and Grammar*. Boston, MA: Houghton Mifflin.

Fry, E. (1998). The most common phonograms. *The Reading Teacher, 51*(7), 345–350.

Fry, Edward Bernard et al., *The Reading Teacher's Book of Lists* (2002). Englewood Cliffs, NJ: Prentice Hall.

Harris, A.J. & Jacobson, M.D. (1982). *Basic Reading Vocabularies*. New York, NY: Macmillan.

McRel Basic Core Words by Grade Level.

Mangieri, J. N. & Block, C. C. (1999). Dolch Basic Sight Word Assessment. In Mangieri, J. & Block, C. C. Nobel Reading Program. Media, PA: Nobel Learning Communities.

Robb, L. (2002). *Easy Mini-Lessons for Building Vocabulary*. NY: Scholastic.

Spears, Richard A. *Essential American Idioms* (1999).Chicago: NTC/Contemporary Publishing Group.

Stanford Assessment Test (Stanford Nine) (2003 edition). San Antonio, TX: The Psychological Corporation.

Texas Assessment of Knowledge & Skills. (2003). Grades 3–6 Core Words. Austin, TX: State Department of Education.

Texas, California, Maine, Florida, Illinois, New Jersey and Colorado State Curriculum Guides and Benchmarks (2002). Grades 3–6 Core Words. State Departments of Education.

How to Use
Powerful Vocabulary for Reading Success

A FLEXIBLE PROGRAM

Powerful Vocabulary for Reading Success is flexible. You may use it as a complete independent vocabulary program for students in grades 3–6 or as a supplement to your current reading program. Based upon your objectives, you may find certain adaptations of its content helpful.

As an Independent Vocabulary Program
If you wish to use *Powerful Vocabulary for Reading Success* as your primary vehicle for teaching vocabulary, we recommend that you teach its lessons in the order in which they occur in the program. This will enable students to use the more basic skills they acquired in the initial lessons to learn more difficult words and vocabulary concepts in the later lessons.

As a Supplement to a Reading Program
If you wish to use this program as a supplement to your current reading program, present the lessons in the order in which they occur in that program. This means that if you are teaching prefixes in your reading program, use the prefix lesson from *Powerful Vocabulary for Reading Success* at the same time. In addition, if your reading program falls short in teaching a particular vocabulary learning strategy such as using context clues, enhance the instruction by using the lessons in this program when you are teaching that strategy in your reading program.

Another way to use the program is as a bridge between your students' current and targeted levels of performance. For example, if you diagnose that a student is weak in a specific vocabulary area, select the appropriate lesson from *Powerful Vocabulary for Reading Success* to use to build needed skills.

PROGRAM STRUCTURE

Powerful Vocabulary for Reading Success contains four chapters. Each chapter develops a specific set of vocabulary building abilities.

Chapters

Chapter 1—Context Clues
Chapter 1 develops students' skill in using *syntactical clues and parts of speech to determine meaning*. Chapter 1 also introduces the vocabulary building strategy of *using context clues* to build vocabulary. When you teach this chapter, you provide instruction and practice for your students in meeting state standards by asking them to use syntax and context clues to determine meaning.

Chapter 2—Words and Their Parts
Chapter 2 introduces students to the *importance of word parts in determining a word's meaning*. Coupled with this word learning principle is the vocabulary building strategy of *adding the distinct meanings of individual word parts together to determine a larger word's meaning*. When you teach this chapter, you

Introduction • How to Use the Program

provide instruction and practice for your students in meeting state standards that require them to use word parts and structures (prefixes, suffixes, roots, compound words, word families) to determine meaning.

Chapter 3—Content Words

Chapter 3 provides strategies students can use to learn the wide range of content-area words that they will read in content area classes and in reading outside of school. This chapter introduces the word learning principle that *content area words have special features*. For example, they are usually longer than high-frequency words. Students also learn the vocabulary-building strategy that *you can determine the meanings of content area words by thinking about the topic and the relationship of the unknown word to that topic*. When you teach this chapter, you provide instruction and practice for your students in meeting state standards that ask them to determine and apply the meaning of content area words.

Chapter 4—Words and Their Histories

Chapter 4 introduces several new word learning principles about unusual words in our language. These principles relate to the idea that *some words have special sounds, histories, spellings, or inferential meanings*. It presents a three-part vocabulary building strategy. That strategy is (1) *to use a word's spelling or sound clues*, (2) *think about a word's history*, and (3) *create a mnemonic device that has personal meaning*. When you teach this chapter, you provide instruction and practice for your students in meeting state standards that ask them to understand word origins, homophones, commonly confused words, and idioms.

Lessons

Here are the key features of the program's lessons:

Key Features in the Student Edition

Words in Context Every lesson provides all the vocabulary words in the context of a high-interest nonfiction or fiction selection. This allows you to encourage students to use the Word Learning Principle and Vocabulary Building Strategy to determine the meaning of the vocabulary words, while you guide them and record their thinking on a transparency. The steps to do so are described in the teacher's edition. (Chapters 1, 3, and 4 begin with this part. In Chapter 2, students determine word parts before they read the words in context.)

Be a Word Architect Chapter 2 begins with a special section called "Be a Word Architect." This provides you with the opportunity to show students how words are built and have them use the parts of a word (prefixes, suffixes, roots, etc.) to determine the word's meaning.

Connect Words and Meanings Every lesson provides the definitions of the vocabulary words in an interactive format. This helps you to make mastery of these definitions an active learning opportunity, since students have to choose the meanings that match the words.

Purposeful Activities Engaging activities help students deepen their knowledge of the meanings of the vocabulary words by using these words in meaningful ways. Students connect the vocabulary words to their own lives and experiences and apply them to meaningful situations. As they interact with the vocabulary words, they make inferences about each word's meaning and explain their reasoning.

Review and Extend Activities These activities provide an opportunity for students to review what they have learned and to extend their understanding. The activities expand students' knowledge because they teach related language concepts or related words. They deepen students' understanding of the lesson's words and they broaden their acquisition of similar words.

Independent Activities Activities at the bottom of workbook pages invite students to use the vocabulary words independently in a variety of contexts. These activities help students move beyond definitions as they process meanings and interact with the words. Students become active word learners as they find other related new words in real-world situations and use the new words as well as the vocabulary words in writing, reading, speaking and listening, art, games, and dramatizations.

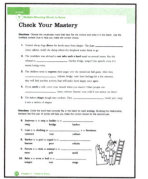

Check Your Mastery You can check students' word mastery at the end of each lesson through a short test. This assessment provides practice using a variety of standardized test formats and includes self-assessment.

Key Features in the Teacher's Edition

Mystery Word of the Week This introductory activity promotes a positive attitude toward vocabulary learning. Each day, begin by writing the mystery word of the week clue on the board or on a chart. This clue is a sentence containing a blank for the mystery word. Explain to students that every day of the week you will give them a new clue to help them identify the mystery word. At the end of the week, they will act like detectives, and, using all of these clues as well as the word learning principle and vocabulary building strategy, try to determine the word.

Think Alouds Suggested Think Alouds allow you to model thinking strategies to determine the meaning of words. Model using the word learning tip and vocabulary building strategy in a particular lesson before you ask students to

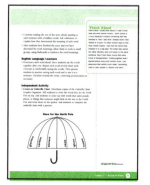

use them independently. Also model the thinking involved in completing activities. Think Alouds build students' ability to know how to independently learn the words in a lesson as well as unfamiliar words with similar features that they encounter in the future. Have

Introduction • How to Use the Program   13

students use these thinking processes to complete the subsequent work for that day either independently, in pairs, or in small groups.

English Language Learners Many lessons provide special support for English language learners. The activities in this section give these learners extra practice both independently and collaboratively.

Independent Activities Although the content of these activities varies from lesson to lesson, they do have two common purposes: (1) to enhance the lesson's vocabulary building content; and (2) to reteach concepts and content for less able and EL learners. You may elect to use one or more of these activities each day or as needed. These activities provide extra learning opportunities for all students because they use an array of learning modalities.

Review and Share Each day begins with opportunities for students to share the results of their independent work from the previous day. This facet of instruction provides continuity and positive reinforcement as well as additional occasions for students to discuss, read, and use the vocabulary words in context.

Tests Mastery assessment occurs at two levels: (1) an objective test that measures students' grasp of the lesson's content; and (2) students' self-assessment through a variety of journal writing prompts.

Flashcards Reproducible flashcards provide extended and varied practice opportunities. The key to the success of the flashcards is that, used purposefully, they add a manipulative practice opportunity to help students develop automaticity with their learning of new words. (The flashcards are included as blackline masters in the back of the teacher's edition.)

ROUTINES FOR USE

Personal Word Journal
At the start of the year, ask students to set up a Personal Word Journal. This can be a simple notebook that they decorate and make their own. Each day, they will be completing independent activities in their journals as well as reflecting on their thinking about their learning.

Mystery Word of the Week
The purpose of the Mystery Word of the Week activity is to get students talking about and thinking about words. You can use the Mystery Word of the Week in a variety of independent and collaborative ways:

- Each day, read the clue and list the words that students think may be the mystery word below the blank. Talk about the strategies they are using to come up with choices. Then at the end of the week, have students review all the words that they have listed and choose the best answer.

- Ask students to write their guesses each day in the personal word journals. Tell them to explain their reasoning.

- On the first day, invite students to generate as many words as they can that might be the mystery word. After they receive the second clue, have them review their choices from the first day. Which words would they remove from the list of possibilities? Which words would they add? Encourage them to share their reasoning. Continue this process until students have seen all five clues and made their final guess.
- After the fourth clue, ask students to vote on which word they believe is the mystery word. Then, after they receive the fifth clue, ask them if they have changed their minds. If they have, ask them to explain how the new information they received changed their answer.
- Divide the class into teams. Each day, the teams can huddle together for one minute and then collectively offer only one guess that day as to what word is the mystery word.

Regardless of the way in which you elicit guesses, the final step of the Mystery Word of the Week activity should always occur on the last day of the lesson. On this day, reveal the mystery word and discuss it. Ask students who correctly guessed the word to tell *how* the word learning principle and vocabulary building strategy helped them identify the correct word.

At times, students will come up with a different word choice that fits all the clues. Accept this word as long as it makes sense in the sentences and students can explain their reasoning.

Flashcards

After you introduce the words and students complete the first activity, distribute flashcards. Allow students to work with a partner or in small groups to reinforce word meanings.

In addition, allow early finishers and students who need extra help to use the flashcards during the week so that they can master the meaning of the words.

OPTIONS FOR USE

Each lesson section takes approximately fifteen to twenty minutes to complete. One or more sections may be taught each day, spread out over a week, or used flexibly to accommodate your particular schedule and curriculum requirements.

Five Day Plan

Chapter 1: Context Clues

Lesson Sections	When to Use
Read Words in Context	Day 1
Connect Words and Meanings	homework
Use Words in Context	Day 2
Put Words Into Action	Day 3
Review and Extend	Day 4
Check Your Mastery	Day 5

Chapter 2: Words and Their Parts

Lesson Sections	When to Use
Be a Word Architect	Day 1
Connect Words and Meanings	homework
Learn Words in Context	Day 2
Use Words in Context	Day 3
Review and Extend	Day 4
Check Your Mastery	Day 5

Chapter 3: Content Words

Lesson Sections	When to Use
Learn Words About a New Subject	Day 1
Connect Words and Meanings	homework
Use Content Words	Day 2
Put Words Into Action	Day 3
Review and Extend	Day 4
Check Your Mastery	Day 5

Chapter 4: Words and Their Histories

Lesson Sections	When to Use
Read Words in Context	Day 1
Connect Words and Meanings	homework
Use Words in Context	Day 2
Put Words Into Action	Day 3
Review and Extend	Day 4
Check Your Mastery	Day 5

THREE DAY PLAN

CHAPTER 1: CONTEXT CLUES

Lesson Sections	When to Use
Read Words in Context	Day 1
Connect Words and Meanings	Day 1 homework
Use Words in Context	Day 2
Put Words Into Action	Day 2 homework
Review and Extend	Day 3
Check Your Mastery	Day 3

CHAPTER 2: WORDS AND THEIR PARTS

Lesson Sections	When to Use
Be a Word Architect	Day 1
Connect Words and Meanings	Day 1 homework
Learn Words in Context	Day 2
Use Words in Context	Day 2 homework
Review and Extend	Day 3
Check Your Mastery	Day 3

CHAPTER 3: CONTENT WORDS

Lesson Sections	When to Use
Learn Words About a New Subject	Day 1
Connect Words and Meanings	Day 1 homework
Use Content Words	Day 2
Put Words Into Action	Day 2 homework
Review and Extend	Day 3
Check Your Mastery	Day 3

CHAPTER 4: WORDS AND THEIR HISTORIES

Lesson Sections	When to Use
Read Words in Context	Day 1
Connect Words and Meanings	Day 1 homework
Use Words in Context	Day 2
Put Words Into Action	Day 2 homework
Review and Extend	Day 3
Check Your Mastery	Day 3

Delivery of the Program

Powerful Vocabulary for Reading Success can be used in many different educational settings. If used in regular classrooms, it can be highly effective as:

- structured activities for students when they arrive at school.
- an opening instructional experience at the beginning of the language arts block of time in each class day.
- an activity to end every day's literacy lesson.
- a supplemental program to meet whole class, small group, or individual student needs.
- meaningful instruction for students who finish other assignments early.
- homework assignments.

If used in pull-out, after-school, or summer programs, *Powerful Vocabulary for Reading Success* can effectively be used as:

- a tutorial literacy program.
- an individualized educational plan (IEP).
- a developmental program for ELL.
- an out-of-level, enrichment program to extend on-grade level and gifted students' vocabulary abilities
- an out-of-level, extended program to build below-grade level students' vocabulary abilities

CHAPTER 1

Context Clues

Lesson 1	Nouns to Know	20
Lesson 2	Verbs to Know	27
Lesson 3	More Verbs to Know	34
Lesson 4	Adjectives to Know	41
Lesson 5	More Adjectives to Know	48
Lesson 6	Adverbs to Know	55
Lesson 7	Multiple-Meaning Words to Know	62
Lesson 8	Synonyms to Know	69
Lesson 9	Antonyms to Know	76
Lesson 10	Putting It Together	83

Research Base

- **Word Learning Tip** Frequently occurring words can be learned by using syntax.
- **Vocabulary Building Strategy** Use context clues to determine word meaning.
- **Research-Based Lists** Chapter 1 includes words students are expected to know at Grade 5 as identified by lists of high-frequency words, such as the Harris-Jacobson and the Francis-Kucera lists. Many of these words appear on standardized tests. The words are organized by parts of speech. This chapter also teaches frequently occurring multiple-meaning words, synonyms, and antonyms.

LESSON

1 Nouns to Know

Materials Needed
- Student Workbook, p. 6
- Transparency 1
- Umbrella Chart Graphic Organizer, p. 228

Vocabulary Words
advantage
agent
challenge
foundation
genius
mainland
mechanic
nuisance
obstacle
precaution
pursuit
rival
scheme
target
vehicle

Read Words in Context

Getting Started

Mystery Word of the Week Clue 1

The explorer carried a _____ filled with clothes, food, and equipment.

- See page 14 for routines for using the Mystery Word of the Week Clue. The mystery word of the week is *bundle*.

Model/Teach

- Have students turn to page 6 in their workbooks.

- After students read the Word Learning Tip, explain that a noun is a word that names a person, place, or thing. It may have the article *a*, *an*, or *the* in front of it. Often it comes right before a verb. When it shows more than one person, place, or thing, the noun may end in *-s -es*, or *-ies*. Ask students to give examples of nouns.

- Direct students to look at the Vocabulary Building Strategy. Tell them that they can often use the words surrounding an unfamiliar word (its *context*) to help them determine what the new word means. Some writers use synonyms (words that mean the same thing) or phrases after some nouns to give the definitions.

- Read the complete story aloud once, directing students to follow along.

- Tell students that you are going to read the story a second time. This time you want them to think about the words in boldface and try to determine what they mean.

- Ask students to read the first paragraph silently as you read it aloud. Then do the **Think Aloud** on page 21.

- Place Transparency 1 on the overhead projector. Explain to students that as you continue to read the story, you will pause so that they can discuss each boldface word. Tell them that you want them to use the Word Learning Tip and Vocabulary Building Strategy to determine the meaning of each word. Let students know that you are going to write down their thinking on the transparency as they discuss each boldface word.

20 Chapter 1 • Context Clues

- Continue reading the rest of the story aloud, pausing at each sentence with a boldface word. Ask volunteers to explain how they determined the meaning of each word.
- After students have finished the story and you have discussed the word meanings, allow them to work in small groups, using flashcards to reinforce the word meanings.

English Language Learners
- Pronounce each word aloud. Have students say the words together, after you. Repeat each word several times until everyone is comfortable saying the words. Then partner students to practice saying each word and to use it in a sentence. Circulate around the room, correcting pronunciation as necessary.

Independent Activity
- **Create an Umbrella Chart** Distribute copies of the Umbrella Chart Graphic Organizer. Tell students to write the words *Race for the North Pole* on top. Ask students to come up with words that name people, places, or things that someone might find on the way to the North Pole and write them on the spokes. Ask students to complete the umbrella chart with a partner.

Race for the North Pole

glaciers, caribou, blizzard, seals, igloos, tundra

Think Aloud

Here's what I would think about if I didn't know what the word *vehicle* means. I think *vehicle* is a noun because it names something that they traveled in. Now I add what I already know—that *vehicle* is a noun—to other context clues to find what *vehicle* means. I see that the *vehicle* they traveled in is a dog sled. The writer also names two other vehicles, *cars and trucks*, in the same sentence. Now I have three nouns that name forms of transportation. Putting together what I learned about nouns and context clues, I can determine that *vehicle* must mean "something used to carry people or objects over land."

Answer Key
See page 209 for definitions.

Lesson 1 • Nouns to Know   21

LESSON 1: Nouns to Know

Connect Words and Meanings

Materials Needed
- Student Workbook, pp. 7–8

Think Aloud

I want to share an easy way I determined to complete puzzles like this one. It's a two-step process. First, I count the number of blanks and look for words with the same number of letters. Here, the first word has five letters. *Agent* and *rival* both have five letters. Next, I read the definition and see which of the words it fits. I'm looking for the word that means a "person who arranges things for other people or represents other people." I know that an *agent* is a person who does something for another person, while a *rival* competes against another person. This tells me that *agent* is the correct choice.

Answer Key

1. **a**gent 2. foun**d**ation 3. **v**ehicle
4. ch**a**llenge 5. **n**uisance 6. **t**arget
7. m**a**inland 8. **g**enius 9. m**e**chanic
10. **a**dvantage 11. D 12. C 13. A
14. B 15. A 16. scheme, advantage
17. mechanic, vehicle
18. rival, obstacle

Getting Started

Mystery Word of the Week Clue 2

The _____ was tied with heavy string so it would not come undone and spill everything onto the ground.

⭐ **Review and Share** Invite students to share the words they generated for the **Umbrella Chart** activity on page 21 in the teacher's edition. Post their charts on the bulletin board.

Model/Teach

- Have students turn to page 7 in their workbooks.
- Before students begin the activity, do the **Think Aloud**.
- After you have modeled finding the meaning of the word and filling in the blank, have students complete the rest of the puzzle on their own.
- Ask students to share their responses. Make sure that they explain their thinking, as you did in the Think Aloud.
- Finally, have students complete the activities on page 8 and work in pairs to discuss their responses.

Independent Activities

⭐ **Create a Chant** Have students complete the activity on page 8 in their workbooks. Making vocabulary chants and rhymes will allow them to use their words in context and to create mnemonics. Keep the groups small (no more than five students each).

- **Play Password** Partner students to play a game of "Password" with the vocabulary words. Students take turns generating synonyms to help their partners guess the vocabulary word. Have partners switch roles often as they play. Students should use all the vocabulary words.

Use Words in Context

Materials Needed
- Student Workbook, p. 9

Getting Started

Mystery Word of the Week Clue 3

The _____ was about the size of a large pillow or package. It was made of cloth.

Think Aloud

Read the first sentence silently as I read it aloud. "Name two reasons why you would want to travel in a **vehicle** such as a car while exploring a new place." If I didn't know what the word *vehicle* means, I'd use this clue: I see that the little word *a* comes before it. I know this indicates that the word is a noun and that the word names a person, place, or thing. Now I look for clues in the sentence that help me understand what *vehicle* means. I see the phrase "travel in." Since you travel in an object, a vehicle must be something used for carrying people or objects or moving them from place to place. I see the phrase "such as a car," so I know I'm right. Now I can answer the question: I would want to travel in a vehicle such as a car while exploring a new place because it would help me move fast and keep me safe.

⭐ **Review and Share** Invite students to share their rhymes and chants from the **Create a Chant** activity on page 8. Ask them to discuss the following questions: Which chants will help them remember these new words? Why? How did writing songs help them learn to use the new nouns?

Model/Teach
- Have students turn to page 9 in their workbooks.
- Before students begin the activity, share the **Think Aloud** with the class.
- After you have modeled finding the meaning of the word, have students work on their own to complete the rest of the items.

English Language Learners
- Partner English language learners to alternate reading the sentences and finding the vocabulary words and context clues. For example, the first student can read sentence 2. Then the partner can circle the vocabulary word *advantage* and underline the context clue *a better chance*. Together, they can create a sentence using the vocabulary word. Monitor students as they work.

Independent Activity

⭐ **Letter in a Bottle** Direct students to complete the Letter in a Bottle activity on page 9 of their workbooks. Remind them to be sure to include the essential information someone would need to find them.

Answer Key

Students' responses will vary. See page 218 for sample sentences.

Lesson 1 • Nouns to Know

LESSON 1: Nouns to Know

Put Words Into Action

Materials Needed
- Student Workbook, p. 10
- Idea Web Graphic Organizer, p. 229

Think Aloud

The directions remind me that nouns are words that name people, places, or things. I have to put the nouns into different groups according to what they name. Some of the nouns can fit into more than one group. I'll have to think carefully about each noun to decide what group or groups it fits into. I'll try it with *agent*. An *agent* is someone who represents others, so I'll put that word in the people column.

Answer Key

Students' responses may vary slightly. For example, some might consider *nuisance* a thing instead of a person. Accept all reasonable answers.
People 1. agent 2. genius 3. mechanic 4. nuisance 5. rival;
Places 6. mainland;
Things 7. advantage 8. challenge 9. foundation 10. nuisance, 11. obstacle 12. precaution 13. pursuit 14. scheme, 15. target 16. vehicle

Getting Started

Mystery Word of the Week Clue 4
"I carry my possessions in a _____!"
"It looks like a package," his partner replied.

⭐ **Review and Share** Partner students to share each other's notes and check that all words were used correctly in the activity on page 9. Create a display of the notes, perhaps around a small bottle.

Model/Teach
- Have students turn to page 10 of their workbooks.
- Use the **Think Aloud**.
- After you have modeled how to do the activity, ask students to complete it on their own and then share their responses.

English Language Learners
- Choosing the correct article for a noun poses special difficulties for many English language learners. Explain that all nouns can take the definite article *the*, but we use the indefinite article *a* for nouns that begin with a consonant sound (as in *baseball, book, paper, history*), and the indefinite article *an* for nouns that begin with a vowel sound (as in *apple, egg, island, onion*). Arrange students in small groups to write the correct indefinite article for each vocabulary word, say the words and articles, and explain their choices.

Independent Activity
⭐ **Create a Job Description** Distribute copies of the Idea Web Graphic Organizer. Suggest that before students start to write a job description, they create an idea web of qualities someone would need for this job.

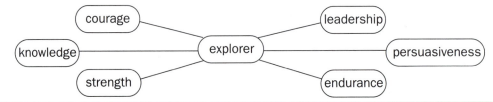

Review and Extend

Materials Needed
- Student Workbook, p. 11
- 5 Ws and H Graphic Organizer, p. 230

Getting Started

Mystery Word of the Week Clue 5

"Why are you carrying a cloth _____ rather than a leather suitcase or knapsack?" people asked the explorer.

Think Aloud

Read the first sentence with me silently as I read it aloud: "Good explorers should be **remarkably smart and gifted people** when it comes to solving problems." First, I notice the phrase in boldface, *remarkably smart and gifted people*. The vocabulary word I want has to mean the same thing or something close to this. Which word could replace *remarkably smart and gifted people*? I look at the word list to find words that name people. I find *agent*, *genius*, *rival*. An *agent* and a *rival* can be remarkably smart and gifted, but they don't have to be. Only a *genius* has to be remarkably smart and gifted, because that's what a *genius* is! So that's the word I need. Now I have to make the word *genius* plural because it names the plural word *people*. To make a noun plural, I have to add *-s* or *-es*. I remember that when a word ends in *s*, you should add *-es*, not just *-s*. So my answer is *geniuses*!

★ **Review and Share** Invite students to share the job descriptions they wrote for the **Create a Job Description** activity on page 10. Put all the descriptions together to make a Want Ad section of a newspaper. You can paste these on a background made of actual pages from the classified section of your local newspaper.

Model/Teach

- Have students turn to page 11 of their workbooks and read the boxed material.
- After answering any questions students have about the boxed information, use the **Think Aloud** and then have them start the activity.
- Remind students that you have modeled completing an item by using what you know about nouns and context clues. Ask them to complete the rest of the activity on their own.

Independent Activities

★ **Write a News Story** Have students complete the Write a News Story activity on page 11 in their workbooks. Suggest that before they begin, they jot down answers to the 5 Ws and H questions: Who? What? Where? When? Why? and How? Pass out the 5 Ws and H Graphic Organizer.

- **Create a Dialogue** Write the vocabulary word *challenge* on the chalkboard. Add an *-s* to make it plural. Then arrange students in small groups to discuss the challenges they have faced and how they have overcome them.

Answer Key

Mystery Word of the Week: bundle.
Also accept *parcel* and any other word that fits the context.

1. geniuses **2.** rivals **3.** obstacles
4. nuisances **5.** targets

Lesson 1 • Nouns to Know

LESSON 1 Nouns to Know

Check Your Mastery

Materials Needed
- Student Workbook, p. 12

Student Self-Assessment

Journal Writing Have students write in their journals telling what they learned about nouns this week.

Answer Key
1. C 2. C 3. A 4. C 5. A
6. foundation 7. scheme 8. agent
9. mechanic 10. advantage

Give the Test
- Have students open their workbooks to page 12.
- Tell students that the Check Your Mastery activity has two parts.
- Read aloud the directions for the first five questions: "Read each item below. Think about the meaning of the boldface word. Then fill in the circle by the item that best answers the question."
- Tell students that there are four choices for each boldface word. Their task is to choose the item that best answers the question about the boldface word and fill in the corresponding circle.
- Model how to answer the question by writing the following item on the chalkboard and reading it aloud:

  What advantage might one swimmer have over another?
  - Ⓐ bigger hands and feet
  - Ⓑ a prettier bathing suit
  - Ⓒ a poor coach
  - Ⓓ less time spent in the water

- Ask students to explain the thinking they would use to answer this question.
- Read aloud the directions for items 6–10: "Write the vocabulary word that best answers each question." Explain that their job is to show that they understand what the vocabulary words mean by showing how to use them.
- Model how to answer a question by writing the following sentence on the chalkboard:

  If you wanted to get a really smart person to help you, who would you call?

- Ask students to answer the question. Have them explain their responses by telling how they used the context clue *really smart person* to define the vocabulary word *genius*.
- Tell students that after they finish this activity, they should reread their answers and check their work.
- Review the Check Your Mastery activity out loud with students.
- Tally students' correct responses.

LESSON 2

Verbs to Know

Read Words in Context

Getting Started

Mystery Word of the Week Clue 1

The farmer tried to _____ his wife, kids, horse, and cows into his small hut, but it was a tight squeeze!

- See page 14 for routines for using the Mystery Word of the Week Clue. The mystery word of the week is *cram*.

Model/Teach

- Ask students to turn to page 13 in their workbooks.
- Direct students to read the Word Learning Tip. Explain that a verb is a word that shows actions or feelings. Often a verb comes right after a noun or pronoun. Sometimes a verb ends in *-s*, *-ed*, or *-ing*. It may have a helping word in front of it such as *may*, *can*, *will*, *shall*, *must*, *could*, or *would*. Tell students that they can use these clues to learn unknown words. Then ask them to give examples of verbs.
- Point out the Vocabulary Building Strategy. Explain to the class that they can often use a word's *context* (the surrounding words and phrases) to help them determine what a new word means.
- Read the complete story aloud once, directing students to follow along in their books.
- Explain to the class that you are going to read the story a second time. This time you want them to think about the words in boldface and try to determine what they mean.
- Have the class read the first paragraph silently as you read it aloud. Before moving on to the second paragraph, do the **Think Aloud** on page 28.

Materials Needed
- Student Workbook, p. 13
- Transparency 1

Vocabulary Words
apologize
assemble
boost
coax
concentrate
consult
devote
irritate
manage
refer
reject
reveal
topple
transport
weaken

LESSON 2 Verbs to Know

Think Aloud

Here's what I would think about if I didn't know what the word *concentrate* means. I see that it has the helping word *could* in front of it, so I think it might be a verb. When I look again, I see that it is telling me about something that the farmer could not do, so now I am sure it is a verb. At this point, I add what I already know—that *concentrate* shows what the farmer could not do—to other context clues to determine what the word means. Now I look at the second part of the sentence: It tells me that his house was noisy. So I start to think about the things that I wouldn't be able to do if my house were very noisy. I know one thing right away—I wouldn't be able to keep my mind focused on what I had to do. That's probably it. When you can't concentrate, you can't keep your mind focused on something. Putting together what I learned about verbs and context clues, I can determine that *concentrate* must mean "to focus on something; to gather all your thoughts and efforts."

Answer Key
See page 209 for definitions.

- Place Transparency 1 on the overhead projector. Tell students that as you continue to read the story, you will pause so that they can discuss each boldface word. You want them to think about the Word Learning Tip and the Vocabulary Building Strategy. They should share their thinking with you, telling you the meaning of each word and how they determined its meaning. Write their responses on the transparency.

- After students have discussed the meaning of each boldface word and how they knew it, divide the class into small groups. Pass out flashcards. Give them the opportunity to use the flashcards to reinforce word meaning.

English Language Learners
- Have students take turns pointing to a vocabulary word as you pronounce it, while the whole group repeats the word after you. Then ask students to write down the pronunciation to help them remember it. For example, for *assemble* they might write "ay-sem-ble" or "ah sem bl." Arrange students in small groups to compare pronunciation guides and practice using them to say the words. Walk around the room, correcting pronunciation and usage as necessary.

Independent Activity
- **Play Match-Up with Verbs** Create two sets of index cards with 15 cards each. Write one vocabulary word on the front of each index card in the first set. Then write the definition for each word on the front of the other index cards. Shuffle each deck of cards and place the two decks in the middle of a table, blank sides up. Divide the class into two teams. Ask the first student from one team to pick a card from each deck and tell whether the word and definition match. If they do not match, the student continues turning over definition cards until a match is made. The team gets a point if the student identifies the correct match. Remove the two cards once a correct match is made. Then give the second team a turn. Continue taking turns until all the cards are used. The team with the most points wins.

Connect Words and Meanings

Getting Started

Mystery Word of the Week Clue 2

"I do not want to _____ all these people and animals in one small room," his wife said. "There are too many to pack in!"

⭐ **Review and Share** Give students an opportunity to talk about the **Match-Up** game they played for the activity on page 28 of the teacher's edition. Which words did they find easiest to match to their definitions? Which matches did they find the most difficult to make? What clues did they use to help them make these matches? Ask students to talk about what this activity taught them about verbs.

Model/Teach

- Have students turn to page 14 in their workbooks.
- Before students begin the activity, do the **Think Aloud**.
- After you have modeled finding the meaning of the word and written the answer, have students complete the rest of the activity on their own and share their responses.
- Ask students to complete the second activity, on page 15.

Independent Activities

⭐ **Create a Billboard** Suggest to students that the easiest words to illustrate for the activity on page 15 in their workbooks might be *topple, irritate, transport,* and *weaken* because the letters can be written to show physical action. Words that show mental activity, such as *concentrate,* might be harder.

- **Conversation Starters** Partner students and give them a conversation starter that uses one of the vocabulary words, such as "Yesterday, I was *irritated* because. . ." Have students continue the conversation by taking turns providing sentences that complete the starter. Challenge students to use as many vocabulary words as they can. Tell them that they can repeat words if they need to and that they can use other verbs, too.

Materials Needed
- Student Workbook, pp. 14–15

Think Aloud

I want to share a good method I have for completing matching activities: the process of elimination. This means I answer the questions that I find easiest first and the ones that I find hardest last. I start by reading all the vocabulary words to see which ones I know. Read down the left-hand column with me: I'm not sure what *irritate* means, but I think that *weaken* means "to feel sick." I look down the right column to find the closest definition. Read with me. Choice G, "to lose strength," is very close to my definition, "to feel sick." I skim the rest of the right column to see if I can find a closer definition, but choice G is the best. Now I write G next to item 2 to show that it's my answer.

Answer Key
1. D 2. G 3. E 4. I 5. C 6. B
7. F 8. A 9. J 10. H 11. A 12. C
13. B 14. A 15. C 16. B 17. D
18. C

Lesson 2 • Verbs to Know   29

LESSON 2 — Verbs to Know

Use Words in Context

Materials Needed
- Student Workbook, p. 16

Think Aloud

Let me show you how I would go about completing this activity. Please read the first sentence to yourself as I read it aloud: "Every day, I (1) _____ with people, giving them advice and helping them solve their problems." I see that the missing word comes after the pronoun *I*, so I know that it must be a verb—a word that tells something about actions or feelings. Now I look for context clues in the sentence to learn what specific action or feeling I need here. The second part of the sentence—"giving them advice and helping them solve their problems"—tells me that I need a word that is related to "advice." Now I see three words in parentheses—*consult, boost,* and *transport*. I know that when I consult with my coach, she gives me advice and when I consult an encyclopedia, it gives me the information I need. So *consult* must mean "to go for information or advice." I try the word to see if it make sense in the sentence: "Every day, I *consult* with people, giving them advice and helping them solve their problems." Yes, it does, so that is the word I will write in the blank.

Answer Key
1. consult 2. irritated
3. concentrate 4. manage 5. devote
6. reveal 7. coaxed 8. assembled
9. toppled 10. apologize

Getting Started

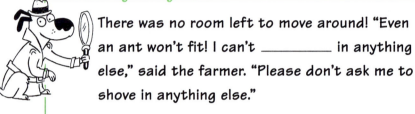

Mystery Word of the Week Clue 3

There was no room left to move around! "Even an ant won't fit! I can't _____ in anything else," said the farmer. "Please don't ask me to shove in anything else."

★ **Review and Share** Display students' verb pictures from the **Create a Billboard** activity on page 15 on a bulletin board. Ask them to talk about which words they found easiest to illustrate and which they found the most difficult.

Model/Teach

- Have students turn to page 16 in their workbooks.
- Before students begin the activity, share the **Think Aloud** with the class.
- After you have modeled how to fill in the missing words, have students work on their own to complete the rest of the items and then share their responses.

English Language Learners

- Arrange English language learners in small groups to take turns reading the sentences aloud with expression. Tell them that they should fill in the blank with any word that they know makes sense in the context. As students generate synonyms, have them look at the list of three choices to find the word that best matches. If time permits, talk to students about the subtle shades of meaning among the words and why English uses so many synonyms.

Independent Activity

★ **Make a Thank-You Card Using Verbs** Direct students to complete the thank-you card activity on page 16 in their workbooks. Allow students to illustrate their cards if they wish.

Put Words Into Action

Materials Needed
- Student Workbook, p. 17
- Problem-Solution Chart, p. 231

Getting Started

Mystery Word of the Week Clue 4
Just when the farmer thought he could not _____ one more animal into his house, the Wise Woman told him to jam in the pigs and chickens!

★ **Review and Share** Give students the opportunity to share the thank-you cards they created for the activity on page 16. Post them on the bulletin board and celebrate students' creativity and originality.

Model/Teach

- Have students turn to page 17 of their workbooks.
- Use the **Think Aloud** to model the thinking involved in completing the activity.
- After you have modeled the thinking involved in completing this activity, have students complete it on their own.
- Allow students time to trade work and talk about how their pictures or statements match the captions.

English Language Learners

- Arrange students in small groups and have them use total physical response to act out as many of the vocabulary words as they can. One student should act out a word while the rest of the group guesses it. The student who guesses the word becomes the next actor. Make sure that everyone gets a chance to act out a word.

Independent Activity

★ **Write a Story Using Verbs** Distribute copies of the Problem-Solution Chart. Suggest that students use it to brainstorm ideas for their story in the activity on page 17.

Think Aloud

This looks like a fun activity, but it involves a lot of thinking. I know that first, I have to choose a verb that fits in the caption: "Look at the farmer speak gently to the animals and _____ them into the house!" I know that the animals probably don't want to go into the house; it's not where they normally live and there is not much space inside. I bet the farmer has to be pretty persuasive to get those animals inside, so I know I am looking for a verb that tells me something like that—he persuaded them or he urged them. Now I look through my vocabulary words and find the word *coax*. I remember that when you coax someone, you gently urge that person to do something. That fits in the caption: "Look at the farmer speak gently to the animals and coax them into the house." Now I have to draw a picture to show what the caption describes or write a sentence that the farmer might say. So my picture or sentence has to show the farmer persuading the animals to go inside.

Answer Key
1. coax 2. assemble 3. irritate
4. topple 5. apologize 6. reveal

Student's responses will vary. See page 218 for sample sentences.

Lesson 1 • Verbs to Know   31

LESSON 2: Verbs to Know

Review and Extend

Materials Needed
- Student Workbook, p. 18

Think Aloud

Read the first item with me: "The fifth graders are really working hard and **spend most of their time** helping animals. They are _____ time to this activity." I see the clue in boldface—*spend most of their time*. If I spend most of my time doing something, what am I doing with my time? I'm dedicating my time, I'm spending my time, I'm giving my time. I look down the list and find the word *devote*, which I remember means "to give time and effort to some activity." Now I have to think about what form to put the verb in. I know this is something they are continuing to do, so this tells me that I should use the ongoing form of the verb. Looking at the chart, I see that the ending -ing is added to verbs to show ongoing action. Since *devote* ends in -e, I will drop the extra e and write *devoting* in the blank.

Answer Key
Mystery Word of the Week: cram
Accept *pack, crowd,* or any other verb that fits the context.

1. devoting 2. concentrating
3. consulted 4. managed 5. transporting

Getting Started

Mystery Word of the Week Clue 5
"I do not want you to _____ anything else in," said the Wise Woman. "Now it is time to empty out your house."

 Review and Share Have students share the stories they wrote for the **Write a Story Using Verbs** activity on page 17. Create a class storybook with all the stories.

Model/Teach
- Direct students to turn to page 18 of their workbooks and read the boxed information about verb tense.
- After you have answered any questions they have about tense, use the **Think Aloud** to model the thinking involved in completing this activity.
- Have students complete the rest of the activity on their own and then share their responses.

English Language Learners
- English verb tenses are often difficult for English language learners to master. Have students practice conjugating the vocabulary words. Students can work in small groups to write the verbs and their conjugations on a chart such as the one below.

	Present Tense	Past Tense	Ongoing Action
I	assemble	assembled	am assembling
you	assemble	assembled	are assembling
he, she, it	assembles	assembled	is assembling
we	assemble	assembled	are assembling
they	assemble	assembled	are assembling

Independent Activity

Use Verbs to Write Bumper Stickers Ask students to complete the activity on page 18 in their workbooks on separate pieces of paper. You might prefer to have them work in small groups. Give extra points to any group that can use all 15 verbs.

Chapter 1 • Context Clues

Check Your Mastery

Materials Needed
- Student Workbook, p. 19

Give the Test

- Direct students to open their workbooks to page 19.
- Explain to the class that the Check Your Mastery activity has two parts.
- Read aloud the directions for the first five questions: "Read each sentence below. Choose the word that best fits in each blank. Write the word in the blank." Point out to students that each item has three choices. They must choose the word that *best* fits the context and write it in the blank.
- Model how to answer the question by writing the following item on the chalkboard and reading it aloud:

  If you politely convince someone to help you learn to swim, you _____ (*boost, coax, consult*) them into doing you the favor.

- Ask students to choose the word that best fits in the blank. Have them justify their choices by explaining what context clue they used. Guide students to understand that the clue "politely convince" shows that the correct choice is *coax*.
- Read aloud the directions for items 6–10: "Circle the letter of the correct answer to each of the questions below." Explain that on this part of the page, students must show that they understand the meaning of the vocabulary words by providing an example for each sentence.
- Model how to answer this type of question by writing the following sentence on the chalkboard:

  Which of the following would you probably **reject** if you didn't like heights?
  A. riding on a rollercoaster C. riding in a car
  B. swimming in a lake D. broccoli

- Ask students to answer the question. Have them explain their response by telling how they used the context clue *didn't like heights* to define the core word *reject*.
- Review the Check Your Mastery activity out loud with students.
- Tally students' correct responses.

Student Self-Assessment

Journal Writing In their journals, have students rate their success in mastering the words. Which words do they feel they could use as part of their everyday vocabulary? Which words do they feel they still need to practice? Why?

Answer Key
1. assemble 2. irritate 3. weaken
4. devote 5. concentrate 6. C
7. B 8. B 9. A 10. D

Lesson 2 • Verbs to Know

LESSON 3 — More Verbs to Know

Read Words in Context

Getting Started

Mystery Word of the Week Clue 1

Beverly enjoys going to the farmer's market where she can _____ the peaches carefully to make sure they are ripe.

- See page 14 for routines for using the Mystery Word of the Week Clue. The mystery word of the week is *examine*.

Model/Teach

- Ask students to turn to page 20 in their workbooks.
- Invite students to read the Word Learning Tip aloud. Remind them that a verb is a word that shows actions or feelings. Point out that a verb often comes right after a noun or pronoun. A verb can end in *-s*, *-ed*, or *-ing*. However, some verbs have an irregular past-tense form. Ask students to give examples of verbs with irregular past-tense forms (for example, *draw/drew*, and *teach/taught*).
- Have a volunteer read the Vocabulary Building Strategy. Explain that students can use surrounding words, phrases, and sentences to help them determine what a new word means.
- Read the complete story aloud once, directing students to follow along in their books.
- Explain to the class that you are going to read the story a second time. This time, you want them to think about the words in boldface and try to determine what they mean.
- Direct students to read the first paragraph silently as you read it aloud. Then do the **Think Aloud** on page 35.
- Tell students: "As we continue to read the story, I will pause so we can discuss each boldface word. Please think about the Word Learning Tip you are using to find the meaning of each word. Also think about the Vocabulary Building Strategy. Share your thinking with me. Tell me what the word means and how you knew this."

Materials Needed
- Student Workbook, p. 20
- Transparency 1

Vocabulary Words
approve
associate
attempt
broadcast
conquer
dedicate
emerge
flourish
organize
overwhelm
pursue
resemble
restore
surrender
withdraw

Chapter 1 • Context Clues

- Place Transparency 1 on the overhead projector. Explain that you are going to record students' thinking as they tell you the meaning of each boldface word.

- After you have finished reading the story a second time and discussed the meanings of the words, use a set of flashcards to reinforce meanings.

English Language Learners

- Write *restore* and *conquer* on the chalkboard. Point to each word and pronounce it. Model for students how to write these words in the past tense by adding *-ed*. Say *restored* and *conquered*, having students repeat the words several times with you. Make sure students do not add an extra syllable for the letters *ed*. Explain that the words *flourished, organized, overwhelmed,* and *surrendered* follow this pattern. Then explain that if a verb ends in *e*, you add *-d*, not *-ed*, to form the past tense. Write the words *emerged, organized, pursued,* and *restored* on the chalkboard. Say each word aloud and have students repeat it after you.

Independent Activity

- **Be a Word Sleuth** Give students the opportunity to thumb through magazines, newspapers, and cookbooks for recipes and other sets of directions. Ask them to list ten verbs that they find. Have them write these verbs in their personal word journals. If they find one of their vocabulary words, they should star it.

Think Aloud

Here's how I would determine what *attempt* means. I look at the sentence and see that this is something Ricardo wants to do, so I know that the word is a verb. Now I look at the words that come after *attempt*: to cook her favorite dish. *Attempt* is going to tell me something about this action. I also see that he's done this before and been successful, so maybe he thinks he can do this now, but he is not quite sure. Putting all these ideas together, I think that *attempt* may mean something like *try*. I substitute the word *try* for *attempt*, so the sentence reads: "Now he wants to try to cook her favorite dish—tacos." The sentence makes sense, so I know I determined the correct meaning of *attempt*.

Answer Key
See page 209–210 for definitions.

Lesson 3 • More Verbs to Know

LESSON 3 — More Verbs to Know

Connect Words and Meanings

Materials Needed
- Student Workbook, pp. 24–25

Think Aloud

My first clue, number 4 Across, is "to chase after." I find the box labeled 4 and count the boxes to see that my answer is going to have six letters. Now I look at my vocabulary words. Only two of them have six letters: *emerge* and *pursue*. I remember that *emerge* has something to do with coming into the open, like emerging from behind the trees or the sun emerging from behind the clouds, so that word doesn't fit the definition. I also remember that *pursue* has to do with tracking something down or going after something, like pursuing a dream or pursuing a criminal. That fits the meaning of "to chase after," so I write *pursue* in the boxes.

Answer Key
Across 4. pursue 5. conquer
6. resemble 8. broadcast 9. withdraw
10. associate 13. overwhelm
14. approve **Down** 1. dedicate
2. surrender 3. flourish 7. organize
10. attempt 11. restore 12. emerge

1. pursue 2. flourish 3. organize
4. emerge 5. associate 6. dedicate
7. restore 8. conquer

Getting Started

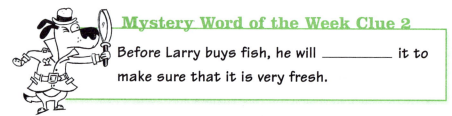

Mystery Word of the Week Clue 2
Before Larry buys fish, he will _____ it to make sure that it is very fresh.

Review and Share Invite students to share the words they found for the **Be a Word Sleuth** activity on page 35 in the teacher's edition. Create a word wall of the vocabulary words. Add these new verbs to the wall also.

Model/Teach
- Have students turn to page 24 in their workbooks.
- Before students begin the activity, do the **Think Aloud**.
- After you have modeled how to complete the crossword puzzle, have students finish it on their own.
- Have students turn to the next activity, complete it, and share their responses.

Independent Activities

Create an Activity Goal Have students complete their paragraphs about creating an activity goal for themselves in their personal word journals. Before they begin, suggest that they brainstorm a list of goals and then star the one they want to pursue. Remind students to use at least five vocabulary words if possible, along with several new verbs.

- **Play Rivet** If time permits, give students the opportunity to work in pairs to play Rivet. One student selects a vocabulary word and draws blank lines on a piece of paper to indicate each letter in the word. This student then fills in the word one letter at a time, pausing after writing each letter. The other student tries to guess the word as each letter is filled in. As an extra challenge, ask the student guessing the word to give its definition in order to win. Once the student guesses the word, the partners change roles.

36 Chapter 1 • Context Clues

Use Words in Context

Materials Needed
- Student Workbook, p. 23

Getting Started

Mystery Word of the Week Clue 3
The head chef likes to _____ every dish before it leaves the kitchen.

⭐ **Review and Share** Have students share their paragraphs about their **activity goal** from the activity on page 22. After sharing paragraphs, give the class the opportunity to talk about the kinds of activities they'd like to learn how to do and some of the steps they can take to accomplish their goals.

Model/Teach

- Have students turn to page 24 in their workbooks.
- Before students begin the activity, share the **Think Aloud** with the class.
- After you have modeled how to complete an item, have students work on their own to complete the rest of the items and share their responses.

English Language Learners

- Write *associate* and *dedicate* on the chalkboard. Point to each word and pronounce it. Ask students to clap out the number of syllables in each word. Then model for students how to write these words in the past tense by adding -d. Say *associated* and *dedicated*. Point out that the ending has the sound -tid. Have students repeat the words several times and clap out the number of syllables.

Independent Activity

⭐ **Write a Restaurant Ad** Ask students to complete their ads for the activity on page 24 in their workbooks on a separate piece of paper, referring to their journal notes as needed. If they have difficulty choosing the kind of restaurant, encourage them to think about a favorite one they've eaten in or perhaps one they have seen on television. Remind students to use at least five vocabulary words and to underline each one.

Think Aloud

Read the first item to yourself as I read it aloud: "Don't **pursue** a bear that's grabbed your roast beef dinner. Why not?" If I didn't know what the boldface word *pursue* means, I would think about the other words in the sentence that I do know. *Bear* is a good context clue. I know that a bear is large and fierce, and I definitely wouldn't want to chase one who has grabbed my dinner! Therefore, I can determine that *pursue* must mean "to chase after." Now I can use the word *pursue* correctly when I answer the question: "I wouldn't pursue a bear because bears are fierce and much bigger than I am!"

Answer Key
Students' responses will vary. See page 218 for sample sentences.

Lesson 3 • More Verbs to Know

LESSON 3 — More Verbs to Know

Put Words Into Action

Materials Needed
- Student Workbook, p. 24

Think Aloud

Let's look at the television screens together. They show what happens in an episode of *The Pie Factory Show*. I see that two chefs are beginning to make apple pies. They seem to have a lot of mishaps but finally they wind up with two beautiful pies. I can tell from the pictures that if I were watching this show, I would probably think it was pretty funny. Here's how I would begin my description for a television guide: "In this humorous episode from *The Pie Factory*, two chefs *attempt* to make apple pies. Notice that I used the vocabulary word *attempt*."

Answer Key

Students' descriptions will vary. See page 218 for sample description.

Getting Started

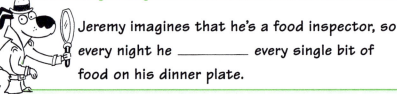

Mystery Word of the Week Clue 4
Jeremy imagines that he's a food inspector, so every night he _____ every single bit of food on his dinner plate.

★ **Review and Share** Collect the **restaurant ads** from the activity on page 23 and display them on a bulletin board. Give students an opportunity to look at all the ads. Lead a class discussion about which ads interest the students enough to make them want to go to that restaurant. Have the class take a vote on which five ads are the most persuasive.

Model/Teach

- Have students turn to page 24 of their workbooks.
- Tell students that they are going to look at some pictures and then write a sentence about each picture in which they include a vocabulary word.
- Use the **Think Aloud**.
- After you have modeled how to complete the activity, have students finish it on their own. Ask them to share their sentences.

Independent Activities

★ **Put on a Cooking Skit** Direct students to complete the Put on a Cooking Skit activity on page 24 in their workbooks. Remind them to use five vocabulary words and three new verbs in their script. Encourage students to keep the skits very brief so that all the groups will have an opportunity to present their skits. Give each group an opportunity to rehearse their presentation.

- **Script Rewrite** After each group has had a chance to rehearse their presentations, give them an opportunity to revise their scripts if they'd like. Point out that often during a rehearsal, writers discover that the dialogue is too long or doesn't work exactly the way it was intended. Now is the time to fix it!

Review and Extend

Materials Needed
- Student Workbook, p. 25

Getting Started

Mystery Word of the Week Clue 5

"These are beautiful! Absolutely perfect!" says Melody after she bends close to the cake to _____ the flowers on it.

★ **Review and Share** Provide additional time for students to **perform the skits** they prepared for the activity on page 24. Remind them to speak clearly during their performance. As groups perform, encourage the class to imagine they are viewers who will decide if the show airs or not. After each skit, give students an opportunity to discuss the show's strengths and weaknesses.

Model/Teach

- Direct students to turn to page 25 of their workbooks and read the boxed information.
- After you have answered any questions students may have about irregular verbs, use the **Think Aloud**.
- Have students complete the rest of the activity on their own.

English Language Learners

- Write *withdraw* on one side of a flashcard and *withdrew* on the other side. Repeat the process for the word *broadcast*. Pair students with greater English fluency with those students who are less fluent. Have students take turns reading the present and past tense of these words. If students are comfortable speaking English, invite them to create sentences using these words. For additional practice, use the following irregular verbs (*teach/taught, see/saw, say/said, make/made, read/read*).

Independent Activity

★ **Invent a Dish** Before students begin, have them work with a partner to discuss ideas for signature dishes. Tell them that the dishes can be serious—something they would really like to make—or funny—unusual combinations that tickle their funnybones.

Think Aloud

I want to show you my thinking as I choose the correct verb and write it in the past tense. Here's the first item: "The television station **showed** a program about a barbecue contest. They _____ the show on Saturday night." I'm looking for a verb that tells that a television station put on a program. I know that the vocabulary word that fits that context is *broadcast*, so now I have to determine what the past tense of *broadcast* is. Let me try to add *-ed*: "They *broadcasted* the show on Saturday night." I know that's not right; I've never heard the word used like that before—so I think *broadcast* is an irregular verb. When I look back at the box, I see that the past tense of *broadcast* is the same as the present tense: *broadcast*—so this is the form I will put in the sentence. I then circle *Irregular*.

Answer Key

Mystery Word of the Week: examine
Accept other words that fit the context, too.

1. broadcast 2. Irregular
3. organized 4. Regular
5. attempted 6. Regular
7. overwhelmed 8. Regular
9. withdrew 10. Irregular

LESSON 3

More Verbs to Know

Check Your Mastery

Materials Needed
- Student Workbook, p. 26

Student Self-Assessment

Journal Writing In their journals, have students rate their success on this lesson. Out of a score of 10, how would they assess their mastery? Why? How could they have done better?

Answer Key
1. conquer 2. restore 3. attempt
4. withdraw 5. overwhelm
6. associate 7. broadcasts
8. dedicated 9. resembled
10. flourish

Give the Test
- Have students open their workbooks to page 26.
- Explain to the class that the Check Your Mastery activity has two parts.
- Read aloud the directions for the first part. Then explain that each sentence contains two pairs of words. The words in the first pair have the same or similar meanings. To complete the sentence, they should find the word that has the same or similar meaning to the first word in the second pair. Tell students they have three choices for each word. Their job is to choose the word with the closest meaning and write it in the blank.
- Model how to answer the question by writing the following item on the chalkboard and reading it aloud:

    Do well is to **prosper** as **grow well** is to _____.

- Ask students to choose the word that best fits in the blank. Point out that *do well* and *prosper* mean the same thing. *Grow well* and *flourish* also mean the same thing.
- Read aloud the directions for items 6–10: "Read each sentence. Choose the word that best fits and write it on the line."
- Model how to answer this type of question by writing the following sentence on the chalkboard:

    Jake always likes to eat at this seafood restaurant because the building _____ (*restores, resembles, organizes*) a big ship.

- Ask students to choose the word that best fits in the sentence. Have them explain their choice by telling which context clues helped them.
- Direct students to reread their answers and check their work.
- Review the Check Your Mastery activity out loud with students.
- Arrange students in small groups to discuss the questions they did not answer correctly. Have students write new sentences using the correct vocabulary word for each item they missed.
- As a class, talk about how the Word Learning Tip and the Vocabulary Building Strategy helped them choose the correct response.

Chapter 1 • Context Clues

LESSON 4

Adjectives to Know

Read Words in Context

Getting Started

Mystery Word of the Week Clue 1

The _____ dog barked and barked, waking up the whole neighborhood!

- See page 14 for routines for using the Mystery Word of the Week Clue. The mystery word of the week is *ferocious*.

Model/Teach

- Ask students to turn to page 27 in their workbooks. Direct them to read the Word Learning Tip aloud. Remind students that an adjective is a word that describes a noun or a pronoun and answers one of these four questions: *What kind? Which one? How many? How much?* Point out that an adjective usually comes before the noun or pronoun it describes or after a linking verb. Also tell students that some adjectives end in *-ant, -ent, -ar, -ent, -ic, -ile, -ive,* and *-ous*. Suggest that they circle the words in their vocabulary list with these endings.

- Invite a student volunteer to read the Vocabulary Building Strategy aloud. Explain to students that they can often use surrounding words and phrases to help them understand what a new word means.

- Read the complete story aloud once, directing students to follow along in their books.

- Tell students that you are going to read the story a second time. This time you want them to think about the words in boldface and try to determine what they mean.

- Have students read the first paragraph silently as you read it aloud. Then do the **Think Aloud** on page 42.

- Explain to students that as you continue to read the story, you will pause so they can discuss each boldface word. Ask them to think about the Word Learning Tip to determine the meaning of each word. Also, ask them to think about the Vocabulary Building Strategy. Encourage them to share their thinking with you and to tell you what the word means and how they knew this.

Materials Needed
- Student Workbook, p. 27
- Transparency 1

Vocabulary Words
adventurous
assorted
beloved
confident
distinguished
easygoing
fragile
fragrant
heroic
massive
mature
mischievous
outstanding
peculiar
shrewd

LESSON 4: Adjectives to Know

Think Aloud

Here's how I would determine what *assorted* means. My first clue is its placement in the sentence. It comes just before the noun *shapes*. I know that an adjective often comes before the noun it describes. I also know that an adjective answers the questions *What kind? Which one? How many? How much? Assorted* tells me <u>what</u> <u>kind</u> of shapes, so now I am sure that it is an adjective. Now, I add what I already know—that *assorted* is an adjective that describes what kind of shapes—to other context clues to determine what the word means. The second half of the sentence reads: "both big and small." *Assorted* must mean "many different kinds." This makes sense in the sentence, so I know I am correct.

- Place Transparency 1 on the overhead projector. Explain to students that you are going to jot down the words that show their thinking as they tell you the meaning of each boldface word.
- Continue reading the rest of the story aloud, pausing at each sentence with a boldface word. Ask students to explain how they determined the meaning of each word. Make certain they describe the facts about adjectives and context clues that they used to determine each word's meaning. Write their responses on the transparency.
- Pair students. Have them use flashcards to reinforce meanings.

English Language Learners
- Write the words *fragile* and *easygoing* on the board. Underline the *g* in *fragile* and the first *g* in *easygoing*. Point to *fragile*. Pronounce it several times with the students. Explain that the *g* in *fragile* is pronounced like a *j* [fraj il]. Point to *easygoing*. Explain that in this word the first *g* is pronounced like the *g* in *get*. Say all vocabulary words and meanings with students.

Independent Activity
- **Create a Chart** Have students create a chart in their personal vocabulary journals. On the chart, they should list vocabulary words to describe a pet they have or would like to have. They should arrange the adjectives in two categories: Adjectives That Describe Your Pet the Best and Adjectives That Describe Your Pet the Least. Then they should add three new adjectives to describe their real or ideal pet.

Answer Key
See page 210 for definitions.

Connect Words and Meanings

Getting Started

Mystery Word of the Week Clue 2

People should not have as a pet a _____ dog who frightens the neighbors.

⭐ **Review and Share** Invite some volunteers to share the **charts** they created for the activity on page 42 in the teacher's edition. Recreate the chart on the chalkboard, and have a volunteer write the vocabulary words that students used to fill in their charts. Lead a class discussion about the variety of words that students used in their charts.

Model/Teach

- Have students turn to page 28 in their workbooks.
- Before students begin the activity, do the **Think Aloud**
- After you have modeled how to do this activity, ask students to complete the rest of it on their own and share their responses.
- Ask students to do the activities on page 29.

Independent Activities

⭐ **Write a Letter** Encourage students to think about qualities they have that would make them good volunteers. Ask them to jot these down before they start the activity. Then have students complete their letters. Remind them to use at least three vocabulary words and at least two new adjectives.

- **Illustrate Words** Ask each student to choose a vocabulary word. Tell them to draw a picture that shows what this word means. For example, for the word *fragile*, they might draw a delicate glass vase, and for the word *beloved* they might draw a child hugging a dog. Then they should write a sentence using the word under their picture.

Materials Needed
- Student Workbook, p. 28–29

Think Aloud
I notice there are three steps to this activity. Right away, I put the steps into my own words. This is what I have to do: read the definition, find the matching word, and write the word in the puzzle. After I've filled in all the words, I'll look at the boxes that go down the page to find another vocabulary word. I look at the first definition. The word means *strange* or *odd*. I look at the vocabulary list to see if I notice a word that fits this definition. I see *peculiar*. I remember that if someone behaves in a peculiar way, that person acts odd. So I write *peculiar* in the puzzle boxes.

Answer Key
1. pe**c**uliar
2. her**o**ic
3. disti**n**guished
4. **f**ragrant
5. frag**i**le
6. outstan**d**ing
7. **e**asygoing
8. adve**n**turous
9. assor**t**ed
10. confident

11. beloved 12. massive
13. mature 14. mischievous
15. shrewd 16. heroic
17. mischievous 18. adventurous
19. mature 20. beloved

Lesson 4 • Adjectives to Know

LESSON 4 — Adjectives to Know

Use Words in Context

Materials Needed
- Student Workbook, p. 30

Think Aloud

Please read the first question silently to yourself as I read it aloud: "How could a cute puppy get into **so much trouble** and cause so many problems?" I know that I need to find a word that suggests "so much trouble." First, I look for other context clues in the sentence that might tell me more about a puppy. I see the words *cute* and *problems*. I put these words together with "so much trouble." Then I ask myself which word describes a cute puppy getting into trouble and causing problems? I try the word *mischievous* in the sentence. It makes sense. Now I can answer the question: "A *mischievous* puppy could chew my shoes."

Answer Key
Students' responses will vary. See page 218–219 for sample sentences.

Getting Started

Mystery Word of the Week Clue 3
The animal shelter takes in _____ animals that have not been tamed.

★ **Review and Share** Invite volunteers to share the **letters** that they created for the activity on page 29. Then have a class discussion about the variety of words that students chose to describe themselves. Discuss with them the placement of the adjectives in the sentences in their letters. Did they place the adjectives before or after nouns or pronouns? Add these adjectives to the word wall.

Model/Teach
- Have students turn to page 30 in their workbooks.
- Before students start, do the Think Aloud .
- After you have modeled how to use context clues to choose the correct adjective and write a sentence answering the question, have students work on their own to complete the activity and then share their responses.

Independent Activities

★ **Create a Lost Pet Ad** Have students complete Create a Lost Pet Ad. Remind them to write an accurate description of the lost pet and to use at least five vocabulary words and three new adjectives.

- **Brainstorm Adjectives** Tell students to think about how they would feel if their pet were lost. (If they don't have a pet, encourage them to use their imaginations.) Then ask them to jot down adjectives that describe their feelings. Next have them imagine that someone found their pet. They should brainstorm adjectives that describe their new feelings. Create two columns on the chalkboard. On the top of one column, draw a smiley face. On the top of the other, draw a frowning face. Ask students to provide adjectives that fit in each column. (If you prefer, have students create this chart in their journals and work in pairs to fill it out.)

44 Chapter 1 • Context Clues

Put Words Into Action

Materials Needed
- Student Workbook, p. 31
- Idea Web Graphic Organizer, p. 229

Getting Started

Mystery Word of the Week Clue 4
The wolves seemed quite _____ as they howled and snorted and showed their teeth.

⭐ **Review and Share** Invite volunteers to read the lost pet **ads** they created for the activity on page 30. Display the ads around the classroom, giving students an opportunity to read and discuss them. Then lead a class discussion about which ads the class thinks would be the most effective in helping to find a lost pet.

Model/Teach
- Have students turn to page 31 of their workbooks.
- Use the **Think Aloud**.
- After you have modeled how to complete the activity, have students finish it on their own and work in pairs to share their responses.

Think Aloud

Here's how I would complete this activity. First, I would read the directions. I read that I have to think of a public figure and write clues about his or her identity. I have to use one vocabulary word in each clue. First, I think I'll decide who I want to write about. I just read a book about Jane Goodall, who studies and cares for chimpanzees in Africa. I really like what she does, so I'll write about her. Now I need to choose the vocabulary words that I want to use. I think about Jane Goodall and all her accomplishments and what kind of a person she is. I decide to use the words *adventurous*, *beloved*, *confident*, *heroic*, and *outstanding*. To write my first clue, I decide to use the word *adventurous*: "She is an *adventurous* person who studies chimpanzees." This sentence uses the vocabulary word *adventurous* to show what Jane Goodall likes to do: have exciting experiences.

Independent Activity

⭐ **Write a Character Sketch** Before students complete the activity, have them brainstorm adjectives to describe the person they admire. Distribute copies of the Idea Web Graphic Organizer and suggest that they use it to come up with ideas.

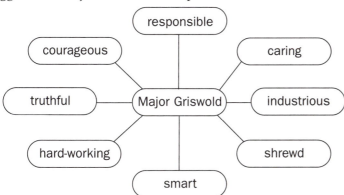

Answer Key
Students' responses will vary.
See page 219 for sample sentences.

Lesson 4 • Adjectives to Know

LESSON 4: Adjectives to Know

Review and Extend

Getting Started

Mystery Word of the Week Clue 5

The tigers made loud roaring sounds and were very _____ as they roamed across the savannah.

Review and Share Have volunteers share the **character sketches** they wrote for the activity on page 31. Invite students to discuss which vocabulary words they chose to use in their character sketches. You may want to make a list of words the students chose to use in their sketches to see which were chosen most often in their descriptions of people they admire.

Model/Teach

- Direct students to turn to page 32 of their workbooks and read the boxed information.
- Use the **Think Aloud** to demonstrate the thinking you would use to complete the activity.
- Tell students that you have modeled completing the first item by using what you know about adjectives and context clues. Have students complete the rest of the activity on their own. Then ask them to share their responses.

Independent Activities

Write a Tall Tale Remind students that tall tales are stories that exaggerate details and events. For example, if the dog pulled 50 pounds, a tall tale might claim that he pulled 5,000 pounds! Suggest that students might want to create a list of details to exaggerate before they start writing to complete the activity.

- **Find New Words** Challenge students to find additional words with these adjective endings. Encourage them to look through textbooks, newspapers, magazines, and books for these words. However, warn them that these letters do not always indicate that the word is an adjective, so they also have to check the context.

Materials Needed
- Student Workbook, p. 32

Think Aloud

Let me show you the thinking I would do to complete this activity. Read the first item with me as I read it aloud: "**Brave** and well-trained dogs made it possible to get medicine to faraway places in Alaska." I see that the word *brave* is boldface, so I know I am looking for a word that means something similar to it. Well, a dog that is brave and does something like get medicine to people could be described as heroic. I write this word in the first blank and I write the ending -ic in the second blank.

Answer Key
Mystery Word of the Week: ferocious
Accept other words that fit the context, too.

1. heroic 2. -ic
3. confident 4. -ent
5. massive 6. -ive
7. adventurous 8. -ous
9. fragile 10. -ile

Check Your Mastery

Materials Needed
- Student Workbook, p. 33

Give the Test

- Have students open their workbooks to page 33.

- Explain to the class that the Check Your Mastery activity has two parts.

- Read aloud the directions for the first five questions: "Circle the letter of the correct answer to each question below." Explain that on this part of the page, students must show they understand the meaning of the vocabulary words by providing a definition of the boldface word in each question.

- Model how to answer the question by writing the following item on the chalkboard and reading it aloud:

    What would you do with something that is *fragile*?
        A. handle it roughly   **C.** sit on it
        B. handle it carefully   **D.** throw it on the floor

- Ask students to choose the word that best fits. Have them explain their choices by explaining which context clue helped them to select the correct definition.

- Read aloud the directions for the second part of the activity: "Read each item below. For each, fill in the blank with the word that fits best." Point out to students that they must choose the word that *best* fits the context and write it on the line.

- Model how to answer this type of question by writing the following sentence on the chalkboard:

    Eddie's _____ (*heroic, assorted, fragrant*) dog bravely rescued a stranger from an icy lake.

- Ask students to choose the word that best completes the sentence. Have them explain their choices by telling how they the used context clues in the sentence to help them find the answer.

- Direct students to reread their answers and check their work after they finish this activity.

- Review the Check Your Mastery activity orally with students.

- Put students in small groups to discuss the questions they did not answer correctly.

- Tally students' correct responses.

Student Self-Assessment

Journal Writing In their journals, ask students to tell which three adjectives they think will be the most useful to know. Ask them to also explain why they chose the adjectives they did.

Answer Key
1. D 2. B 3. C 4. A 5. B
6. Mature 7. easygoing 8. beloved
9. massive 10. distinguished

LESSON 5
More Adjectives to Know

Read Words in Context

Materials Needed
- Student Workbook, p. 34
- Transparency 1
- Idea Web Graphic Organizer, p. 229

Vocabulary Words
annual
billowy
breathtaking
convenient
dense
distant
ebony
genuine
luminous
perilous
sincere
spectacular
spotless
unique
wondrous

Getting Started

Mystery Word of the Week Clue 1

The _____ child stubbornly refused to put on her shoes and go to the picnic.

- See page 14 for routines for using the Mystery Word of the Week Clue. The mystery word of the week is *obstinate*.

Model/Teach

- Direct students to page 34 in their workbooks.

- Ask them to read the Word Learning Tip aloud. Remind students that an adjective is a word that describes a noun or a pronoun and usually comes before the noun it describes or after a linking verb. This location is a clue to meaning. Explain that adjectives answer one of these four questions: *What kind? Which one? How many? How much?*

- Invite a student volunteer to read the Vocabulary Building Strategy. Explain to students that they can often use a new word's *context* (the surrounding words and phrases) to help them determine what it means.

- Read the complete story aloud once, directing students to follow along in their books.

- Explain to the class that you are going to read the story a second time. This time you want them to focus on the words in boldface and try to understand what they mean.

- Ask students to read the first paragraph silently as you read it aloud. Then do the **Think Aloud** on page 49.

48 Chapter 1 • Context Clues

- Place Transparency 1 on the overhead projector. Tell the class that as you continue to read the story, you will pause so they can discuss each adjective in boldface. Explain that you want them to apply the Word Learning Tip and the Vocabulary Building Strategy to determine the meaning of each word. You will call on student volunteers to share their thinking, telling what each word means and how they knew this.

- Continue reading the rest of the story aloud, pausing at each sentence with a word in boldface. As students explain their thinking, record it on the transparency.

- Ask students to identify three words from the word list that are closely related in meaning (*breathtaking, spectacular,* and *wondrous*). Explain that these words are synonyms, or words that mean almost the same thing, although there are shades of difference. The word *breathtaking* means "exciting; thrilling; very beautiful." It suggests that something is so beautiful or exciting that it takes your breath away, such as a breathtaking view. The word *spectacular* means "remarkable" or "dramatic and exciting." Something that is spectacular is really sensational and impressive, such as spectacular fireworks. *Wondrous* means "marvelous." Something that is wondrous fills you with wonder and amazement, such as a tiny carousel made entirely of crystal.

- After students have finished reading the story, have pairs use flashcards to reinforce word meanings.

Independent Activities

Create an Idea Web Distribute copies of the Idea Web Graphic Organizer. Ask students to write the key words *A Family Tradition* in the middle circle. Then they should brainstorm adjectives that describe this topic and write them in the outer circles. Urge them to come up with at least three new adjectives.

- **Make a Word Chain** Arrange students in small groups to write the vocabulary words and their definitions on index cards, reading the words and definitions to each other as they work. Have students staple the cards together to create a chain. Tape this garland across the back of the room.

Think Aloud

Let me tell you how I would determine what *annual* means. First I look at its placement in the sentence. It comes before the noun *vacation*. This tells me that it is probably an adjective describing vacation. I also know that an adjective answers questions like *What kind? Which one? How many? How much?* Now I look for other context clues to tell me more specifically what *annual* means. The second sentence tells me that the family goes on a long or a short trip "every year." I know that *annual* tells me *what kind* of vacation, so I think that *annual* must mean "yearly" or "once a year." I try this meaning in the sentence to see if it makes sense: "Amber and her family take a yearly vacation." That makes sense, so now I am sure that *annual* means "yearly."

Answer Key
See page 210 for definitions.

LESSON 5
More Adjectives to Know

Connect Words and Meanings

Materials Needed
- Student Workbook, pp. 35–36

Think Aloud

I use a two-step method to complete matching activities. My first step is to try to define each word on the left for myself before looking at the choices of definitions on the right. Next, I look for the choice in the right-hand column that is closest to my definition. For example, the first vocabulary word in the left column is *spotless*. Now, I think *spotless* means "having no spots" or "without stains." I look down the right-hand column to find the definition that is closest to mine. I read item H, "perfectly clean," which is close to "having no spots or stains." I skim the rest of the choices and find none that comes closer to the meaning of *spotless*. Now I write 1 for *spotless* next to item H.

Answer Key
1. H 2. E 3. A 4. J 5. G 6. C
7. F 8. B 9. I 10. D 11. annual
12. luminous 13. spectacular (also accept *breathtaking* and *wondrous*)
14. billowy 15. sincere (also accept *genuine*) 16. breathtaking (also accept *spectacular* and *wondrous*)
17. distant 18. genuine

Getting Started

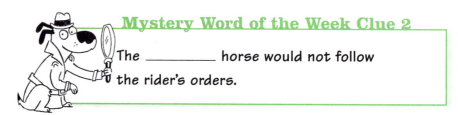

Mystery Word of the Week Clue 2
The _____ horse would not follow the rider's orders.

⭐ **Review and Share** Invite volunteers to share the adjectives they generated for the **Create an Idea Web** activity on page 49 in the teacher's edition. Ask them to use each adjective in a sentence about a family vacation and to write the adjective on the chalkboard.

Model/Teach
- Have students turn to page 35 in their workbooks.
- Before students begin the activity, do the **Think Aloud**
- After modeling how to complete the first item, have students do the rest of the items on their own. Ask them to share their responses.
- Have a student volunteer read the directions for the second activity. Then ask students to complete the second activity and share their answers.

Independent Activities

⭐ **Make a Vacation Brochure** Before students start the activity on their own, ask them to talk about travel brochures. (If possible, bring some in to the class.) What type of information does a travel brochure contain? What would make someone want to travel to a special place? After your conversation, have students complete the activity.

- **Do a Round Robin** Arrange students in small groups. Have students take turns choosing a word, defining it for the group, and explaining how they remember the definition. Ask everyone to repeat the words and definitions. Help students with any words they cannot define.

Use Words in Context

Materials Needed
- Student Workbook, p. 37

Getting Started

Mystery Word of the Week Clue 3

The _____ defendant insisted she was innocent despite all the evidence against her.

⭐ **Review and Share** Invite volunteers to show and talk about the **vacation brochures** they wrote for the activity on page 36. Then create a class bulletin board display of their work.

Model/Teach

- Have students turn to page 37 in their workbooks.
- Before students begin the activity, do the **Think Aloud**.
- After modeling how to complete the first item, have students do the rest of the items on their own. Ask students to share their responses.

English Language Learners

- Partner English language learners with more proficient English speakers to do the Words in Context activity. For instance, the English language learners can read the second sentence. Then their partners can circle the vocabulary word *perilous* and underline the context clue, *very risky*. The first student can then use the clue to define the word and write the answers on the blanks.

Independent Activity

⭐ **Describe a Family Tradition** Have students complete the activity on page 37 of their workbooks. Remind them to use at least three vocabulary words in their description and to circle each one. Ask them to provide context clues for the new adjectives they use.

Think Aloud

Here's how I would go about this activity. First, I would read the directions. They tell me that I have to name two things in each item and write my answers in the blanks. They also tell me that in order to answer I have to be able to determine what each adjective in boldface means. So I read the first item: "Name two **convenient** household items that make people's lives easier." The context clue "makes people's lives easier" helps me to determine that the adjective *convenient* means "easy to use." Then I ask myself what things make life easier around the house. I answer a vacuum cleaner and a microwave, and write these two things in the blanks for 1 and 2.

Answer Key
Sample answers:
1. vacuum cleaner
2. microwave
3. mountain climbing
4. off-trail skiing
5. jungle
6. fog
7. moon
8. Australia
9. fingerprints
10. me
11. a true friendship
12. leather
13. my father
14. my teacher
15. full moon
16. rainbow

Lesson 5 • More Adjectives to Know

LESSON 5 — More Adjectives to Know

Put Words Into Action

Materials Needed
- Student Workbook, p. 38

Think Aloud

There are four things I must do to complete the activity. First, I look at the picture on the left. Second, I read the definition next to the picture. Third, I choose a vocabulary word that matches the picture and the definition. Last, I write a sentence about the picture using the adjective. Now, I study the first picture. I am looking for visual clues to help me choose the vocabulary word. I see a group or people. I read the banner, "Once-a-Year Chung Reunion." Then I read the definition "yearly." Putting all these clues together, I choose *annual* and write it in the blank. Finally, I write a sentence using *annual* that describes the picture: "The Chung family has a good time at their annual reunion."

Answer Key
1. annual **3.** luminous **5.** billowy
7. spotless **9.** ebony
Students' responses for 2, 4, 6, 8, and 10 will vary. See page 219 for sample sentences.

Getting Started

Mystery Word of the Week Clue 4
This word is on the same page in the dictionary as *observe* and *obtain*.

★ **Review and Share** Guide students to talk about the **Describe a Family Tradition** activity they completed on page 37. Which adjectives did they use? How did using adjectives make their writing more precise and interesting?

Model/Teach

- Ask students to turn to page 38 in their workbooks.
- Before students begin the activity, share the **Think Aloud** with the class.
- After modeling how to complete the first item, have students do the rest of the items on their own. Ask them to share their responses.

English Language Learners

- In Spanish, *ge* represents a strong guttural sound with no equivalent in English. The English *h* has a sound that most closely matches this Spanish consonant. As a result, some students may pronounce *genuine* as *henuine* and so misspell it. Arrange students in small groups to practice saying *genuine* and other words they find difficult to pronounce.

Independent Activity

★ **Write an E-Mail** If students have difficulty completing the activity, give them frame sentences such as: All the family felt _____ regret that you could not be at the picnic. (sincere). When it got dark, we had a(n) _____ fireworks display. (spectacular).

52 Chapter 1 • Context Clues

Review and Extend

Materials Needed
- Student Workbook, p. 39

Getting Started

Mystery Word of the Week Clue 5

A synonym for this word is *stubborn*.

Model/Teach

- Direct students to turn to page 39 of their workbooks and read the boxed material.

- You may wish to point out that *unique* cannot be used for comparison because it means "one of a kind." The word *ebony* is not used to compare either, since it means "made of a heavy dark wood," or "dark or very black in color like ebony wood."

- Before students begin the activity, do the **Think Aloud**.

- After modeling how to complete the first item, have students do the rest of the items on their own. Ask students to share their thinking and their responses.

Think Aloud

I begin this task by reading the directions. They tell me to choose the correct form of the adjective in parentheses and use the context of each sentence to determine how many things are being compared. I read the first item: "This year's party decorations are ____ (*more spectacular/most spectacular*) than last year's." Following the directions, I look to see if I am comparing two or more things. Since I am comparing two things—this year's party decorations and last year's party decorations—I write *more spectacular* in the blank because *more* is used to compare two.

English Language Learners

- Making comparisons is difficult for many English language learners. For extra practice, ask students to fill in the following frame sentences, using each adjective in the lesson in its correct form. (They should not use *unique* or *ebony*.)

This _____ is more _____ than that one.

This _____ is the most _____ of all three.

Independent Activity

Write a Comparison Have students complete the diary entry activity. Ask them to read their entries in small groups, pointing out which forms of the adjectives they used and why.

Answer Key
Mystery Word of the Week: obstinate
Accept other words that fit the context, too.

1. more spectacular
2. most convenient
3. more sincere
4. most luminous
5. denser
6. more wondrous

Lesson 5 • More Adjectives to Know

LESSON 5
More Adjectives to Know

Check Your Mastery

Materials Needed
- Student Workbook, p. 40

Student Self-Assessment

Journal Writing In their journals, ask students to write about which activities in this lesson helped them the most and why.

Give the Test
- Ask students to open their workbooks to page 40.
- Explain to the class that the Check Your Mastery activity has two parts.
- Read aloud the directions for the first five questions: "Circle the letter of the item that best completes each sentence below." Tell students that there are three choices and their task is to pick the one that fits the meaning of the word.
- Model how to answer this type of question by writing the following item on the chalkboard and reading it aloud:

  A **breathtaking** sight would make you feel—
  A. filled with wonder and amazement
  B. unhappy and sad
  C. terrified that something bad will happen

- Ask students to tell which item best completes the sentence and to explain that answer.
- Then read aloud the directions for items 6–10: "On the lines below, write the vocabulary word that best completes each sentence." Tell students it is their task to use context clues in the sentence to find the best vocabulary word.
- Model how to answer this type of question by writing the following sentence on the chalkboard:

  A _____ (spotless, luminous, genuine) light is one that shines brightly.

- Ask students to choose the vocabulary word that best completes the sentence. Guide them to explain their choice by pointing out that the phrase "shines brightly" is a context clue that suggests the adjective *luminous*.
- After students finish all the items, they should reread them and check their answers.
- Have students talk with a partner about the items they got wrong and why they might have made the wrong choices.
- Tally students' correct responses.

Answer Key
1. A 2. B 3. A 4. C 5. B
6. unique 7. spotless 8. perilous
9. genuine 10. sincere

LESSON 6

Adverbs to Know

Read Words in Context

Getting Started

Mystery Word of the Week Clue 1

Knights of King Arthur's Round Table fought _____ to defend honor, justice, and truth.

- See page 14 for routines for using the Mystery Word of the Week Clue. The mystery word of the week is *chivalrously*.

Model/Teach

- Have students turn to page 41 in their workbooks.
- Ask students to look at the Word Learning Tip. Explain that an adverb tells more about a verb, an adjective, or an adverb. Direct them to look at the vocabulary list and circle all the adverbs that end in *-ly*.
- Ask a student volunteer to read aloud the Vocabulary Building Strategy. Remind students that as they read, they can use the words they know in a sentence to help them determine the meanings of any adverbs they have never seen before.
- Explain that you are going to read a passage about King Arthur. Create a concept web on the chalkboard. Ask students what they know about King Arthur. Write their ideas in the concept web.
- Read the complete story aloud once, having students follow along in their books.
- Tell students that you are going to read the story again, this time paying particular attention to the words in boldface.
- Before you read the story the second time, do the **Think Aloud** on page 56.
- Place Transparency 1 on the overhead projector. Tell students that as you continue to read the story, you will stop to talk about the meaning of each boldface word. You want them to think about the Word Learning Tip and the Vocabulary Building Strategy. Ask students to let you know the thinking they do to determine what each word means.

Materials Needed
- Student Workbook, p. 41
- Transparency 1

Vocabulary Words
clearly
earlier
eventually
everywhere
firmly
frequently
immediately
largely
mostly
naturally
outside
practically
precisely
rapidly
widely

LESSON 6 Adverbs to Know

Think Aloud

I want to tell you what I think when I come to a word that I don't know so that you can do something like it. Read along silently in your workbook as I read aloud. "When you imagine knights in shining armor, **immediately**, one name springs to mind—King Arthur." Here's what I would think about if I didn't know the word *immediately*. I think the word may be an adverb because it has an *-ly* ending. As I read, I'm thinking about what this word is telling me. It's telling me *when* the name springs to mind, so now I know it must be an adverb. I also see another clue in the sentence. The verb *springs* suggests that something happens very quickly. Now, I add these two ideas together. I think, "When would something *spring* to mind?" I think that something would *spring* to mind at once. So *immediately* must mean "at once."

- Continue reading the rest of the story aloud, pausing at each sentence with a boldface word. Ask student volunteers to explain how they determine the meaning of each word. Write their responses on the transparency.
- Ask students to indicate the two words that are synonyms and mean almost the same thing. Explain that both *largely* and *mostly* indicate "almost all." For example, you could say "The audience was largely made up of children," or "The audience was mostly may up of children." *Practically* is also close in meaning. It means "very nearly but not quite" as in "We are practically finished" as well as "in a way that is practical."
- After students have finished the story, have them work with a partner. They can use flashcards to reinforce meaning.

English Language Learners
- Explain that words are made up of syllables. Some words, such as *be*, *my*, and *for*, contain only one syllable. Other words, such as *swiftly*, *afterwards*, and *courageously* contain more than one syllable. Say each vocabulary word aloud and have students repeat it after you. After you say each word, ask students to tell you how many syllables it has. Then say the word again as students clap each time they hear a syllable.

Independent Activity
- **Find New Words** Allow students to work in small groups to find five new adverbs that they particularly like in books or magazines. In their personal word journal, they should list each word, tell what they think it means, and write the sentence in which they found the word. They should also explain how they knew each word was an adverb.

Answer Key
See page 210–211 for definitions.

Connect Words and Meanings

Getting Started

Mystery Word of the Week Clue 2
In King Arthur's court, a knight was behaving _____ when he was polite and courteous to women and children.

★ **Review and Share** Give students the opportunity to share the new adverbs they found for the activity on page 56 in the teacher's edition. Ask them to tell why they particularly liked each word. Build a word wall. Include the new adverbs students found as well as the vocabulary words.

Model/Teach

- Have students turn to page 42 in their workbooks.
- Before students begin the crossword puzzle, do the `Think Aloud`.
- Instruct students to complete both activities on their own.

Independent Activities

★ **Create a Favorite Story Poster** Before students start this activity, ask student volunteers to name stories they particularly like and why they like these tales. Tell students who have the same favorite story to work together to create a poster.

- **Compare Characters' Actions** Begin a discussion about characters in books or movies who are arch rivals or enemies. Have students brainstorm a list of such characters. Then tell students to create a two-column chart in their personal word journal, writing the name of one character at the top of one column and the rival or enemy at the top of the other column. Ask them to list adverbs in each column that tell how that character acts.

Materials Needed
- Student Workbook, pp. 42–43

Think Aloud

I want to show you the thinking that I do to complete a crossword puzzle. I know that I must use the clues to find which vocabulary word goes in each set of boxes. The number of boxes tells me how long the word is. I'm going to start by looking at the first clue under Across: *not moving, bending, or giving way easily under pressure; solidly.* I think I'm looking for a word that tells *how* something is done. The clue has the number 4 in front of it, so I find the set of boxes that begins with the box labeled 4. There are six boxes in this set. This tells me that the word I am looking for has six letters. *Mostly, firmly,* and *widely* have six letters, so these are my choices. *Mostly* tells me about how *much* was done, so this isn't my answer. *Firmly* seems to fit; it would explain how something was done, but let me try the next word just to be sure. *Widely* tells me to what extent—like something is widely known—so that's not my answer. I write *firmly* in the boxes and move on to my next clue.

Answer Key
Across 4. firmly **7.** eventually
10. naturally **11.** largely
13. precisely **14.** rapidly

Down 1. frequently **2.** mostly
3. widely **5.** practically **6.** earlier
8. clearly **9.** outside **12.** everywhere
15. immediately

1. frequently **2.** practically (or mostly or largely) **3.** earlier **4.** firmly
5. immediately **6.** rapidly **7.** eventually
8. naturally **9.** clearly **10.** precisely

Lesson 6 • Adverbs to Know

LESSON 6 Adverbs to Know

Use Words in Context

Getting Started

Mystery Word of the Week Clue 3

For a knight to receive the high praise of fighting _____, he had to demonstrate fairness, courage, nobility, and courtesy on the battlefield.

⭐ **Review and Share** Give students the opportunity to tell about their **favorite stories** and about the **posters** they created for the activity on page 43. Display the posters around the room.

Model/Teach

- Have students turn to page 44 in their workbooks.
- Before students start the activity, do the **Think Aloud**.
- After you have modeled using trial and error, have students complete the rest of the activity on their own. Ask students to share their responses and explain their thinking.

English Language Learners

- Remind students that an adverb can modify or tell more about a verb, an adjective, or another adverb. English language learners may need special practice in identifying which word the adverb modifies. Read the first three sentences in the activity aloud with students. Pause after each item. Ask students to tell you which word the missing adverb will tell more about (1. asked, 2. true, 3. ruled).

Independent Activity

⭐ **Create a Banner** If it is available, allow students to use pieces of construction paper to create their banners. As an alternative, some software programs have banner-making tools you might use. If neither of these is available, have students work with plain paper.

Materials Needed
- Student Workbook, p. 44

Think Aloud

I want to show you the thinking that I do to choose a word to fit in the blank. Read along silently in your workbook as I read aloud the first item: "One question is asked ____ (immediately, frequently, precisely) or over and over: How much of the story of Arthur is true and how much is imaginary?" I see the clue "over and over," so I think that the missing word is going to tell me *how often* this question is asked. Now I look at my choices: *immediately*, *frequently*, and *precisely*, and try to fit them in the blank. The word *immediately* tells me when, not how often, so I can rule that word out. My next choice is *frequently*. It's telling me that the question is asked very often. The third choice is *precisely*. This choice doesn't make sense, since precisely is telling me how, not how often. So I know *frequently* is correct and I write it on the line.

Answer Key
1. frequently 2. clearly 3. firmly
4. eventually 5. everywhere
6. outside 7. widely 8. precisely
9. largely 10. rapidly

Put Words Into Action

Materials Needed
- Student Workbook, p. 45

Getting Started

Mystery Word of the Week Clue 4

Only the most gallant, honorable, and respectful defenders of women and the poor could claim accolades for fighting and behaving _____.

⭐ **Review and Share** Ask students to talk about the **banners** they created for the activity on page 44. Invite them to explain why they chose the colors, motto, and adverbs they did. Display the banners around the classroom.

Model/Teach
- Have students turn to page 45 in their workbooks.
- Use the **Think Aloud** to model how to sort the words.
- After you have modeled sorting the words, ask students to sort the rest of the words on their own and then share their responses.

Independent Activities

⭐ **Sort New Words** Allow students to work with a partner to complete this activity. Suggest that a good place to search for words is in their favorite books. However, they can also recall adverbs that they learned from listening to their friends or watching television or movies.

- **Be a Director** Tell students to imagine that they are directing a movie of their favorite story. Their job is to work with their lead actor. Challenge students to come up with five adverbs they would use to tell the actor how to speak the lines.

Think Aloud

I want to model for you the type of thinking I do to sort my words. My first adverb is *clearly*. First I try to use this word in a sentence. "I can see *clearly* that I'm going to need a new car soon." Now I run though my questions. Is this word telling me *where* I can see that I'm going to need a new car? No. Is this word telling me *when* I can see that I'm going to need a new car? No. Is it telling me *how* I can see this? Yes. *Clearly* does tell me *how* I can see that I'm going to need a new car. Now I look to see if there is a clue on the scroll labeled How that *clearly* fits. Here it is: "not in a hidden way but ____," so I write *clearly* in the blank.

Answer Key
Where?
1. everywhere 2. outside
When?
3. earlier 4. eventually
5. immediately
How?
6. firmly 7. naturally 8. rapidly
9. clearly 10. precisely
How often? or How long?
11. frequently
How much? or To what extent?
12. mostly 13. largely
14. practically 15. widely

LESSON 6: Adverbs to Know

Review and Extend

Materials Needed
- Student Workbook, p. 46

Think Aloud

I know that in this activity I'm going to form an adverb from an adjective. Read the first item with me: "The black knight is riding from the castle and coming straight at you. Luckily, your horse is **rapid**. How should you move to get out of his way?" I see the adjective *rapid* in boldface. I know I can add *-ly* to *rapid* to form the adverb *rapidly*. Does this word answer the question? Yes, if the black knight was coming at me, I would certainly get out of his way *rapidly*.

Answer Key
Mystery Word of the Week:
chivalrously
Accept other words that fit the context, too.

1. rapidly 2. firmly 3. clearly
4. frequently 5. precisely

Getting Started

Mystery Word of the Week Clue 5

Knights were rewarded for honoring the Code of Chivalry, or behaving _____.

⭐ **Review and Share** Ask students to share the words they added to the **sorting charts** on page 45. Invite them to tell where they found each word and why they chose it. Then add these words to the word wall.

Model/Teach

- Have students turn to page 46 in their workbooks and read the boxed information.
- After you have discussed how to form adverbs from adjectives, use the **Think Aloud** to model how to complete the activity.
- After you have modeled answering a question, have students complete the activity on their own and then share their responses.

Independent Activities

⭐ **Write a Story** You might have students brainstorm ideas for their story before they start. Draw the concept web shown below on the chalkboard. Suggest that students copy it in their journals and fill it in to get ideas. Then they should write their stories.

What Character Is Like — Character — What Character Does

- **Increase Your Vocabulary** Challenge students to find the meaning of each of the following adverbs: *completely, automatically, generously, personally, sincerely*. Tell them to first think of the meaning of the adjective. Then add the words "in a way that is." For example, *generous* would mean "in a way that is unselfish."

Check Your Mastery

Materials Needed
- Student Workbook, p. 47

Give the Test

- Have students open their workbooks to page 47.
- Ask a volunteer to read the directions aloud.
- Explain to students that, from the three words that appear after each blank, they should choose the one that best fits the context and write it on the line.
- Model how to complete the questions by writing the following on the chalkboard:

    Hector has been in jousts in all parts of the country.
    He has traveled _____ (*everywhere, mostly, precisely*).

- Ask students to choose the word that best fits in the blank. Point out that the words *in all parts of the country* are a good clue that they should use the adverb *everywhere*.
- Ask whether students have any questions. Then have them complete the sentences.
- Remind students that after they finish the test, they should read it over to make sure the words they chose fit the context.
- Tally students' correct responses and share their responses.

Student Self-Assessment

Journal Writing Have students write in their personal word journals, telling what they learned about adverbs. How are adverbs different from adjectives?

Answer Key
1. frequently 2. everywhere
3. earlier 4. clearly 5. Naturally
6. mostly 7. widely 8. practically
9. precisely 10. immediately

Lesson 6 • Adverbs to Know

LESSON 7
Multiple-Meaning Words to Know

Read Words in Context

Materials Needed
- Student Workbook, p. 48
- Transparency 1

Vocabulary Words
- bridge
- bureau
- cabinet
- contract
- harbor
- mold
- peer
- pelt
- range
- refrain
- rest
- rung
- steer
- temper
- vent

Getting Started

Mystery Word of the Week Clue 1

In the morning, Carlos always has a few slices of crisp, hot _____ with butter.

- See page 14 for routines for using the Mystery Word of the Week Clue. The mystery word of the week is *toast*.

Model/Teach

- Have students turn to page 48 in their workbooks.

- Direct students to the Word Learning Tip. Explain that some words have more than one meaning, and the meanings may be very different. Identifying a multiple-meaning word's part of speech can help in determining what the word means in a particular sentence. For example, the simple word *jar* can be a noun that means "a container," or it can be a verb that means "to disturb or bother." Ask students to provide other examples of multiple-meaning words.

- Ask a volunteer to read the Vocabulary Building Strategy to the class. Explain that with a multiple-meaning word, students must make use of the word's context, or they will not be able to determine which meaning the writer intended. Then they must choose the meaning that fits the context. Be sure students understand that a word's *context* is the words and sentences that surround it.

- Read the complete story aloud once, directing students to follow along in their books.

- Tell the class that you are going to read the story a second time. This time you want them to think about the words in boldface and use context clues to decide which meaning is intended.

- Ask students to read the first paragraph silently as you read it aloud. Do the **Think Aloud** on page 63.

62 Chapter 1 • Context Clues

- Place Transparency 1 on the overhead projector. Then explain to students that, as you continue to read the story, you will pause so that they can talk about each boldface word. You want them to use the Word Learning Tip and the Vocabulary Building Strategy to determine the meaning of each word and share their thinking with you.

- Continue reading the rest of the story aloud, pausing at each boldface word. Ask students to explain how they determined the meaning of each word. Make certain they describe their thinking about parts of speech and context clues. Write their responses on the transparency.

- Explain to students that *cabinet* and *bureau* are close in meaning. Read aloud the sentences from the story containing these words. Explain that a cabinet is a piece of furniture with shelves and drawers. A bureau is a piece of furniture with drawers, too, but it is used specifically for storing clothes.

- After students have finished reading the story, have pairs use flashcards to reinforce word meanings.

Independent Activities

⭐ **Multiple Meaning Word Challenge** Ask students to change the three vocabulary words in the story that were used as verbs into nouns (*pelts, peer, vents*) or to select three nouns and change them into verbs. Have them write three sentences or more in which these vocabulary words mean something very different from what they did in the story. Suggest they use a dictionary to find each word's different meanings.

- **Understand Different Pronunciations** Write the word *contract* on the chalkboard. Ask a student volunteer to provide a sentence using *contract* as a noun. Say the word again, this time questioning which syllable is stressed (the first one). Explain that *contract* has a very different meaning when used as a verb. The verb *contract* means "to get." Say the following sentence: *The nurse wore a mask so that he would not contract the patient's disease.* Ask students what syllable is stressed when *contract* is a verb (the second one). Then have students search through magazines and newspapers to try to find other words that are pronounced differently as nouns and verbs.

Think Aloud

Let me share how I would determine what meaning the word *contracts* has in the first sentence in the passage. I know that *nouns* are words that name people, places, and things. The word *contracts* here seems to be naming some things Carlos's parents have gotten. I remember also that some nouns are made plural by adding –s to the end of the noun. Now that I know *contracts* is a plural noun, I look for clues in the surrounding sentences that will help me understand its meaning. The next sentence says: "These written agreements give them the right to graze their steer on public land." The phrase *written agreements* is the clue to the meaning of *contracts* that I am looking for. It tells me that in this context, *contracts* means the same thing as "written agreements."

Answer Key
See page 211 for definitions.

LESSON 7: Multiple-Meaning Words to Know

Connect Words and Meanings

Materials Needed
- Student Workbook, pp. 49–50

Think Aloud

I want to share with you my thinking as I do this activity. Let's do the first item together. I see that *range* has two very different meanings, and that both of these meanings are for a noun. *Range* can be an area of open land used for a special purpose, or it can be a cooking stove. Now I read the sentence: "Carmella put the kettle on top of the range." I'm supposed to determine which meaning of *range* fits in this context. I think about what Carmella wants to do. She probably wants to boil some water. Well, she wouldn't put a kettle on some open land; that wouldn't make the water boil. She would put it on top of a stove. So that second meaning of *range* fits this context. I write "B" for this meaning in the blank.

Answer Key
1. B 2. B 3. B 4. A 5. A 6. B
7. A 8. A 9. A 10. B 11. B 12. B
13. A 14. A 15. B

Getting Started

Mystery Word of the Week Clue 2

On the range, Carlos can _____ his bread by placing it over the campfire.

⭐ **Review and Share** Ask volunteers to share the **sentences** they created for the activity on page 63 in the teacher's edition. Post the sentences on the bulletin board and add the words to the word wall.

Model/Teach
- Have students turn to page 49 in their workbooks.
- Before students begin the activity, do the **Think Aloud**.
- After you have modeled completing the first item, have students do the rest on their own. Encourage students to share their responses and the thinking behind them.

English Language Learners
- Write the word *bureau* on the chalkboard. Underline the letters *eau* and say *oh*. Explain that in this word, these letters work together to form the sound of long *o*. Then write the word *beautiful* on the chalkboard and underline the letters *eau*. Explain that in this word, these letters work together to form the sound *yoo* that you hear in *few*.

Independent Activity

⭐ **Make a Collage** Guide students to use a dictionary to find as many meanings as they can for the words they are illustrating. One student in each group can look up the word while others create or find pictures to convey its meaning. Still others can write labels for the collage.

64 Chapter 1 • Context Clues

Use Words in Context

Materials Needed
- Student Workbook, p. 51

Getting Started

Mystery Word of the Week Clue 3

At weddings, the best man usually raises his glass to _____ the bride and groom.

- **Review and Share** Invite volunteers to share the **collages** they created for the activity on page 50. Ask others to identify the word being illustrated. Display the collages around the classroom.

Model/Teach

- Have students turn to page 51 of their workbooks.
- Before students start the activity, do the **Think Aloud**.
- After you have modeled how to complete the first item, have students do the other items on their own. Invite them to share their responses and the thinking behind them.

Independent Activities

- **Write a Story** Have students complete the bad-day story activity in their journals. If they have trouble finding ideas, ask them to recall the plots of some comic Western movies they have seen. Encourage them to use exaggeration to make the cowboy's bad day seem really bad.
- **Use Context Clues** Arrange students in pairs. Ask one student to write a sentence using one of the vocabulary words, making sure that the context gives clues to the word's meaning. Have the other student identify the vocabulary word and give its meaning in that sentence. The second student can then write a sentence using the same word but with a different meaning.

Think Aloud

The directions tell me that studying the context is the key to filling in the correct vocabulary word in each blank. In that case, I will read the first sentence to look for clues that will help me find the word that fits in the first blank: "I've been riding the _____ for twenty-five years because I like wide open spaces." The phrase "wide open spaces" is the clue I am looking for. It matches one of the meanings of a word on my vocabulary list: *range*. To make sure *range* fits in the context, I read the sentence with it in the blank: "I've been riding the *range* for twenty-five years because I like wide, open spaces." *Range* makes sense in the sentence, so I will write it in the blank marked number 1.

Answer Key

1. range 2. refrain 3. rest
4. temper 5. bureau 6. cabinet
7. peer 8. pelt 9. steer 10. harbor

LESSON 7 — Multiple-Meaning Words to Know

Materials Needed
- Student Workbook, p. 52
- Word Map Graphic Organizer, p. 232

Think Aloud

Here's how I would fill in the word map for *refrain*. I have learned that *refrain* can mean "repeated words," so I write that in the blank for the first meaning. Since repeated words are a thing, I know that *refrain* used in this way is a noun. I write *noun* in the first blank under "Part of Speech." I know that *refrain* can also mean "leave off or stop." I write that definition in the second blank under "Meaning." This meaning of *refrain* expresses an action, so I'll write *verb* in the second blank under "Part of Speech." I can also consult the glossary or a dictionary if I'm unsure of a meaning or part of speech. Now, I'll make up sentences to write in the blanks at the bottom of the map: Meaning #1: The song's *refrain* is repeated at the end of every stanza. Meaning #2: We *refrain* from watching TV on school nights.

Answer Key
1. a structure over a river
2. a card game 3. noun
4. noun 7. to strike or beat
8. animal skin 9. verb 10. noun
Students' responses to 5, 6, 11, and 12 will vary. See page 219 for sample sentences.

Put Words Into Action

Getting Started

Mystery Word of the Week Clue 4
On New Year's Eve, many people drink a _____ to the New Year.

★ **Review and Share** Invite volunteers to read the **bad-day stories** they wrote for the activity on page 51. Ask class members to identify the multiple-meaning words in the stories and use the context to determine their meanings.

Model/Teach
- Have students turn to page 52 in their workbooks.
- Before students begin the activity, do the **Think Aloud** to model completing a word map for the word *refrain*. (This is just an example and not one of the words in the student activity, since there are only two word maps for students to fill out.)
- After you have modeled how to complete the activity, have students do the word maps on their own. Invite them to share their responses and the thinking behind them.

English Language Learners
- Some vocabulary words are often combined with prepositions. For example, *refrain from*, *peer into*, *steer away from*, *range over*, and many others. Partner English language learners with more English-proficient students for practice using these combinations in sentences.

Independent Activities

★ **Make More Maps** Distribute copies of the Word Map Graphic Organizer. Arrange students in groups of five so that each student can write about one word. Before students start, find out which words each group has chosen to write about. If all the words are not being used, ask for volunteers to focus on the unused words.

Chapter 1 • Context Clues

Review and Extend

Materials Needed
- Student Workbook, p. 53
- 5 Ws and H Chart Graphic Organizer, p. 230

Getting Started

Mystery Word of the Week Clue 5

The mystery word can be used as a noun or a verb.

★ **Review and Share** Have volunteers share the **word maps** they created for the activity on page 52. Try to display at least one map for every vocabulary word.

Model/Teach

- Direct students to turn to page 53 of their workbooks and read the boxed information.

- Answer any questions students have about the boxed information before they start the activity. Then do the **Think Aloud**.

- After you have modeled how to complete the first item, have students do the other items on their own. Ask them to share their responses and the thinking behind them.

English Language Learners

- Arrange students in small groups to write one vocabulary word on an index card and its multiple definitions on other index cards. Students can tape the words at the top of wire coat hangers and the definitions below so that they dangle. Display the mobiles around the room to help students remember the words and their definitions.

Independent Activity

★ **Write Interview Questions** Distribute copies of the 5 Ws and H Chart Graphic Organizer. Suggest that students use these questions to write their own interview questions. You may want to have partners work together. One student can ask the questions while the other answers them, then they can switch roles.

Think Aloud

To start this activity, first I read the directions and the first item: "The campers **got** poison ivy when they walked unprotected in the woods. Philip _____ it whenever he forgot to wear his gloves." Next, I look at the context clue "got" in boldface and use it to choose a verb from the vocabulary list. I know that *contract* as a verb means "get." But before I write *contract* in the blank, I notice that *got* is in the past tense. I will have to add an *-ed* to the end of *contract*. Now, I write *contracted* in the blank and read the whole item: "The campers got poison ivy when they walked unprotected in the woods. Philip contracted it whenever he forgot to wear his gloves." Yes, that makes sense. *Contracted* is the correct choice.

Answer Key

Mystery Word of the Week:
toast
Accept other words that fit the context, too.

1. contracted 2. molded
3. pelted 4. contracts
5. steered

LESSON 7 Multiple-Meaning Words to Know

Check Your Mastery

Materials Needed
- Student Workbook, p. 54

Student Self-Assessment

Journal Writing In their journals, have students explain why multiple-meaning words are tricky to use and what strategies they have learned for determining the meanings of these kinds of words in the future.

Give the Test
- Have students open their workbooks to page 54.
- Explain to students that the Check Your Mastery activity has two parts.
- Read aloud the directions for the first part: "Choose the vocabulary word that best fits the context and write it in the blank. Use the boldface context clue to help you make the correct choice."
- Model how to answer the first type of question by writing this sample item on the chalkboard and reading it aloud:

   Sleet and hail **beat** down on the cars. The frozen hailstones _____ (*pelt, mold, bridge*) the windshields.

- Ask students to choose the word that best fits in the blank. Have them explain their choice of *pelt* by using the context clue *beat*.
- Read aloud the directions for the second activity: "Circle the word that correctly fits in the blank for each analogy. Studying the relationship between the first pair of words will help you make the correct choice for the second pair."
- Model how to answer the second type of question by writing this sample item on the chalkboard and reading it aloud:

   Rise is to **fall** as **work** is to _____.

- Ask students to choose the word that best fits in the blank. Have them explain how understanding the relationship of the first pair of words (they are opposites) helped them choose *rest* as the correct word to complete the second part of the analogy.
- Direct students to reread their answers and check their work.
- Review the Check Your Mastery activity orally with the students.
- Have students talk with a partner about the questions they got wrong.
- Tally students' correct responses.

Answer Key
1. steer 2. temper 3. vent
4. contract 5. mold 6. rung
7. cabinet 8. peer 9. pelt
10. range

Read Words in Context

LESSON 8 — Synonyms to Know

Getting Started

Mystery Word of the Week Clue 1
It would not be wise to _____ or eliminate the laws that protect the prairie dogs.

- See page 14 for routines for using the Mystery Word of the Week Clue. The mystery word of the week is *abolish*.

Model/Teach

- Direct students to turn to page 55 in their workbooks.
- Ask students to read the Word Learning Tip aloud. Point out that a *synonym* is a word that means the same or nearly the same as another word. Ask students to provide synonyms for words in their everyday vocabulary such as *happy, angry, wonderful*.
- Invite a student to read the Vocabulary Building Strategy aloud. Explain to students that they can often use context clues to help them determine what a new word means.
- Read the complete story aloud once, directing students to follow along in their books.
- Tell the class that you are going to read the story again. This time you want them to think about the words in boldface and try to determine what they mean by using context clues.
- Ask students to read the first paragraph silently as you read it aloud. Then do the **Think Aloud** on page 70.
- Tell the class that as they continue to read the story, you will pause so they can discuss each boldface word. Encourage them to think about the Word Learning Tip to help understand the meaning of each word. Also, ask them to think about the Vocabulary Building Strategy. Invite them to share their thinking with you and to tell you what the word means and how they knew this.

Materials Needed
- Student Workbook, p. 55
- Transparency 1

Vocabulary Words
approval
bustle
civil
commotion
consent
corridor
drenched
fumble
glory
gnarled
gravity
knotty
hallway
honor
mishandle
pesky
polite
seriousness
soaked
troublesome

LESSON 8: Synonyms to Know

Think Aloud

Here's what I would think about if I didn't know the meaning of the word *gravity*. First I think about the situation. One prairie dog has given a warning call. There could be badgers around. I see the word *danger*. This is all very serious. In fact, as I read the sentence, I see that the word *seriousness* follows *gravity*. This is a clue that *gravity* and *seriousness* are synonyms. They both mean that something is really important. I see another context clue. When I look at the word *gravity*, I see the smaller word *grave*. This supports my ideas. If something is *grave*, it shouldn't be taken lightly.

- Place Transparency 1 on the overhead projector. Tell students that you are going to jot down the words that show their thinking as they determine the meaning of each boldface word.

- Continue reading the rest of the story aloud, pausing at each sentence with a boldface word. Ask volunteers to explain how they determined the meaning of each word. Make certain they describe the facts about context clues that they used to understand each word's meaning. Write their responses on the transparency.

- Pair students. Have them use flashcards to reinforce meanings.

Independent Activities

- **Play Synonym Match** Ask students to turn to page 55 and pair the twenty vocabulary words into ten sets of synonyms without looking at any words in the story. They can use a dictionary or the glossary. Challenge them to find the two words in the synonym list that are also multiple-meaning words (*bustle*, *gravity*), and have them write sentences that use the multiple meanings of these words.

- **Play the Concentration Game** Have pairs of students write each vocabulary word in a sentence on a separate index card. Then ask them to arrange the twenty cards on a table, blank side up, and take turns turning over two cards at a time. If a match of two synonyms is made, the student takes the cards.

Answer Key
See page 211 for definitions.

Connect Words and Meanings

Getting Started

Mystery Word of the Week Clue 2

The town council voted to _____, or do away with, the tax on clothing.

★ **Review and Share** Have pairs compare the ten sets of **synonyms** they created for the activity on page 70 of the teacher's edition. Invite volunteers to share their sentences. Ask students to read aloud their sentences with the words *bustle* and *gravity*.

Model/Teach

- Have students turn to page 56 in their workbooks.
- Before students begin the activity, do the **Think Aloud**.
- After you have modeled using a clue to find a word, have students complete the rest of the crossword puzzle on their own.
- Then ask them to complete the activity on page 57 independently.

English Language Learners

- Write *drenched* and *soaked* on the chalkboard. Invite English language learners to draw pictures that show the words *drenched* and *soaked*. Then ask them to write a sentence in which they use either *drenched* or *soaked* to tell about their pictures. Give students an opportunity to discuss the pictures and read their sentences in small groups.

Independent Activity

★ **Write a Journal Entry** Before students start the activity, conduct a class discussion about explorers who traveled west. Explain that the explorers saw animals and vast stretches of prairie land they had never seen before. Help students to imagine the excitement and curiosity the explorers must have felt when they saw their first prairie dog colony. Then ask them to write their journal entries.

Materials Needed
- Student Workbook, pp. 56–57

Think Aloud

I want to share with you my thinking as I try to complete this crossword puzzle. I know that there are clues for the words that fit in the boxes across and there are clues for the words that fit in the boxes that go down. Let's look at the first clue under Across. The clue says: "acceptance of a plan or idea; a synonym for *consent*." I know that if I accept a plan or idea, I give it my *approval* or *consent*. *Approval* and *consent* mean the same thing. Now let's see if this word fits in the boxes. I find the box with the number 4 in front of it, and I see that the word I am looking for has eight letters. I know this because there are eight boxes. *Approval* has eight letters, so now I know that this is the word I want.

Answer Key
Across 4. approval 8. troublesome 10. soaked 11. honor 12. glory 15. gnarled 16. mishandle 18. polite 19. drenched
Down 1. civil 2. fumble 3. corridor 5. commotion 6. pesky 7. gravity 9. bustle 10. seriousness 13. hallway 14. knotty 17. consent

The order of words below may vary.
1. approval, consent 2. pesky, troublesome 3. civil, polite 4. drenched, soaked 5. gravity, seriousness 6. gnarled, knotty 7. bustle, commotion 8. glory, honor 9. corridor, hallway 10. fumble, mishandle

Lesson 8 • Synonyms to Know

LESSON 8
Synonyms to Know

Use Words in Context

Materials Needed
- Student Workbook, p. 58
- Umbrella Chart Graphic Organizer, p. 228

Getting Started

Mystery Word of the Week Clue 3

Do you support the amendment, or would you like to _____ it?

⭐ **Review and Share** Invite volunteers to read from their **journal entries** from the activity on page 57. If additional synonyms are used in the entries, add them to the word wall.

Model/Teach
- Have students turn to page 58 of their workbooks.
- Use the **Think Aloud**.
- After you have modeled how to complete the activity, have students complete the rest of the items on their own and share their responses.

Independent Activities

⭐ **Debate Your Position** Divide the class into pairs. Before students start the activity, distribute copies of the Umbrella Chart Graphic Organizer. Suggest that they use this chart to list the reasons that they come up with. They should write their position at the base of the umbrella and their reasons along the spokes.

- **Play Five Fingers** Explain to students that English is rich in synonyms. Sketch a hand with five fingers on the chalkboard. Write the word *small* in the center. Challenge students to come up with a synonym for *small* to write on each finger. Continue this activity with the words *large*, *change*, *pleasant*, and *look*.

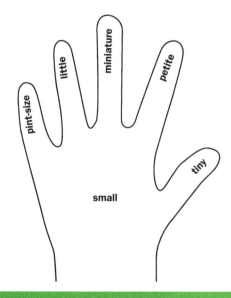

Think Aloud

To answer the first question, I must determine which pair of vocabulary words mean the same as *twisted* and *bumpy*. I picture these words in my mind, and look at the vocabulary words to see which words match. I notice *gnarled* and *knotty*. I know that *gnarled* means "twisted." For example, someone's hands might be gnarled with age. *Knotty* means "something that has a lot of knots." If something is *knotty*, it has a lot of bumps. I decide to use *gnarled* and *knotty*. Now I have to think about something in nature that is *gnarled* and *knotty*. I remember an old oak tree in the park, so I write: "There's an old oak tree in the park that is *gnarled* and *knotty*."

Answer Key
Students' responses will vary. See page 219 for sample sentences.

Put Words Into Action

Materials Needed
- Student Workbook, p. 59

Getting Started

Mystery Word of the Week Clue 4
There is a plan not to _____ or remove restrictions until the populations of the prairie dogs have increased.

⭐ **Review and Share** Invite two students to **debate**, with one student taking the role of the farmers or the other of the wildlife scientists. After the debate, ask the class to evaluate the effectiveness of using synonyms to make a point.

Model/Teach
- Have students turn to page 59 in their workbooks.
- Before students begin the activity, share the **Think Aloud** with the class.
- After you have modeled how to complete the activity, ask students to finish it on their own. You might want to challenge students to replace the word they cross out with another synonym.

English Language Learners
- In Spanish, the *b* and *v* are pronounced with the same sound, like the letter *b* in *balloon*. As a result, some students may have difficulty saying words with the letter *v*, such as *civil, approval, gravity*. Partner those in early speech emergence with more fluent learners to practice pronouncing and spelling these words.

Independent Activity
⭐ **Interview a Wildlife Scientist** Help students create interesting interview questions to ask each other. Encourage them to think about questions using synonyms, such as: Why do some people think prairie dogs are *pesky*? Why don't you think they are *troublesome*? Why do you enjoy observing the *bustle* of the prairie dog colonies?

Think Aloud
Let's look at the words in the first star together. I see the words *honor* and *glory* and I know that they are synonyms. They both deal with the idea of the respect you get when you do something good that is out of the ordinary. Now I look at the other words to see which of them also deal with this idea. *Praise* fits, since you would receive praise if you did something good. *Tribute* also deals with this idea, so it must be a synonym, too. *Blame* doesn't fit. You wouldn't receive blame if you did something good, so this word is not a synonym. I cross it out to indicate my answer.

Answer Key
Star 1 blame
Star 2 pleasant
Star 3 rude
Star 4 peace
Star 5 denial
Star 6 dry

LESSON

8 Synonyms to Know

Review and Extend

Materials Needed
- Student Workbook, p. 60

Think Aloud

This activity involves a lot of thinking, since I have to understand shades of difference between synonyms. Let's look at the first one together. The two synonyms are *fumbled* and *mishandled*. Here's the first sentence: "The team lost the point when he _____ the ball." This seems to be a physical activity, since the player must have dropped the ball. I know that *fumble* is the better word to use with physical activity, so I will write *fumbled* in the blank.

Answer Key
Mystery Word of the Week:
abolish
Accept other words that fit the context, too.

1. fumbled 2. mishandled
3. commotion 4. bustle
5. civil 6. polite

Getting Started

Mystery Word of the Week Clue 5
The meaning of this word is "to end something."

Review and Share Have volunteers reenact their **interviews** for the class. Then invite students to participate in a follow-up question and answer period. Remind students to use vocabulary words in their questions.

Model/Teach

- Direct students to turn to page 60 of their workbooks and read the boxed information.

- Discuss the information about shades of difference. Provide the following additional example: *Bustle* suggests a lot of fuss and bother, such as the *bustle* in the house as your family prepares for your sister's wedding. *Commotion* suggests a more serious situation, such as the *commotion* and confusion after a hurricane.

- Use the **Think Aloud** to model how to complete the activity.

- After you have modeled completing an item, have students finish the rest on their own. Allow time for them to share their answers and discuss their thinking.

English Language Learners

- The silent *-g* in *gnarled* and the pronounced *-g* in *glory* are apt to confuse English language learners, as can the silent *-t* in *bustle* and the silent *-h* in *honor*. Have students work together to say these words, then practice writing them in their personal word journals.

Independent Activity

Find New Synonyms Encourage students to look through magazines, newspapers, and textbooks to find new synonyms. (They can use a dictionary to help them.) Display their synonym lists around the classroom.

Check Your Mastery

Materials Needed
• Student Workbook, p. 61

Give the Test
- Have students open their workbooks to page 61.
- Tell the students that the Check Your Mastery activity has two parts.
- Read aloud the directions for the first part: "Complete each sentence below." Tell students that their task is to complete each sentence in a way that shows that they understand the meaning of the boldface word.
- Model how to answer this type of question by writing the item on the chalkboard and reading it aloud:

    The school monitor tried to quiet the *commotion* after _____.

- Ask a student volunteer to complete this sentence and explain his or her thinking.
- Read aloud the directions for the second activity: "Complete the word analogies below. Write your answers on the lines."
- Model how to answer this type of question by writing the following analogy on the chalkboard:

    Crooked is to **twisted** as **commotion** is to _____.
    A. bustle   B. drenched   C. glory

- Ask a volunteer to complete the item and share his or her thinking.
- Direct students to reread their answers and check their work after they finish this activity.
- Review the Check Your Mastery activity orally with students.
- Students can work with a partner to discuss the questions they did not answer correctly.
- As a class, discuss how the Word Learning Tip and the Vocabulary Building Strategy helped students choose the correct responses.
- Tally students' correct responses.

Student Self-Assessment

Journal Writing In their journals, have students describe how they can find the meaning of synonyms in the future.

Answer Key
Sample answers:
1. grab a towel and dry yourself off.
2. saved someone's life.
3. go on a class trip.
4. aunts and uncles come for dinner.
5. a large circular staircase.
6. A 7. B 8. B 9. A 10. A

Lesson 8 • Synonyms to Know

LESSON 9 Antonyms to Know

Read Words in Context

Materials Needed
- Student Workbook, p. 62
- Transparency 1

Vocabulary Words
allowed
dismiss
distracted
dull
frail
focused
forbidden
glistening
hardy
high-priced
hire
inexpensive
inferior
meaningful
misery
optimist
pessimist
pleasure
senseless
superior

Getting Started

Mystery Word of the Week Clue 1

Derek does not want a job in a _____ city. He wants to stay in a nearby town, close to family and friends.

- See page 14 for routines for using the Mystery Word of the Week Clue. The mystery word of the week is *remote*.

Model/Teach

- Ask students to turn to page 62 in their workbooks.
- Have a volunteer read the Word Learning Tip aloud. Be sure students understand that an *antonym* is a word that means the opposite or nearly the opposite of another word. Point out that true antonyms are the same part of speech.
- Invite a volunteer to read the Vocabulary Building Strategy. Explain to students that they can often use an unfamiliar word's *context* to help them determine what the word means and that antonyms are one kind of context clue.
- Read the complete story aloud once with students following along in their books.
- Tell the class that you are going to read the story a second time. Explain that this time you want them to think about the words in boldface and to try to understand what they mean.
- Do the **Think Aloud** on page 77.
- Place Transparency 1 on the overhead projector. Explain to students that as you continue to read the story, you will pause so they can discuss each boldface word. Explain that you want them to think about how they can use the Word Learning Tip and the Vocabulary Building Strategy to determine the meaning of each word. Ask students to tell you what each word means and how they knew this. Write their thinking on the transparency.

76 Chapter 1 • Context Clues

- Continue reading the rest of the story aloud, pausing at each sentence with a boldface word. Ask students to explain how they determined the meaning of each word, using what they know about context clues and antonyms. Write their responses on the transparency.

- After students have discussed the meaning of each boldface word, divide the class into groups. Allow them time to use flashcards to reinforce word meanings.

English Language Learners

- In Spanish, the letters *c* (before *e* or *i*), *s*, and *z* have the same sound as the letter *s* in *sent*. So English words with these letters might present problems to Spanish speakers. Arrange students in small groups and ask them to identify vocabulary words with these letters. Say the words for students and have them echo your pronunciation.

Independent Activity

- **Sort Antonyms** Ask students to fold a piece of paper in half. On the left side, have them write "Positive Words," and on the right, "Negative Words." Then ask them to list the antonyms on the vocabulary list under one of the headings. Tell students that there are no hard-and-fast rules for assigning the words, but they should be able to defend their choices.

Think Aloud

This is my method for determining what *high-priced*, the boldface word in the first sentence, means. I read the first two sentences. I think about the Word Learning Tip and I look for clues in the context to the meaning of *high-priced*. I know the sentences are contrasting costs, so I think that they may contain antonyms. The first clue is "even though he doesn't have much money." This tells me that the bicycle Christopher wants costs a lot of money. The next sentence tells me that the bicycle that Christopher does *not* want is "inexpensive." I conclude that *inexpensive* is an antonym of *high-priced* and that *inexpensive* means "doesn't cost a lot of money."

Answer Key
See page 212 for definitions.

LESSON 9 Antonyms to Know

Connect Words and Meanings

Materials Needed
- Student Workbook, pp. 63–64

Think Aloud

Here is how I would complete this matching activity. I read the first word in the left-hand column: *misery*. I think about the meaning of *misery*. I know it's something you feel after something terrible has happened. When you feel misery, you feel pain and sadness mixed together. Now I look in the right-hand column for an antonym, or a word that means the opposite of pain and sadness. Looking down this column, I find the word *pleasure*. I know that *pleasure* is what I experience when I feel good or happy. That's the opposite idea, so *misery* and *pleasure* must be antonyms. To indicate my choice, I write the letter C in the blank next to *misery*.

Answer Key
1. C 2. D 3. B 4. A 5. H 6. G
7. J 8. F 9. I 10. E

1. dismiss 2. optimist 3. glistening
4. superior 5. frail 6. forbidden
7. meaningful 8. pleasure
9. distracted 10. inexpensive

Getting Started

Mystery Word of the Week Clue 2

Marissa traveled to a _____ country miles from home. She lost touch with everything that was near and dear.

★ **Review and Share** Ask volunteers to share the antonym lists they made for the **Sort Antonyms** activity on page 77 in the teacher's edition. Work with students to create a master list of these words. Encourage them to discuss and reach a consensus on the designation of each antonym as "positive" or "negative."

Model/Teach
- Have students turn to page 63 in their workbooks.
- Before students begin the activity, do the **Think Aloud**.
- After you have modeled how to do the first item, have students do the rest on their own. Invite them to share their responses and their thinking.
- Ask students to complete the activity on page 64.

Independent Activities

★ **Have a Silent Dialogue** To help students complete the activity, tell them they can determine the definition of a word they don't know by using its antonym as a clue to its meaning. Suggest they check all their definitions in the glossary.

- **Study Word Parts** Tell students that breaking words into their parts (prefixes, roots, and suffixes) can help them determine word meanings. For example, the prefix *in-* means "not," so *inexpensive* means "not expensive." The suffix *-ful* means "full of," so *meaningful* means "full of meaning." Ask students what they think the suffix *-less* means in *senseless*. Then have groups search through books and magazines to find other words with these suffixes, and discuss their meanings.

78 Chapter 1 • Context Clues

Use Words in Context

Materials Needed
- Student Workbook, p. 65

Getting Started

Mystery Word of the Week Clue 3

Professor Ling travels long distances to _____ places looking for butterflies. He cannot find what he is studying close to home.

⭐ **Review and Share** Invite volunteers to read aloud the results of the **silent dialogues** they created for the activity on page 64. Have them compare definitions and explain the ways they arrived at these word meanings.

Model/Teach

- Ask students to turn to page 65 in their workbooks.
- Before students begin the activity, do the **Think Aloud**.
- After you have modeled how do the first item, have students do the rest on their own. Invite them to share their responses and their thinking.

Independent Activities

⭐ **Write Instructions** Before students begin the activity, divide the class into small groups and ask each group to talk about different goals that they have. Then tell students that they can write their how-to instructions in paragraph form or as a numbered, step-by-step list.

- **Sentence Challenge** Challenge students to write a sentence using two pairs of antonyms. For example: *The optimist found pleasure in everyday things, while the pessimist saw only misery*. Use all the vocabulary words if possible.

Think Aloud

This how I would approach this activity. The directions tell me that the words in boldface do not make sense in the context of the passage. The word that does make sense is the antonym of the boldface word. I read the first item: "To grow **frail** (1)_____ plants that are strong and healthy, there are several things you must do." No, *frail* does not make sense here. Plants that are "strong and healthy" are not *frail*. In fact, they are the opposite of *frail*. I look at the vocabulary list and find the word *hardy*. I know that if something is hardy, it's strong. *Frail* and *hardy* are antonyms. I'll put *hardy* in the blank in the first sentence and see if it fits the context: "To grow *hardy* plants that are strong and healthy, there are several things you must do." Yes, *hardy* makes sense in the context. So, I'll write *hardy* in the blank for item 1.

Answer Key
1. hardy 2. focused 3. high-priced
4. superior 5. glistening
6. forbidden 7. misery
8. pessimist 9. hire
10. meaningful

Lesson 9 • Antonyms to Know

LESSON 9: Antonyms to Know

Put Words Into Action

Materials Needed
- Student Workbook, p. 66

Think Aloud

Let me show you the thinking I do to complete this activity. Let's look at the first question: "How would an **optimist** and a **pessimist** look at their chances of winning a contest?" I know that an *optimist* has a positive attitude and always sees the bright side of things, while a *pessimist* has a negative attitude and always sees the downside of things. So I would answer the question like this: An optimist would think that he or she will win the contest, while a pessimist would think he or she has no chance of winning.

Getting Started

Mystery Word of the Week Clue 4

In the dictionary, this word is on the same page as remember and remove.

⭐ **Review and Share** Ask students to share the **instructions** they wrote for the activity on page 65. Then make a class booklet of instructions for achieving your goals.

Model/Teach
- Ask students to turn to page 66 in their workbooks.
- Before students begin the activity, do the **Think Aloud**.
- After you have modeled how to write answers to questions, have students complete the activity. Invite them to share their responses.

English Language Learners
- Since *h* is silent in Spanish, Spanish-speaking students may have difficulty pronouncing words like *hire*, *hardy*, and *high-priced*. After modeling the pronunciation for them, have students say, spell, and write the words in small groups until they achieve fluency.

Independent Activity

⭐ **Write Headlines** Ask students to look at headlines in school and local newspapers. Remind them that headlines have to be short and catchy, and that most have at least one action word. Challenge students to create headlines using pairs of antonyms from the vocabulary list.

Answer Key
Students' responses will vary. See page 219 for sample sentences.

80 Chapter 1 • Context Clues

Review and Extend

Materials Needed
- Student Workbook, p. 67

Getting Started

Mystery Word of the Week Clue 5

Karim is a(n) _____ relative of my grandmother, but we have no closer relatives in this country.

★ **Review and Share** Have students exchange the **headlines** they wrote for the activity on page 66. Ask them to underline the vocabulary word or words in each headline. Then display the headlines around the room.

Model/Teach

- Direct students to turn to page 67 in their workbooks and read the boxed information.
- After discussing how to use antonym clues, demonstrate how to complete this activity with the **Think Aloud**.
- After you have modeled doing the first item, have students complete the rest on their own. Invite them to share their responses and their thinking.

Independent Activities

★ **Give a Speech** Have students work in pairs to write and present their speeches. Remind them that as a presenter of an award, they must describe what the person achieved and why the achievement was special.

- **Create a Comic Strip** Have individuals create a comic strip telling the story of someone working toward a goal. Suggest that they create three or four frames to show what happens. They should use speech balloons to show what the characters say. Challenge them to use three or four vocabulary words in their comic strips. Then arrange students in small groups to discuss their comic strips and the vocabulary words they used.

Think Aloud

The directions for this activity tell me that the words in boldface are antonym clues that will help me choose the correct vocabulary word to fill in the blank. I read the first item: "Staying _____ on your goals helps prevent you from becoming **distracted** and losing your sense of purpose." I know that the word I am looking for must mean the opposite of *distracted*, so it must mean "having a sense of purpose or focus." I remember that *focused* is one of my vocabulary words. It means the opposite of *distracted*. Now I'm going to try *focused* in the blank to see if it makes sense: "Staying focused on your goals helps prevent you from becoming distracted and losing your sense of purpose." That makes a lot of sense, so *focused* is the word I will write in the blank.

Answer Key
Mystery Word of the Week:
remote
Accept other words that fit the context, too.

1. focused 2. pessimist 3. misery
4. inferior 5. meaningful

See page 219 for sample bonus sentence.

Lesson 9 • Antonyms to Know

LESSON 9 Antonyms to Know

Check Your Mastery

Materials Needed
- Student Workbook, p. 68

Student Self-Assessment

Journal Writing Have students write about how knowing antonyms can help them learn unfamiliar words when they read.

Give the Test
- Have students open their workbooks to page 68.
- Tell the students that the Check Your Mastery activity has two different parts.
- Read the directions to the first part aloud: "Choose the word that best fits each sentence below. Write the word in the blank." Explain to students that their task is to choose from the three words in parentheses and identify the one that best fits the context.
- Model how to answer the items in the first activity by writing the following on the chalkboard and reading it aloud:

  Since it was the last day of school before summer vacation, the class waited eagerly for the teacher to _____ (*dismiss, hire, focused*) them.

- Ask a student volunteer to complete this item and to explain the thinking that went into choosing the correct word.
- Read aloud the directions for the second activity: "Fill in the blank with the vocabulary word that best completes each sentence. Use the clue in the boldface to help you choose the correct word."
- Model how to answer the items in the second activity by writing this sample item on the chalkboard and reading it aloud:

  A **weak** plant can become _____ if it receives the right amount of sunlight, moisture, and nutrition.

- Ask students to choose the word that best fits in the blank. Have them explain how they used the antonym clue *weak* to choose the correct word *hardy*.
- When students have finished, remind them to recheck their work.
- Review the Check Your Mastery activity out loud with students.
- Students can work in small groups to discuss the questions they answered incorrectly. Have students write the definitions for any vocabulary word they missed.
- As a class, talk about how the Word Learning Tip and the Vocabulary Building Strategy helped students choose the correct response.
- Tally students' correct responses.

Answer Key
1. focused 2. frail 3. inexpensive
4. senseless 5. dismiss 6. optimist
7. hire 8. glistening 9. pleasure
10. forbidden

LESSON 10

Putting It Together

Read Words in Context

Getting Started

Mystery Word of the Week Clue 1

Alex did a search on the Internet to gather information because he found Venice _____.

- See page 14 for routines for using the Mystery Word of the Week Clue. The mystery word of the week is *intriguing*.

Model/Teach

- Direct students to turn to page 69 in their workbooks.
- Have a volunteer read the Word Learning Tip aloud. Be sure students understand that, in this lesson, they are putting together everything that they have learned about nouns, verbs, adjectives, and adverbs. Explain that knowing what part of speech a word is can help them determine what that word means.
- Ask a student volunteer to read the Vocabulary Building Strategy to the class. Explain to students that they can often use the words that are around an unknown word to help them determine what that word means.
- Read the complete passage aloud once, directing students to follow along in their books.
- Explain to the class that you are going to read the passage a second time, and that this time you want them to think about the words in boldface and try to determine what they mean.
- Invite students to read the first paragraph silently as you read it aloud. Then do the **Think Aloud** on page 84.
- Tell the class that as you continue to read the passage, you will pause so they can discuss each boldface word. Ask them to think about the Word Learning Tip to help them determine the meaning of each word. Also, encourage them to think about the Vocabulary Building Strategy. Invite them to share their thinking with you about how they determined the meaning of each word.

Materials Needed
- Student Workbook, p. 69
- Transparency 1

Vocabulary Words
casually
dignity
gigantic
impressive
patience
perish
reassure
suitable
thrive
vividly

LESSON 10 Putting It Together

Think Aloud

Here's what I would do if I didn't know what *impressive* means. My first clue is its placement in the sentence: *impressive* comes right before the noun *city*. This tells me that *impressive* is an adjective because an adjective often comes before the noun it describes. Now I add what I know—that this word is an adjective that describes Venice—to other context clues to determine what *impressive* means. The rest of the sentence tells about extraordinary canals and majestic buildings. These are reasons why Venice is impressive so I think the words *extraordinary* and *majestic* are connected to the meaning. The next sentence has a good context clue: "Many people visit it each year and are dazzled by its amazing places." *Dazzled* is an excellent clue! It means impressed or amazed! I also see the word *amazing*. When I add all these ideas together, I think that *impressive* is an adjective that means "amazing or having a strong and striking effect." This is logical because it makes sense in the passage.

Answer Key
See page 212 for definitions.

- Place Transparency 1 on the overhead projector. Tell students that you are going to jot down the words that show their thinking as they determine the meaning of each boldface word.

- Continue reading the rest of the passage aloud, pausing at each sentence with a boldface word. Ask students to explain how they understood the meaning of each word. Write their responses on the transparency.

- Pair students. Have them use flashcards to reinforce meanings.

English Language Learners
- The *th-* sound does not exist in Spanish, so Spanish-speaking students may have difficulty pronouncing *thrive*. To help students, write *th-* on the chalkboard. Have students repeat the *th-* sound several times. Then write *thrive*, *the*, *then*, *there*, and *therefore* on the board. As you point to each word, have students repeat it after you.

Independent Activity
- **Create a Travel Guide** Work with students to create a "Community Travel Guide." Brainstorm favorite fun and interesting places where students and family members enjoy going on weekends. Have small groups choose one place about which to write and illustrate one page for the guide. One half of their pages should consist of writing, and the other half should be filled with their illustrations. Ask them to use five vocabulary words.

Connect Words and Meanings

Getting Started

Mystery Word of the Week Clue 2
From the _____ information that Alex researched, he learned this fact: Venice was once a powerful trading center.

⭐ **Review and Share** Ask a volunteer from each group to share the page their group created for the **Community Travel Guide** activity on page 84 in the teacher's edition. If time permits, have students brainstorm a list of additional words that could be used to describe these places. Add these words to the word wall.

Model/Teach

- Ask the class to turn to page 70 in their workbooks.
- Before students begin the activity, do the **Think Aloud**.
- After you have modeled how to find the meaning of a word and use it in a sentence, ask students to complete the rest of the items on their own. Then invite them to share their responses.
- Ask students to complete the activity on page 71 independently.

Independent Activities

⭐ **Write a Letter** Display a world map if possible. Then brainstorm with students different cities they might like to visit, and write a list of their names on the chalkboard. If some students name cities that are not familiar to the others, point out where the cities are on a map. Encourage students to choose a variety of different cities.

- **Make a List** Tell students to imagine that they are going on a three-day vacation and are old enough to drive a car. Ask them to write about how they prepared for the trip in order to be assured that they and the car would be ready to go. Instruct them to use two words from this week's lesson and three words from Lesson 1.

Materials Needed
- Student Workbook, pp. 70–71

Think Aloud

Let me share with you the thinking I do to complete this activity. Let's read the first definition together: "to do well; to flourish or prosper." The word *to* in the definition is a clue that I am looking for a verb. Next I look at the three words choices. I think the word that fits this definition is *thrive*. For example, my flowers *thrive* or do well on the windowsill. So I circle the letter A to show that *thrive* is my answer.

Answer Key
1. A 2. A 3. A 4. C 5. C 6. B
7. C 8. B 9. A 10. A 11. suitable
12. perish 13. thrive 14. reassure
15. casually 16. impressive
17. gigantic 18. vividly

Lesson 10 • Putting It Together

LESSON 10 Putting It Together

Use Words in Context

Materials Needed
- Student Workbook, p. 72

Think Aloud

Let's read the first item together: "Name two activities that you need **patience** to do well." I'm pretty sure that *patience* means to stay calm and not get angry when I get frustrated with something. So, I need to think of two activities where I need to practice *patience*. Well, I know that I need to be very patient when I try to kick a soccer ball, since it takes a long time to become good. I also need patience when I go in-line skating because I'm a beginner and I make a lot of mistakes. Those are definitely two activities that require my *patience,* so I write them in the blanks.

Answer Key
Sample responses:
1. playing the piano
2. in-line skating
3. milk 4. cheese
5. grass 6. flowers
7. sneakers 8. hiking boots
9. *Number the Stars*
10. *Hatchet* 11. Coretta King
12. my parents
13. my grandfather
14. my next-door neighbor
15. New York 16. Chicago

Getting Started

Mystery Word of the Week Clue 3

Alex looked for more _____ facts about Carnival in Venice because he wanted more information about the amazing costumes people wear.

⭐ **Review and Share** Invite volunteers to share the **letters** they wrote for the activity on page 71. Before students begin, ask them to tell a few words about why the particular city they chose is their favorite.

Model/Teach

- Have students turn to page 72 of their workbooks.
- Use the **Think Aloud** to model how to complete the activity.
- After you have modeled how to complete the activity, ask students to finish it on their own and then share their responses.

English Language Learners

- Pair more fluent English language learners with those in early speech emergence. Write *gigantic* on the chalkboard. Have pairs brainstorm different words that mean the same as *gigantic*, such as *huge*, *big*, and *large*. Invite them to say sentences using *gigantic* correctly. Then have them select two or more words from the list that are difficult and repeat the process.

Independent Activity

⭐ **Guess the Mystery Place** Take a few minutes to discuss the rules for this guessing game. Point out to students that the places should be familiar to all students and that each person can ask five questions. If partners cannot guess the places, have students choose new places to use for the game.

86 Chapter 1 • Context Clues

Put Words Into Action

Materials Needed
- Student Workbook, p. 73

Getting Started

Mystery Word of the Week Clue 4

Alex found out that a long time ago, people in Venice wore masks every day. He found this fact to be the most _____ of all.

⭐ **Review and Share** Guide students to talk about the **Guess the Mystery Place** activity they completed on page 72. Which vocabulary words did they use in their questions and answers, and why did they use them?

Model/Teach
- Have students turn to page 73 in their workbooks.
- Before students begin the activity, share the **Think Aloud** with the class.
- After you have modeled how to fill out a card, have students work on their own to complete the activity. If time permits, you may have them "interview" other words.

English Language Learners
- Pair more fluent learners with those in early speech emergence. Write *casually* and *vividly* on the chalkboard under the heading "Adverbs." Point out that adverbs often end in the letters *-ly*. Have students make a word web for adverbs in their personal word journals, and add the words *casually* and *vividly*.

Independent Activity

⭐ **Stage a Newscast** Give students an opportunity to rehearse their newscasts for the activity on page 73 of their workbooks. Make sure that the speeches and questions include words from the list.

Think Aloud

I want to model for you how I would interview these words. I'm going to use the word *gigantic* to show you my thinking. The first question I'll ask *gigantic* is "What do you mean?" In the blank, I'll write *huge, very large*. Next, I'll ask *gigantic*, "What words are your opposites?" Since the opposite of gigantic is *tiny* or *very small*, I'll write that in the blank. Third, I'll ask *gigantic*, "What part of speech are you?" Since the word describes nouns and pronouns, *gigantic* must be an adjective. I'll write that in the third blank. Fourth, I'll ask *gigantic*, "How could I use you in a sentence?" I'll write a sentence to answer that question: "We saw a gigantic mountain." Last, I'll ask *gigantic*, "What other words are in your 'family'?" I know that *giant* and *gigantic* are related, so I write *giant* in the blank.

Answer Key
Sample answers:
1. honor, respect
2. contempt, disdain
3. noun 5. undignified
6. prosper, flourish
7. fail, falter 8. verb
10. thrived or throve

Students' responses for 4 and 9 will vary. See page 219 for sample sentences.

Lesson 10 • Putting It Together

LESSON 10 Putting It Together

Materials Needed
- Student Workbook, p. 74

Think Aloud

Read the first item silently with me as I read it aloud. "Glassblowers **clearly** and _____ imagine how an object will look as they blow the glass." The first thing that I have to do is determine what part of speech *clearly* is. I know that adverbs often end in *-ly*, which *clearly* does. I also know that adverbs add meaning to verbs, adjectives and other adverbs. Since *clearly* comes just before the verb *imagine*, I know that *clearly* is an adverb and the word I am looking for should be an adverb, too. Now I have to choose a word that is an adverb that means the same thing as *clearly*. I look at the vocabulary words and see the word *vividly*. Let me try that word in the sentence: "Glassblowers clearly and vividly imagine how an object will look as they blow the glass." *Vividly* fits the context, so I write *vividly* in the blank and I circle the word *adverb*.

Answer Key
Mystery Word of the Week: intriguing
Accept other words that fit the context, too.
1. vividly 2. adverb 3. impressive
4. adjective 5. thrive 6. verb
7. suitable 8. adjective 9. reassure
10. verb

Review and Extend

Getting Started

Mystery Word of the Week Clue 5
Alex learned more interesting and _____ facts about Venice and its mask history from a book that his father bought him.

 Review and Share Invite volunteers to present their **newscasts** for the class. Encourage students to answer questions in character.

Model/Teach
- Direct students to turn to page 74 in their workbooks.
- Use the Think Aloud .
- Have students complete the remaining items on their own. Then ask them to share their responses.

Independent Activities

Write About What Was Impressive For the activity on page 74 in their workbooks, have students list different events they've seen that they think are *impressive*. Write their ideas on the chalkboard. Give them an opportunity to choose an event and then write sentences that show why it was impressive. As an extra challenge, ask them to use three words from Lesson 4.

- **Talk About It!** Have students work in small groups and talk about events that have taken place in their lives that they *vividly* remember. Encourage them to use all adjectives and adverbs from this lesson as well as Lessons 4, 5, and 6 as they converse. Ask one member in each group to list all adjectives and adverbs used.

Chapter 1 • Context Clues

Check Your Mastery

Materials Needed
- Student Workbook, p. 75

Give the Test

- Have students open their workbooks to page 75.
- Tell students that the Check Your Mastery activity has two parts.
- Read aloud the directions for the first five questions: "Complete each analogy. Write the word that best fits in the blank." Tell students there are three choices. Their job is to choose the word that best completes the analogy.
- Model how to complete an analogy by writing the following item on the chalkboard and reading it aloud:

   Honor is to **respect** as **nobility** is to
   dignity   perish   thrive

- Ask students to choose the correct word to complete the sentence. Students should say that *honor, respect,* and *nobility* are synonyms for *dignity*. Thus, *dignity* is the correct choice.
- Then read aloud the directions for items 6–10: "Circle the letter of each correct answer." Explain that students must show they understand the meaning of the vocabulary words by providing an example for each sentence.
- Model how to answer this type of question by writing the following on the chalkboard and reading it aloud:

   Which of the following animals is likely to be gigantic?
   A. an ant   **C.** a mouse
   B. a cat   **D.** an elephant

- Ask students to choose the animal that best answers the question. Only an elephant is gigantic, since all the other choices identify small animals.
- Review Check Your Mastery out loud with students.
- Tally their correct responses.

Student Self-Assessment

Journal Writing Ask students to think about all of the words they have mastered in this chapter. Tell them to summarize the Word Learning Tip and Vocabulary Building Strategy they will use in the future.

Answer Key

1. thrive 2. gigantic 3. perish
4. suitable 5. reassure 6. A 7. A
8. C 9. B 10. B

CHAPTER 2

Words and Their Parts

Lesson 11 Words With Prefixes
(*bi-*, *multi-*, *oct-/octa-/octo-*, *tri-*) **92**

Lesson 12 Words With Suffixes
(*-an/-ian*, *-er/-or*, *-ee*, *-ist*) **99**

Lesson 13 Words With Roots
(*cur/curs*, *micro*, *mort*, *scope*) **106**

Lesson 14 Compound Words With
Brain, *Head*, *Heart*, and *Foot* **113**

Lesson 15 Word Families
(*name*, *nomen/nomin*, *onym*) **120**

Lesson 16 Word Families (*graph*) **127**

Research Base

- **Word Learning Tip** Many students have difficulty decoding long words. The challenge is reduced when the students are taught to look for morphological units within them that carry meaning.

- **Vocabulary Building Strategy** By adding the separate meanings of word parts within a word, the complete meaning of many unknown words can be determined.

- **Research-Based Lists** Chapter 2 focuses on words with prefixes, suffixes, and roots, as well as compound words and other multisyllabic words. To discern the meanings of words in these lessons, students will have to use their knowledge of word parts to determine meanings. For example, the student will know the word *state*, but to determine the meaning of *tristate*, an unfamiliar word, he or she must know that the prefix *tri-* means "three," so *tristate* means "involving three states."

LESSON 11

Words With Prefixes
(*bi-, multi-, oct-/octa-/octo-, tri-*)

Be a Word Architect

Materials Needed
- Student Workbook, p. 78

Vocabulary Words

biannual
biceps
bifocals
binoculars
biweekly
multicolored
multimillionaire
multitude
octagonal
octopus
triangular
triathlon
tricycle
tripod
tristate

Getting Started

Mystery Word of the Week Clue 1

The tour guide's talents can be described as _____ because he can do so many different things.

- See page 14 for routines for using the Mystery Word of the Week Clue. The mystery word of the week is *multifaceted*.

Model/Teach

- Ask students to turn to page 78 in their workbooks.

- Request that they read the Word Learning Tip. Tell students that many big words are made of smaller words. Explain that students can often understand new words by learning these word parts and looking for them in new words. The words in this lesson contain *prefixes*, a word part added to the beginning of a word or word root to change its meaning.

- Ask students to take a look at the Vocabulary Building Strategy. Point out that they can find the meaning of new words by putting together the meaning of the prefix and the word or word root to which it was added. The meaning of the new word is based on the meanings of both parts.

- Explain that a root is a word part that usually comes from Latin or Greek. For example, the root *ped* or *pod* means "feet." When you add the prefix *tri-* to it (*tri* + *pod* = *tripod*), you form the word *tripod*, which is a stool or stand with three feet.

- Write the prefixes *bi-, tri-, oct-/octa-/octo-* and *multi-* on the chalkboard. Tell students that *oct-, octa-* and *octo-* are different spellings of the same prefix. Explain that each of these prefixes shows a number or a general amount. Then explain each prefix and its specific meaning: *bi-* = two; *tri-* = three, *oct-/octa-/octo-* = eight, and *multi-* = many.

- Have students look at the chart showing these prefixes in their workbooks. Tell students that when they see an unfamiliar word with one of these prefixes, they immediately know one thing about the word, because the meaning of the prefix is part of the meaning of the unfamiliar word.

- Ask a student to read the directions for the activity aloud, then do the **Think Aloud**.

- Have students work on their own to complete the activity. Ask volunteers to share their responses and explain their thinking.

- Ask students to try to think about the meaning of each word. Have them put the meaning of the word parts together to try to determine the meaning of each unfamiliar word. Explain that they should try to think creatively as they do this. Some words will be easy to decipher, such as *tricycle*. Some will be harder, such as *multitude*. Explain the meaning of each word, but do not mark students' responses as right or wrong at this point. The purpose is to encourage the students to use the Word Learning Tip and Vocabulary Building Strategy to determine word meanings. This will build word consciousness by allowing them to play with meanings without the worry of being marked incorrect.

- Provide time for students to work in small groups, using flashcards to reinforce word meanings.

English Language Learners

- Explain to students that adding word parts often changes what syllable is accented or stressed in a word. Write the words *octagon* and *octagonal* on the chalkboard. Divide the word *octagon* into syllables: oct a gon. Say the word aloud and ask students to identify which syllable is stressed (the first syllable). Then divide the word *octagonal* into syllables: oct a gon al. Say the word aloud and ask the students to identify which syllable is stressed (the second syllable). Have students work with a partner to practice saying this pair of words aloud.

Independent Activity

- **Find New Words** Provide dictionaries and have students look for words for each prefix. Ask them to write each word in their personal word journal. Lead a class discussion about the variety of words students found and their definitions.

Think Aloud

Let me show you how to complete this activity. Look at the first word with me: *biannual*. I see the prefix *bi-* so I put the word on the branch of the tree labeled *bi-* and I circle the letters *bi*. I'm not exactly sure what the word means yet, but I know that since *bi-* means "two," part of the meaning of *biannual* is "two." So *biannual* must mean "two of something." I've seen the word *annual* before. We have an *annual* party at the end of the school year, or a party once a year. I think that perhaps *annual* is related to anniversary, which is also something that occurs once a year. So if I put all these ideas together, I think that *biannual* must mean "twice a year." *Biannual* can also mean happening once every two years.

Answer Key

bi-
- biannual
- biceps
- bifocals
- binoculars
- biweekly

tri-
- triangular
- triathlon
- tricycle
- tripod
- tristate

oct-, octa-, octo-
- octagonal
- octopus

multi-
- multicolored
- multimillionaire
- multitude

See page 212–213 for definitions.

LESSON 11

Words With Prefixes
(*bi-, multi-, oct-/octa-/octo-, tri-*)

Connect Words and Meanings

Materials Needed
- Student Workbook, pp. 80–81

Think Aloud

I want to share with you my thinking as I complete this activity. Let's look at the first definition: "**triathlon** a long distance race that is made up of three events. Usually, these include swimming, bicycling, and running." I notice the word *three* in the definition. There are three separate events. This ties in with the meaning of the prefix *tri-* in *triathlon*. *Tri-* means "three" and a *triathlon* has three events. Now I look at the question that follows the definition: "If a race is made up of ten events, can it be called a **triathlon**? Explain why or why not." Remembering the meaning of the prefix helps me answer this question: *A race that has ten events is not a triathlon, since a triathlon has three events.* Notice that I used the vocabulary word in my answer.

Answer Key
Students' responses will vary. See page 220 for sample sentences.

Getting Started

Mystery Word of the Week Clue 2
Jennifer loved her job because her tasks were _____. She also entertained visitors by singing the state song!

⭐ **Review and Share** Provide an opportunity for students to share the **new words** and definitions they found for the activity on page 78. Create a prefix word wall. First, have each group write the vocabulary words on an index card and add them to the wall. Then ask volunteers from each group to write the new words they generated on index cards and add them under the appropriate prefix.

Model/Teach

- Have students turn to page 79 in their workbooks.
- Before students begin the activity, do the **Think Aloud**.
- Ask students to complete the rest of the page on their own, and then have them share their responses.

Independent Activities

⭐ **Exploring Word Meaning** Before students begin the activity, write the words "twice a year" and "once every two years" on the chalkboard. Ask students to suggest events that could fit in each column. Explain that the word *biannual* can be used in both situations. Then have students write sentences using the word in their personal word journal.

- **Create a Multicolored Octagonal Structure** Discuss the meaning of *octagonal* with students again. Point out that *octa-* means "eight" and that *-gon* means a geometrical figure that has the number of sides and corners that is specified by the prefix. So, an *octagonal* figure has eight sides and corners. Challenge students to create a multicolored *octagonal* structure in which they write eight sentences using words with the prefix *oct-/octa-*.

94   Chapter 2 • Words and Their Parts

Learn Words in Context

Materials Needed
- Student Workbook, p. 82
- Transparency 1

Getting Started

Mystery Word of the Week Clue 3

At a gem museum, the guide pointed out a _____ ruby. Because it had so many different sides, the ruby glittered brightly.

★ **Review and Share** Ask students to share their sentences from the **Exploring Word Meaning** activity on page 81. Suggest that they write them on sentence strips.

Model/Teach

- Have students turn to page 82 their workbooks.
- Ask students to follow along in their books as you read the story aloud.
- Use the **Think Aloud** before you read the story again.
- Place the transparency on the overhead projector. Tell students that as you read the story again, you will pause at every boldface word. Have students use the Word Learning Tip and Vocabulary Building Strategy to define each word. They should also explain their thinking.
- After you have finished reading the passage a second time, review the meaning of the vocabulary words.

English Language Learners

- Partner more fluent students with those in early speech emergence to play a game. The first player holds up 2, 3, or 8 fingers to show *bi-*, *tri-*, or *oct-*, respectively. The other partner has to point to, or say, a vocabulary word that begins with a prefix that matches the number of fingers. Have partners take turns.

Independent Activity

★ **Write Slogans** Discuss with students different places in your state people might like to visit. Then invite students to write slogans that will make people want to visit these places in their state.

Think Aloud

I'm always glad when I come to a word that has a prefix because it means that I have a good way to understand what the word means, if I don't know it already. Listen carefully while I read the first sentence: "There's so much to do in the **tristate** area in the summer." If I didn't know the word *tristate*, I'd first look to see if it has a prefix. I'm in luck because it begins with the prefix *tri-*. If I divide the word into its parts, I get the prefix *tri-* and the word *state*. I know that *tri-* means "three." That tells me that *tristate* means "three states."

Answer Key
See page 212–213 for definitions.

LESSON 11

Words With Prefixes
(*bi-, multi-, oct-/octa-/octo-, tri-*)

Use Words in Context

Materials Needed
- Student Workbook, p. 83

Think Aloud

Follow along silently as I read the first sentence aloud: "I just bought a kite that has a _____ shape. It has three angles and three sides." I know that the prefix *tri-* means "three," so I'm looking for a vocabulary word that starts with this prefix. I can eliminate *multicolored* right away because it starts with the prefix *multi-*. That leaves the words *triangular* and *tripod*. I rule out *tripod* because I know that a tripod is a stand with three legs. So *triangular* is the correct answer. Just to make sure, I think about the definition for *triangular* which means "having three angles." I know that a kite can be like a triangle, so that's my word choice. I write *triangular* in the blank.

Getting Started

Mystery Word of the Week Clue 4

The _____ tour of Texas involved many different phases, including a visit to the Alamo, a barbecue lunch, and a rodeo.

★ **Review and Share** Lead a class discussion in which students discuss which vocabulary words they used in their **slogans** from the activity on page 82 in their workbooks. Then create a display of students' slogans, and give them a chance to view and discuss them among themselves.

Model/Teach
- Have students turn to page 83 in their workbooks.
- Before students begin the activity, share the **Think Aloud** with the class.
- After you model how to use your knowledge of prefixes and roots to complete each sentence, have students work on their own to complete the activity. Invite volunteers to share their answers.

Independent Activities

★ **Write a Postcard** Invite students to imagine they are on vacation and to write postcards to someone at home. Encourage them to use at least three vocabulary words in their postcards.

- **Word Challenge** Use index cards to make two sets of flashcards. For one set, write *bi-, tri-, oct-/octa-/octo-,* and *multi-*. For the other set, make a card for each root word. Have pairs take turns holding up the top card from each pile. When a student makes a word, he or she must tell the definition. Have pairs continue until they have made five matches.

Answer Key
1. triangular 2. multicolored
3. binoculars 4. tricycle
5. triathlon 6. biannual 7. biceps
8. tripod 9. multitude 10. tristate

96 Chapter 2 • Words and Their Parts

Review and Extend

Materials Needed
- Student Workbook, p. 84

Getting Started

Mystery Word of the Week Clue 5

This word begins with the prefix multi- and means "having many sides or faces." This word is _____.

⭐ **Review and Share** Have students exchange the **postcards** they wrote for the activity on page 83 in their workbooks. Invite students to underline the vocabulary words in their postcards and circle each prefix. Then display the postcards around the room.

Think Aloud

Let's look at the first item together: "If a **tricycle** has three wheels, how many wheels does a **bicycle** have?" The prefix *tri-* in *tricycle* tells me that it has three wheels. What does the prefix *bi-* in *bicycle* tell me? I know that *bi-* means "two," so a *bicycle* would have two wheels. So *two* is the word I write in the blank.

Model/Teach

- Direct students to turn to page 84 in their workbooks.
- Use the **Think Aloud**.
- Have students complete the rest of the activity on their own and share their responses in small groups.
- Then challenge students to complete the second activity on their own.

Independent Activities

⭐ **Write a Sentence** Allow students time to work with a partner to create their sentences. As a special challenge, have them include one vocabulary word as well as the two new words.

- **Create a Word Web** Draw a word web on the chalkboard that has a circle around the word "many" along with two smaller categories for *multiplication* and *multinational*. Challenge students to think of as many words as they can that are associated with these two words. Point out that the words do not have to start with the prefix *multi-*.

Answer Key
Mystery Word of the Week:
multifaceted
Accept other words that fit the context, too.

1. two 2. two 3. three 4. three
5. three 6. eight 7. many 8. two
9. many 10. three

Lesson 11 • **Words With Prefixes**

LESSON

11 Words With Prefixes
(bi-, multi-, oct-/octa-/octo-, tri-)

Check Your Mastery

Give the Test

- Have students open their workbooks to page 85.
- Read aloud the directions for the first five questions: "Circle the letter of the correct answer to each question below." Point out that there are four choices. Students should select the choice that best answers each question.
- Model how to answer the questions by writing the following item on the chalkboard and reading it aloud:

  Which of the following does an octopus have?
  A. a furry coat   **B.** eight limbs   **C.** three eyes   **D.** two big feet

- Ask students to choose the word or phrase that best completes the sentence.
- Read aloud the directions for items 6–10: "Read each item below. Choose the word that best fits in each blank. Write it on the line." Tell students that each sentence has three choices. It's their job to choose the word that best fits the context, and write it in the blank.
- Model how to answer this type of question by writing the sample item on the chalkboard and reading it aloud:

  The doctor put on her _____ (binoculars, bifocals, tripod) so that she could read the report and also see the nurses, who waited for her to look up and give instructions.

- Ask students to choose the word that best fits in the blank. Have them explain their choice.
- Remind students to reread their answers and check their work after they finish this activity.
- Review the Check Your Mastery activity out loud with students.
- Tally students' correct responses.

Materials Needed
- Student Workbook, p. 85

Student Self-Assessment

Journal Writing Have students write in their journals about how knowing just a handful of prefixes can help them define many unfamiliar words. Ask them to describe what new ways they learned for defining and spelling new words.

Answer Key
1. D **2.** C **3.** B **4.** A **5.** C
6. octopus **7.** biceps **8.** triangular
9. multimillionaire **10.** tricycle

LESSON 12

Words With Suffixes
(-an/-ian, -er/-or, -ee, -ist)

Be a Word Architect

Getting Started

Mystery Word of the Week Clue 1

The _____ began his career as a soldier in the army taking orders, so he had little training for being an absolute ruler.

- See page 14 for routines for using the Mystery Word of the Week Clue. The mystery word of the week is *dictator*.

Model/Teach
- Direct students to open their workbooks to page 86.
- Ask students to read the Word Learning Tip. Remind them that many large words contain smaller word parts. Knowing the meaning of these parts—prefixes, roots, and suffixes—can help them uncover what an unfamiliar word means. This is especially helpful with long words. Point out that all the vocabulary words in this lesson contain *suffixes*, a letter or group of letters added to the end of a word or a root to change its meaning and part of speech.
- Tell students to look at the Vocabulary Building Strategy. Explain again that they can find the meaning of new words by looking at their parts, especially their suffixes.
- Write the suffixes *-an/-ian, -er/-or, -ee, -ist* on the chalkboard. Explain that each of these suffixes means "a person who does something." In addition, the suffixes *-an/-ian* and *-er/-or* also means "a native of." All these suffixes turn a word into a noun.
- Tell students that sometimes you add a suffix to a complete word that can stand by itself. Sometimes you add it to a Greek or Latin root that cannot stand by itself as a word. A root needs a prefix or suffix added to it to form a complete word.
- Ask a student to read the directions for the activity aloud. Then use the **Think Aloud** on page 100 to model how to do the activity.

Materials Needed
- Student Workbook, p. 86

Vocabulary Words
African
announcer
artisan
aviator
civilian
employee
janitor
jurist
laborer
mathematician
naturalist
nominee
pedestrian
spectator
veterinarian

LESSON 12
Words With Suffixes
(-an/-ian, -er/-or, -ee, -ist)

Think Aloud

I'd like to show you the thinking that I do to complete this activity. The first word is African. I see the suffix -an, so I place the word on the branch of the tree labeled -an/-ian and I circle the letters -an. I know this word is a noun and that I can use the words "a person who; a native of, or related to" to determine its meaning. I think that African means "a native of Africa" or "a person who comes from Africa."

- Have students work independently to complete the activity. Ask volunteers to share their responses and explain their thinking.

- Ask students to think about the meaning of each word. Have them put the meaning of the word parts together to try to determine the meaning of each unfamiliar word. Explain that they should try to think creatively as they do this. Some words will be easy to define, such as *African*. Some will be harder, such as *janitor*. Explain the meaning of each word, but do not mark students' responses as right or wrong at this point. The purpose is to encourage the students to use the Word Learning Tip and Vocabulary Building Strategy to determine word meanings. This will build word consciousness by allowing students to play with word meanings without the worry of being marked incorrect.

- Divide the class into small groups. Allow them time to use flashcards to reinforce word meaning.

English Language Learners

- Students are likely to find many of these words challenging because they are very long. Say each word aloud for students and have them repeat the word after you several times. Then have students sort the words according to the number of syllables they have: 2, 3, 4, 5, 6.

Independent Activity

⭐ **Learn New Words with Suffixes** Before students begin, ask them what type of books and magazines they think would be most helpful for finding words that name what people do. Suggest that biographies, autobiographies, profiles, and want ads might be very useful.

Answer Key

-an/-ian
Afric(an)   mathematic(ian)
artis(an)   pedestr(ian)
civil(ian)   veterinar(ian)

-er/-or
announc(er)   jan(it)(or)
labor(er)   spectat(or)
aviat(or)

-ee
employ(ee)   nomin(ee)

-ist
jur(ist)   natural(ist)

See page 213 for definitions.

Chapter 2 • Words and Their Parts

Connect Words and Meanings

Getting Started

Mystery Word of the Week Clue 2

The _____ rules the entire country without asking for agreement from others.

⭐ **Review and Share** Provide an opportunity for students to share the **new words** and definitions they found from the activity on page 87 in their workbooks. Add them to the word wall.

Model/Teach

- Direct the class to open their workbooks to page 88.
- Before students begin the activity, use the **Think Aloud**.
- Ask students to complete the rest of the page on their own, and then have them share their responses.

English Language Learners

- Write *spectator* on the chalkboard. Pair more fluent English language learners with those in early speech emergence. Have pairs brainstorm different activities where they might be *spectators* and complete simple sentences, such as: I was a *spectator* at _____.

Independent Activity

⭐ **Understand Word Histories** Read aloud the word history for the root *ped*. Ask students to suggest words based on this root. Then have them complete the activity in their personal word journals.

Materials Needed
- Student Workbook, pp. 88–89

Think Aloud

I want to share with you the thinking that I do to complete this activity. Because of the suffixes in the vocabulary words, I know that each word is going to name a person. I see that a *spectator* is someone who watches an event. Read the sentence stem along with me: "During a football game, a spectator might _____." Well, if a spectator is someone who watches an event, during a football game, a spectator would be sitting in the stands. People sitting in the stands often cheer loudly for their teams. So I'm going to complete the sentence this way: "During a football game, a spectator might cheer loudly for her team."

Answer Key
Students' responses will vary. See page 220 for sample sentences.

Lesson 12 • Words With Suffixes **101**

LESSON 12

Words With Suffixes
(-an/-ian, -er/-or, -ee, -ist)

Learn Words in Context

Materials Needed
- Student Workbook, p. 90
- Transparency 1

Getting Started

Mystery Word of the Week Clue 3
The _____ was not elected to become an absolute ruler, but when the government failed, he took over by force.

Think Aloud

Here's my technique for defining a word I may not know that ends with a suffix. Read the first sentence with me: "'Today is career day for the fifth grade classes,' the **announcer** said over the loudspeaker yesterday morning." If I didn't know the meaning of the word *announcer*, I'll check to see if the word has a suffix. I'm in luck: I see the suffix *-er*. Now I can divide the word into its parts: *announce* and *-er*. I know that *-er* means "a person who." From this, I can determine that *announcer* means "a person who announces or gives information." I'll look back at the sentence to check my thinking: My definition fits. Since the announcer is speaking over the loudspeaker, an announcer must be "a person who reports information."

⭐ **Review and Share** Ask students to share their thinking about how *pedal*, *pedestal*, and *centipede* are related after doing the **word history** activity on page 89. Add these words to the word wall.

Model/Teach
- Direct the class to turn to page 90 in their workbooks.
- Tell students that you are going to read a story that uses all their vocabulary words. Students should follow along in their books as you read the story aloud.
- Use the **Think Aloud** before you read the story again.
- Put the transparency on the overhead projector. Tell students that as you read the story again, you will pause at every boldface word. Direct the class to use the Word Learning Tip and Vocabulary Building Strategy to define each word. Record their thinking on the transparency.
- After you have finished reading the passage a second time, review the meaning of all of the vocabulary words.

Independent Activities

⭐ **Write a Job Description** Explain that a job description contains two parts: It tells what a person in that job does and what qualifications or background this person should have. Then have students complete their job descriptions.

- **Name That Word** Partner students to play a game of "Password" with the vocabulary words. Students take turns generating clues to help their partners guess the vocabulary word. Clues should include the suffix as well as the definition.

Answer Key
See page 213 for definitions.

Chapter 2 • Words and Their Parts

Use Words in Context

Materials Needed
- Student Workbook, p. 91

Getting Started

Mystery Word of the Week Clue 4

The _____ said that he was helping the country, but he did not listen to what other people said and did only what he wanted.

⭐ **Review and Share** Create a display of students' **job descriptions** from the activity on page 90 in their workbooks. Then lead a class discussion in which volunteers talk about the job descriptions they wrote.

Model/Teach

- Ask the class to open their workbooks to page 91.
- Before students begin the activity, share the **Think Aloud** with the class.
- Have students work on their own to complete the activity. Invite volunteers to share their answers.

English Language Learners

- In Spanish, *b* and *v* are pronounced with the same sound, like the letter *b* in *balloon*. As a result, some students may have difficulty saying and spelling words with the letter *v*, such as *veterinarian*, *aviator*, and *civilian*. Partner students to practice pronouncing and spelling these words.

Independent Activity

⭐ **Interview an Artisan** Take a few minutes to discuss with students different items that artisans might create, such as pottery, jewelry, woven items, or glass objects. Then have them work with a partner to think of interview questions that would be appropriate to ask the kind of artisan they have chosen to interview.

Think Aloud

Let's look at the first item together: "Which gift would you give to a **pedestrian**—a world map or a good pair of walking shoes? Explain why." The suffix *-ian* tells me that part of the meaning of this word is "a person who." I also see the root *ped*, which I've learned means "foot." Putting these clues together with what I have learned about the word, I can decide that a *pedestrian* is a person who travels on foot. So which of the two gifts would be more suitable for a pedestrian? A pedestrian probably wouldn't need a world map to walk somewhere. But a pedestrian might need a good pair of walking shoes because he or she walks a lot. Now I write my answer: "I would give a pedestrian a good pair of walking shoes because a pedestrian walks a lot."

Answer Key

Students' responses will vary. See page 220 for sample sentences.

Lesson 12 • Words With Suffixes

LESSON 12
Words With Suffixes (-an/-ian, -er/-or, -ee, -ist)

Review and Extend

Materials Needed
- Student Workbook, p. 92
- Idea Web Graphic Organizer, p. 229

Think Aloud

I see that I am supposed to use the word parts in the boldface words to determine which vocabulary words to put in the blanks. Let's look at the first item: "An **employer** hires an _____ to do a job." I see that *employ* is the smaller word in *employer*. I look at the list of vocabulary words to see which word has the same smaller word in it. I see *employee*. *Employ* means "to hire somebody to work in exchange for money." The suffix *-ee* means "a person who." Since an *employer* is the person who hires somebody to work in exchange for money, an *employee* is the person hired to do a job. I write *employee* in the blank.

Answer Key
Mystery Word of the Week: dictator
Accept other words that fit the context, too.

1. employee 2. jurist 3. aviator
4. announcer 5. janitor 6. spectators
7. mathematician 8. nominee
9. civilian 10. pedestrian

Getting Started

Mystery Word of the Week Clue 5
This word ends with the suffix *-or*.

★ **Review and Share** Ask volunteers to reenact their **interviews** with an artisan from the activity on page 91 of their workbooks. Tell students to listen carefully so they can ask additional questions if they'd like. Encourage a variety of interviews from different artisans.

Model/Teach
- Have students to turn to page 92 of their workbooks.
- Use the **Think Aloud** to model how to do the activity.
- Direct students to complete the rest of the activity on their own and share their responses in small groups.

Independent Activities

★ **Create a Web of Related Words** Distribute copies of the Idea Web Graphic Organizer. Before students start, you might want to model how to complete this activity by creating a web on the chalkboard with the word *employee* in the center. Encourage students to come up with at least two new related words (*employment, employable*).

- **Act It Out** Assign each group one of the following professions to act out: *editor, baker, mariner, astronomer,* and *optometrist.* Give groups an opportunity to brainstorm how they will act out the profession they have been given. Then invite groups to act out their words for the class.

104 Chapter 2 • Words and Their Parts

Check Your Mastery

Materials Needed
- Student Workbook, p. 93

Give the Test

- Ask students to open their workbooks to page 93.
- Read aloud the directions for the first part of the activity: "Circle the letter of your answer to each item below." Tell students that each question has four choices. Their task is to choose the correct choice.
- Model how to answer the question by writing the following item on the chalkboard and reading it aloud:

    When at work, an **artisan** might _____.

    A. make a vase   **C.** operate on a patient

    B. score a touchdown   **D.** act in the play

- Ask students to choose the best response (A). Guide them to explain their choice.
- Read aloud the directions for items 6–10: "Choose the vocabulary word that best completes each sentence. Write it on the line."
- Model how to answer this type of question by writing the sample item below on the chalkboard and reading it aloud:

    If you needed someone to read the daily messages over the loudspeaker, you should ask a student to serve as a(n) _____ (*pedestrian, civilian, announcer*).

- Ask students to choose the word that best fits the blank (*announcer*). Have them explain their choice.
- When everyone has finished working, review the Check Your Mastery activity out loud with students.
- As a class, talk about how the Word Learning Tip and the Vocabulary Building Strategy helped students to choose the correct responses.
- Tally students' correct responses.

Student Self-Assessment

Journal Writing Ask students to describe in their journals how knowing just a handful of suffixes can help them define many unfamiliar words. Ask them to describe what new ways they have learned for defining and spelling unfamiliar words.

Answer Key
1. C 2. D 3. A 4. D 5. A
6. veterinarian 7. artisan
8. mathematician 9. naturalist
10. African

LESSON 13

Words With Roots
(*cur/curs, micro, mort, scope*)

Be a Word Architect

Materials Needed
- Student Workbook, p. 94

Vocabulary Words
curriculum
cursive
excursion
immortal
immortality
kaleidoscope
microscopic
microwave
mortal
mortality
occurrence
periscope
recurring
stethoscope
telescopic

Getting Started

Mystery Word of the Week Clue 1

The museum _____ has an exhibit of ancient Egyptian culture. Last month, the museum had a show on Greek vases.

- See page 14 for routines for using the Mystery Word of the Week Clue. The mystery word of the week is *currently*.

Model/Teach

- Have students open their workbooks to page 94.

- Ask students to look at the Word Learning Tip. Explain that some words are built by attaching other word parts to a root word. When they come across a long word that they don't know, they can look to see if it contains a root they do know. Then they can use this knowledge and their knowledge of other word parts to determine what the entire word means.

- Have students look at the Vocabulary Building Strategy. Tell students that a root is a word to which a prefix or a suffix is added to make a new word. Point out that if students know the meaning of the root and any prefixes or suffixes, they can put the meanings together and come up with a meaning for the entire word.

- Ask students to look at the boxed information and discuss the meaning of each root.

- Use the **Think Aloud** on page 107 to model how to do the activity.

- Have students complete the rest of the activity on their own.

- Invite students to share their responses and explain their thinking.

- Ask students to think about the meaning of each word. Have them put the meaning of the word parts together to try to determine the meaning of each unfamiliar word. Explain that they should try to think creatively as they do this. Some words will be easy to understand, such as *microwave*. Some will be harder, such as *periscope*.

106 Chapter 2 • Words and Their Parts

Explain the meaning of each word, but do not mark students' responses as right or wrong at this point. The purpose is to encourage students to use the Word Learning Tip and Vocabulary Building Strategy to determine word meanings. This will build word consciousness by allowing them to play with word meanings without the worry of being marked incorrect.

- Allow time for groups to use flashcards to reinforce roots and meaning.

English Language Learners
- Help students learn to pronounce the *cur/curs* words by having them repeat the words after you. Direct them to clap out the syllables and raise their voices to indicate the ones that are stressed. Then pair students to practice using the words in sentences.

Independent Activity

Get to the Root of the Matter Urge students to try to identify the meanings of the words by studying their parts before they look them up in the dictionary. (Answers: *incur* means "bring about"; *cursory* means "going over quickly, superficial"; *discursive* means "going here and there, wordy"; and *current* means "happening now, or the movement of water in a river or ocean.")

Think Aloud

I want to show you the thinking that I do as I complete this activity. The first word on the vocabulary list is *curriculum*. When I look at this word closely, I see the root *cur*. I write *curriculum* on the branch of the tree labeled *cur*, and I circle the letters *cur*. I know that all the words I put on this branch of the tree will have something to do with running. I do know that a *curriculum* is a set of courses of study. For example, there is the mathematics curriculum and the science curriculum. I guess you could say that all of the courses in a curriculum run together or are connected in some way. I know that's a little bit of a stretch, but when you use word parts, sometimes you have to think creatively to understand their meaning.

Answer Key
cur/curs
curriculum   occurrence
cursive   recurring
excursion

micro
microscopic   microwave

mort
immortal   mortal
immortality   mortality

scope
kaleidoscope   stethoscope
microscopic   telescopic
periscope

See page 213–214 for definitions.

Lesson 13 • Words With Roots

LESSON 13

Words With Roots
(cur/curs, micro, mort, scope)

Connect Words and Meanings

Materials Needed
- Student Workbook, pp. 96–97

Think Aloud

The definition for *immortal* is "not subject to death; living or lasting forever." I know that the meaning of the root *mort* is death, and I also know that the prefix *im* means "not." Now I want to think a little bit about the word. I know that no one is really immortal, although we all like to believe we are. I also know that sometimes having children makes people feel immortal, since people think they will live on through their offspring. Now I'm going to use both the definition of the word and my thinking about it to try to answer the question: "How can a poet make someone immortal?" I write, "A poet can make a person immortal by writing a poem about him or her so that this person lives on in the minds of all who read the poem."

Answer Key
Students' responses will vary. See page 221 for sample sentences.

Getting Started

Mystery Word of the Week Clue 2

_____, the entrance fee to the museum is five dollars, but it will go up to six dollars next month.

Review and Share Have groups of students create word cards for a Word Wall. Direct students to write each vocabulary word and each **new word** they defined for the activity on page 94 on an index card, underlining the root and providing a definition. As students learn new words with the same roots, have them create cards for those words and add them to the Word Wall.

Model/Teach

- Ask students to turn to page 96 in their workbooks.
- Review the roots and their meaning: *cur/curs* (run, running), *micro* (small), *mort* (death), *scope* (see, watch).
- Ask students to provide a vocabulary word or two for each root.
- Before students start the activity, share the **Think Aloud**.
- Have students complete the rest of the items on their own and invite students to share their responses and their thinking.

Independent Activities

Write a Sentence Give students an example sentence to get them started: *In the Greek myths, it is not an unusual occurrence for a god to have one mortal and one immortal parent.* Ask students to underline the vocabulary words in their sentences, as well as any other words containing roots from this lesson.

- **Write About an Immortal Creature** Myths and folktales are filled with stories of immortal beings. Ask students to choose one immortal creature they have read about. For example, they might choose Thor and his thunderbolts from Norse myths or the plumed serpent Quetzalcoatl from Aztec myths. Ask them to write a paragraph describing this being using at least three vocabulary words.

Learn Words in Context

Materials Needed
- Student Workbook, p. 98
- Transparency 1

Getting Started

Mystery Word of the Week Clue 3

The exhibit _____ includes mummies, jewelry, and models of the pyramids, but the mummies will be moved to another museum soon.

⭐ **Review and Share** Have students make sentence strips with the **sentences** they wrote for the activity on page 97. Post each sentence strip on the bulletin board.

Model/Teach

- Have students open their workbooks to page 98.
- Explain to the class that you are going to read a story that uses all their vocabulary words. Ask students to follow along silently as you read aloud.
- Before you read the story a second time, share the **Think Aloud** to model how to use roots to determine the meanings of unfamiliar words.
- Place the transparency on the overhead projector. Explain to students that as you read the story the second time, you will stop at each boldface word. Ask students to use the Word Learning Tip and Vocabulary Building Strategy to tell you the meaning of each word. You also want them to explain their thinking. Encourage them to think creatively. Record their responses on the transparency.
- After you have finished reading, review the meanings of the vocabulary words.

Independent Activity

- **Create a Museum Brochure** Invite students to create a brochure for the museum exhibit that Charles and Rebecca visit in the passage, using as many vocabulary words as they can. Remind them to tell what the exhibit is, when it takes place, and why people should visit it.

Think Aloud

I want to show you how I think when I come to a word in my reading that I am not sure of. Listen closely while I read the first two sentences of "Off to Egypt!" "'Let's take an **excursion** to the Museum of Natural History,' Rebecca said. 'Sounds like a great trip to me,' Charles replied." I am not sure what *excursion* means, but I recognize some of the word parts that make it up. The first part is the prefix *ex-*, which means "out or out of." Next, I see the root *curs*, meaning "run," and the noun-forming suffix *-ion*. I know that this suffix adds the meaning "act of." I put these three meanings together and come up with this definition for *excursion* "the act of running or going out." Now I have to think a little creatively. If I'm running out, I'm probably going somewhere, so perhaps an *excursion* is a trip. The word *trip* in the second sentence is a context clue that supports my conclusion. *Excursion* is an "outing or trip."

Answer Key
See page 213–214 for definitions.

Lesson 13 • Words With Roots 109

LESSON 13

Words With Roots
(*cur/curs, micro, mort, scope*)

Use Words in Context

Materials Needed
- Student Workbook, p. 99

Getting Started

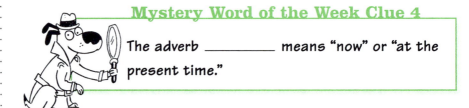

Mystery Word of the Week Clue 4
The adverb _____ means "now" or "at the present time."

★ **Review and Share** Create a display of the brochures students made for the **Create a Museum Brochure** activity on page 109 in the teacher's edition. You may first wish to check each brochure to make sure the vocabulary words are used correctly.

Model/Teach
- Ask students to open their workbooks to page 99.
- Before students do the activity, share the **Think Aloud**.
- Have students work on their own to complete the rest of the items.

English Language Learners
- In Spanish, the sound represented by the letter *k* in English is found only in words of foreign origin. So Spanish-speaking students are likely to have trouble pronouncing and spelling the word *kaleidoscope*. Give them extra practice repeating the word after hearing you or another student say it correctly. Then ask them to write it in a sentence that shows they understand its meaning.

Independent Activities
★ **Write New Questions** To help students develop more questions, suggest that pairs work together and role-play the interview. They can take turns being the museum guide and newspaper reporter, asking and answering each other's questions.

- **Write About Mortal and Immortal** The newspaper columnist Walter Lippman once wrote that human beings are mortal, but ideas are immortal. In their personal word journals, ask students to explain what they think he meant by this statement. They should tell whether they agree or disagree that words are immortal.

Think Aloud

Before you start, I'd like to explain my method for doing this activity. The directions tell me to answer each question using a vocabulary word. I read the first item: "Some pieces of pottery have been broken **into small, almost invisible** pieces. Does it take a lot of work to put all these very tiny pieces back together?" I notice that the question contains a clue as to which vocabulary word I can use in my answer. The clue is "into small, almost invisible pieces." I recall that *microscopic* combines the roots *micro* and *scope* and means "very small or too small to be seen by the eye alone." This gives me the idea to use the vocabulary word *microscopic* in my answer. Now, I have to think about how to answer the question. *It takes a lot of work and effort to put the microscopic pieces back together again.*

Answer Key

Students' responses will vary. See page 221 for sample sentences.

Chapter 2 • Words and Their Parts

Review and Extend

Materials Needed
- Student Workbook, p. 100
- Idea Web Graphic Organizer, p. 229

Getting Started

Mystery Word of the Week Clue 5
The mystery word contains the root *cur*.

★ **Review and Share** Have students trade papers and write answers to the **questions** their partners wrote for the activity on page 99 in their workbooks, using the same vocabulary word in the answers. Ask partners to circle the vocabulary word in each question and answer.

Model/Teach

- Ask students to open their workbooks to page 100 and read the new words aloud.
- Before students start the activity, do the **Think Aloud**.
- Have students complete the activity on their own. Invite them to share their responses and their thinking.

Independent Activities

★ **Create a Superhero** Distribute copies of the Idea Web Graphic Organizer. Suggest that students use it to brainstorm ideas about their superhero. After they have finished the assignment, give them the opportunity to share their paragraphs in small groups. Add new words they coined to the word wall.

- **Identify Parts of Speech** Although some of the words in this lesson look alike because they share the same root, they have different meanings depending on their part of speech and how they are used in sentences. For example, *immortal* and *mortal* are both nouns that can name people, but *immortal* and *mortal* are also adjectives when they describe a noun or pronoun. Ask students to use these four words in sentences. Then have them identify the parts of speech of the rest of the lesson words and use each in a sentence. Call attention to adjective-forming suffixes like *-ic* and *-ive* and noun suffixes like *-ity*.

Think Aloud

Let's look at the first item together so that I can share my thinking with you. "If you write in **cursive**, you write in a _____ (flowing, shaky, broken) script and the letters run together." The word *cursive* has the root *curs*. The meaning of *curs* corresponds to the word *run* in the sentence. Now if the letters run together, would the script be flowing, shaky, or broken? Certainly, they wouldn't be broken, because this is the opposite idea of the letters running together. They might be shaky, but that doesn't really connect with the idea of the letters running together. I think they would be flowing. Sometimes, you speak of running water as flowing. So *flowing* is the word I write in the blank.

Answer Key

Mystery Word of the Week:
currently
Accept other words that fit the context, too.

1. flowing 2. quickly 3. moveable
4. die 5. deathly 6. changing
7. viewing 8. barely 9. small
10. bacteria

LESSON 13

Words With Roots
(*cur/curs, micro, mort, scope*)

Check Your Mastery

Materials Needed
- Student Workbook, p. 101

Student Self-Assessment

Journal Writing Have students write in their journals telling what they learned this week about defining new words by studying their roots. Also have them describe how the word learning tip and the vocabulary building strategy helped them build their vocabularies.

Give the Test
- Have students open their workbooks to page 101.
- Tell the class that Check Your Mastery has two parts. Ask a student volunteer to read the directions for the first part aloud: "Circle the letter that best completes each item below."
- Model how to answer a test item by writing the following on the chalkboard and reading it aloud:

    Someone might use a periscope to _____.

    A. spot another ship   **C.** study germs

    B. look at a photograph   **D.** play a movie

- Ask students to discuss why A is the best choice to complete this item. Explain that they would circle A to show that this is their choice.
- Have a volunteer read the directions for the second activity: "Circle the letter of the choice that best fits in each sentence below."
- Write the following on the chalkboard to demonstrate how to answer this type of question.

    In order to warm up the slice of pizza, I put it in the _____.

    A. stethoscope   **B.** microwave   **C.** microscope

- Ask students to discuss why B is the best choice to complete this item. Explain that they would circle B to show that this is their choice.
- Tell students after they have completed the test to reread all the items and check their answers.
- Review the Check Your Mastery activities orally with students.
- Tally students' correct responses.

Answer Key
1. C 2. A 3. C 4. A 5. C 6. A
7. C 8. A 9. C 10. A

112 Chapter 2 • Words and Their Parts

LESSON 14

Compound Words With *Brain, Head, Heart,* and *Foot*

Be a Word Architect

Getting Started

Mystery Word of the Week Clue 1

The plane had to fight against a strong _____.

- See page 14 for routines for using the Mystery Word of the Week Clue. The mystery word of the week is *headwind*.

Model/Teach

- Ask the class to turn to page 102 in their workbooks.
- Tell students to look at the Word Learning Tip. Explain that compound words are made up of two shorter words that are put together to make a new, longer word. If they know the meanings of the shorter words, they may be able to determine the meaning of the compound word, although sometimes they will have to think creatively.
- Have students look at the Vocabulary Building Strategy. Remind students that if they come upon a compound word in their reading, they should identify the words that make it up and think about what these words mean. Then they may be able to put these meanings together to find a definition for the compound word.
- Before students start the activity, do the **Think Aloud** on page 114 to demonstrate how to do the activity and to think creatively about the meaning of the words.
- After you have modeled how to do the first item, have students complete the rest on their own.
- Invite students to share their responses and explain their thinking. Encourage them to think creatively to try to discover the meaning of the compound words.

Materials Needed
- Student Workbook, p. 102

Vocabulary Words
brainstorm
brainteaser
brainwash
downhearted
footbridge
foothill
footnote
headdress
headline
headlong
headstrong
headwaters
heartbroken
heartland
heartwarming

LESSON 14
Compound Words With *Brain, Head, Heart,* and *Foot*

Think Aloud

Let me show you the thinking that I do to complete this activity. The first compound word is *brainteaser*. I see two smaller words in this word—*brain* and *teaser*—so I write these two words in the blanks. Now I'm going to think about the meaning of the words. I know that *brain* is something that indicates a mental activity, and that something that *teases* you challenges you in a playful way. So I think that a *brainteaser* is something that challenges your mind or makes you think in a playful way. This is what certain types of puzzles do, so they are probably examples of brainteasers.

- Explain that some words will be easy to understand, such as *headline*, and some will be harder, such as *headstrong*. Give the meaning of each word, but do not mark students' responses as right or wrong at this point. The purpose is to encourage them to use the Word Learning Tip and Vocabulary Building Strategy to determine word meanings. This will build word consciousness by allowing students to play with word meanings without the worry of being marked incorrect.

- Allow time for groups to use flashcards to reinforce word meanings.

Independent Activities

 Play the Brain Game You many want to get students started on their lists by giving some examples, such as *brainchild* ("product of a creative mind"), *brainwave* ("electrical impulses in the brain"), and *brainwork* ("mental effort").

- **Understand Figurative Meanings** Students may find it difficult to determine the meaning of some vocabulary words because their definitions are not the literal sum of their individual parts, but a more imaginative or figurative construction. Explore the meaning of *brainstorm* with students. Explain that a *brainstorm* does not involve literal thunder, lightning, and rain. Rather, the word is used to capture the drama of a sudden, powerful idea or thought. Other figurative words include *brainwash*, *heartbroken*, and *heartwarming*.

Answer Key

1. brain, teaser **2.** head, strong
3. heart, broken **4.** foot, hill
5. brain, storm **6.** heart, warming
7. head, waters **8.** brain, wash
9. foot, note **10.** heart, land
11. head, dress **12.** foot, bridge
13. head, long **14.** head, line
15. down, hearted

See page 214 for definitions.

114 Chapter 2 • Words and Their Parts

Connect Words and Meanings

Getting Started

Mystery Word of the Week Clue 2

The bikers were slowed down by the _____ coming from the north.

★ **Review and Share** Invite groups to share the lists of "**brain**" words they made for the activity on page 103 in their workbooks. Ask them to compare their definitions with those in the dictionary. Then have the class prepare a master list or chart.

Model/Teach

- Ask the class to open their workbooks to page 104.
- Use the **Think Aloud** to model the thinking involved in completing this activity.
- After you have modeled how to do the first item, have students do the rest on their own. Invite them to share their responses and their thinking.

Independent Activities

★ **Make a Picture Dictionary** You may want to give students a couple of ideas for sketches. For example, they might draw a small hill next to a huge mountain to show a *foothill* or a thought balloon next to a person's head with the words "What a great idea!" in the balloon for *brainstorm*.

- **Spell Compound Words** Unlike words made with prefixes, roots, and suffixes, most compound words do not change the spelling of the words that are put together to make the compound. However, compound words are sometimes spelled with hyphens or left as two separate words, such as *president-elect* or *folk song*. Tell students that these variations are mainly matters of style and do not change the meaning of the compound word. Ask students to look in newspapers and magazines for examples of open compounds and compound words spelled with hyphens.

Materials Needed
- Student Workbook, pp. 104–105

Think Aloud

Let's look at the first item together so that I can model for you the thinking that I do to complete this activity. The definition tells me that this word deals with making someone accept or believe something by saying it over and over again. It's about changing a person's beliefs "so completely it's as though the beliefs were **washed** from the person's **brain**." The words *washed* and *brain* are in boldface, so I know I should put these two words together to form the compound word *brainwash*. I know that this word does not mean literally that someone goes in with soap and a mop and washes the brain clean. But it's like this in a figurative way. In other words, when you have been *brainwashed*, it's as though people have washed all your own thoughts away. They also replaced your thoughts with ideas they want you to believe. Now that I have thought about the meaning of *brainwash*, I'm going to try to complete the sentence: "If enemy agents brainwash a captured soldier, they might convince the soldier to act against his country."

Answer Key
Students' responses will vary. See page 221 for sample sentences.

Lesson 14 • Compound Words

LESSON 14

Compound Words With *Brain, Head, Heart,* and *Foot*

Learn Words in Context

Materials Needed
- Student Workbook, p. 106
- Transparency 1

Getting Started

Mystery Word of the Week Clue 3

"Let's hope we don't encounter a strong _____," said Malcolm. "If we do, you certainly won't be able to win this sailboat race."

Think Aloud

I want to share with you what I do when I come to an unfamiliar compound word in my reading. Let's read the first sentence from the passage again: "It was a sunny, spring day and Tyrone and his friends were talking about what to do. 'I just had a **brainstorm**,' said Tyrone." If I didn't know what the word *brainstorm* means, I would look at the meanings of the two words that make it up: *brain* and *storm*. I know that *brain* means "mind," and a *storm* is "a sudden, powerful burst of rain, thunder, etc." Putting the two meanings together, I get a sense that a *brainstorm* is "a sudden powerful burst of mental energy" or "a creative idea." This meaning fits with the context since Tyrone is presenting an idea that he really likes—going for a hike.

★ **Review and Share** Work with students to create a class **Picture Dictionary** by collecting and binding together a selection of the drawings which students made for the activity on page 105 in their workbooks. Then place the class Picture Dictionary in the reading corner for students to use for reference.

Model/Teach

- Have students open their workbooks to page 106.
- Explain to the class that you are going to read a story that uses all their vocabulary words. Ask students to follow along silently as you read the story aloud.
- Before you read the story a second time, do the **Think Aloud**.
- Place the transparency on the overhead projector. Tell students to listen carefully as you read the story again, stopping at every boldface word. Ask students to use the Word Learning Tip and Vocabulary Building Strategy to define each word. As they explain their thinking and the meaning of each word, write their responses on the transparency.
- After you have finished reading the passage, have students review the meaning of each compound word.

Independent Activity

- **Write a Dialogue** Ask students what they and their friends like to do on a sunny, spring day. Invite small groups to develop and write dialogues in which a group of friends debate plans for an outing. Ask them to use as many vocabulary words as they can in their dialogues.

Answer Key
See page 214 for definitions.

116 Chapter 2 • Words and Their Parts

Use Words in Context

Materials Needed
- Student Workbook, p. 107

Getting Started

Mystery Word of the Week Clue 4
After the _____ died down, they picked up speed.

⭐ **Review and Share** Ask volunteers to act out the **dialogues** they wrote for the activity on page 116 in their workbooks. Have audience members raise their hands when they hear a vocabulary word.

Model/Teach
- Direct the class to open their workbooks to page 107.
- Before students begin the activity, do the **Think Aloud**.
- Ask students to work on their own to complete the rest of the items.
- Have students share their answers and explain their thinking.

English Language Learners
- Spelling compound words is challenging when the words that are combined end and begin with the same letter, such as in *headdress*. Point out to students that when they combine two words to create a new word, they do not drop or add letters. Give students other examples such as *bookkeeper* and *nighttime*. Have them write the words and then draw a line between the words that make up the compound.

Independent Activity

⭐ **Write a Letter** Review correct letter format with students. Remind students to be brief but clear in presenting their question or problem.

Think Aloud

Here's my method for doing this activity. The directions tell me to answer each question by writing a sentence in which I must use a vocabulary word. I read the first item: "What bright idea did you have on how to spend a rainy day?" I notice that the question contains a clue to which vocabulary word I can use in my answer. The clue is "bright idea." I recall that a *brainstorm*, which combines the words *brain* and *storm*, means "a creative idea" or "burst of thought." This tells me I can use the vocabulary word *brainstorm* in my answer. Now, I have to think about how to answer the question. I remember that I once got the idea on a rainy day to write and put on a play. So, I write this answer on the line following item 1: "One rainy day I had the **brainstorm** to write and put on a play."

Answer Key
Students' responses will vary. See page 221–222 for sample sentences.

Lesson 14 • Compound Words 117

LESSON 14

Compound Words With *Brain, Head, Heart,* and *Foot*

Review and Extend

Materials Needed
- Student Workbook, p. 108
- Idea Web Graphic Organizer, p. 229

Getting Started

Mystery Word of the Week Clue 5

The Mystery Word of the Week contains the word *head.*

Review and Share Have volunteers exchange the **letters** they wrote for the activity on page 107. Ask students to underline the vocabulary words and write replies to their partners' letters. Then have them review each other's work and share it with the class.

Model/Teach
- Direct the class to turn to page 108 in their workbooks.
- Before students start the activity, do the Think Aloud .
- After you have modeled how to sort the first word in the box, have students sort the rest of the words on their own.
- Ask students to share their responses and their thinking.

English Language Learners
- Since students have been taking compound words apart and putting them back together during this lesson, they may assume that any two words can be combined to form a new word. Explain that only some English words can be combined and only in a particular order. Tell them that if they are unsure about whether or not a word is a legitimate compound, they should check a dictionary.

Independent Activities

Make a Word Web Distribute copies of the Idea Web Graphic Organizer. Arrange students in groups of four to brainstorm ideas about the word *heartwarming.* Then bring the class back together and have them share their ideas.

- **Tutor Your Peers** Arrange students in groups of three. Assign each student three of the new compound words in the box and have them work independently to become "experts" on their meaning. Then have students come together to "teach" their words to the rest of the group.

Think Aloud

I read the first new compound word in the box: *headquarters.* Since it is made up of the word *head* and the word *quarters,* I write it on the first line of the chart labeled head. Putting the meanings of the two short words together, I get the meaning of *head,* "at the front of" and *quarters,* coins or places where people live or work. *Headquarters* must mean "the place from which an organization is run or where the most important part of an organization is centered."

Answer Key
Mystery Word of the Week: headwind
Accept other words that fit the context, too.

1. **brainwave** electrical impulse in the brain 2. **brainwork** mental effort 3. **headstand** act of standing on one's head 4. **headquarters** center of operations 5. **headlight** light at the front of a car
6. **headband** strip worn around the head 7. **heartache** emotional pain
8. **heartbeat** rhythm of the pulsing heart 9. **footpath** trail for walkers
10. **footwear** covering for the feet

Chapter 2 • Words and Their Parts

Check Your Mastery

Materials Needed
- Student Workbook, p. 109

Give the Test

- Direct the class to open their workbooks to page 109.
- Explain that the Check Your Mastery activity has two parts and read the directions for the first activity aloud: "Complete the following analogies by filling in each blank with a vocabulary word."
- Model how to complete the analogies by writing the following on the chalkboard and reading it aloud:

  Desert is to **ocean** as **coast** is to _____.

  A. heartland　　**B.** headlong　　**C.** foothill

- Ask students to complete the analogy (or double comparison) with a vocabulary word. Remind them that analogies can be comparisons between two words that are similar or opposites. Guide them to see that the relationship between the first two boldface words is that of opposites. Then they can complete the analogy by choosing a vocabulary word that is the opposite of the third word, *coast*. The answer is *heartland*.
- Now read the directions aloud for the second activity: "Choose the word that best completes each sentence. Circle the letter of your choice."
- Model how to answer the test items in the second part by writing the following on the chalkboard and reading it aloud:

  If you only have a few minutes to read the newspaper, you will probably just read the _____.

  A. footnotes　　**B.** headlines　　**C.** brainteasers

- Ask students to choose the word that best completes the sentence. Then have them explain their choice.
- When students have completed all the items, have them review their responses.
- Review the test orally with the students.
- Tally students' correct responses.

Student Self-Assessment

Journal Writing Suggest that students think and write about how the Word Learning Tip and Vocabulary Building Strategy helped them this week to understand and use compounds made from *brain*, *head*, *heart*, and *foot* to learn more words.

Answer Key

1. downhearted 2. footnote
3. footbridge 4. headdress
5. headstrong 6. C 7. B 8. C
9. C 10. B

LESSON 15

Word Families (*name, nomen/nomin, onym*)

Be a Word Architect

Materials Needed
- Student Workbook, p. 110

Vocabulary Words
acronym
anonymous
antonym
denominator
nameless
namely
namesake
nametag
nominal
nominate
nomination
nominator
pseudonym
rename
synonym

Getting Started

Mystery Word of the Week Clue 1

All the coins in my pocket are the same _____: pennies.

- See page 14 for routines for using the Mystery Word of the Week Clue. The mystery word of the week is *denomination*.

Model/Teach

- Have students turn to page 110 in their workbooks.

- Tell students to read the Word Learning Tip. Point out that when they see a word they don't know, they can check to see if it contains a shorter word they can identify. The shorter word may be attached to word parts or another word. In this lesson, they will learn words that include the word *name*, the root *nomen/nomin*, or the root *onym*. Explain to students that when they see these word parts in an unfamiliar word, they know that the unfamiliar words tells something about names or naming.

- Ask students to look at the Vocabulary Building Strategy. Remind them that they can use the meaning of a word part they already know to help them learn the meaning of an unfamiliar word. To determine the meaning of a bigger word, students can use the meaning "name" or "naming" to help them.

- Ask a student to read the directions for the activity aloud. Use the **Think Aloud** on page 121 to model how to do the activity.

- Have students complete the rest of the activity on their own and share their responses.

- Tell students to look at the branch of the tree for *nomen/nomin*. Point out that all of their vocabulary words use the spelling *nomin* for this root. However, when they read, they may encounter new words in which this root is spelled *nomen* (*nomenclature*).

120   Chapter 2 • Words and Their Parts

- Ask students to try to determine the meaning of the vocabulary words by using their knowledge of word parts. Explain that they should try to think creatively as they do this. Some words will be easy to understand, such as *rename*. Some will be harder, such as *nominal*. As students provide definitions, tell them the meaning of each word. However, at this time do not mark their responses as right or wrong. The purpose is to provide an opportunity for students to use word parts to determine the meaning of unfamiliar words.

- Divide the class into small groups. Allow them time to use flashcards to reinforce word meanings.

English Language Learners

- Write *nametag* on the chalkboard. Invite English language learners to write their names on index cards. Then invite students in early speech production to say: My *nametag* reads _____. Use this activity as an opportunity for English language learners to practice introducing themselves to others. You may also wish to have those in intermediate and advanced fluency write interesting *pseudonyms* for themselves.

Independent Activity

⭐ **Create a Pseudonym** Before students start this activity, discuss some famous pseudonyms with them. For example, Mark Twain is the pseudonym for Samuel Clemens. After working on the steam boats going up and down the Mississippi River, he chose as his pen name "Mark Twain," after the term that means that the depth of the water is twelve feet. After you have discussed famous pseudonyms, have students write paragraphs explaining their pseudonym choices.

Think Aloud

I want to model for you the thinking that I do to complete this activity. Let's look at the first word together: *acronym*. I see the root *-onym*, so I place this word on the branch of the tree labeled *onym* and I circle the letters *onym*. I know that these letters spell a Greek root that means "to name" or "naming." I think an *acronym* is probably some kind of a name. I also see the prefix *acro-*. I'm not sure what this prefix means, but I've seen it before in a word like *acrobat*, which still doesn't help me know what *acronym* means. So I'm going to make a guess as to what this word means and check my guess against the glossary. I find that an *acronym* is a word formed from the first or first few letters of the words in a phrase.

Answer Key

name
- nam(e)less
- nam(e)ly
- nam(e)sake
- (name)tag
- re(name)

nomen/nomin
- de(nomin)ator
- (nomin)al
- (nomin)ate
- (nomin)ation
- (nomin)ator

onym
- acr(onym)
- an(onym)ous
- ant(onym)
- pseud(onym)
- syn(onym)

See page 214 for definitions.

Lesson 15 • Word Families

LESSON 15

Word Families (*name, nomen/nomin, onym*)

Connect Words and Meanings

Materials Needed
- Student Workbook, pp. 112–113

Think Aloud

Let's look at the definition for *pseudonym*: "a false or made-up name." I notice the root *onym* in this word, which I know means "name." So a *pseudo* name is a false name or a made-up name. I know that sometimes writers use a pseudonym. Sometimes, they just don't want their identity to be known. For example, a famous judge may write a mystery story set in a courtroom. She thinks it might affect her reputation if her colleagues—the people she works with—knew that she did this. They might think she was not acting in a way a judge should. So she uses a pseudonym to hide her identity. Now that I have thought about the word *pseudonym*, I'm going to answer the question: "Why might an author use a pseudonym?" *An author might use a pseudonym to prevent people from knowing her true identity.*

Answer Key
Students' responses will vary. See page 222 for sample sentences.

Getting Started

Mystery Word of the Week Clue 2

It is impossible to make seventeen cents from a single _____ of coins.

Review and Share Ask students to share their paragraphs explaining their choices for **pseudonyms** from the activity on page 110 in their workbooks. Add all the "name" words to the Word Wall. Continue to add other new words as students find them.

Model/Teach
- Have students turn to page 112 in their workbooks.
- Before students begin the activity, do the **Think Aloud**.
- Ask students to complete the activity independently and then share their responses.

Independent Activities

Give a Speech Lead a brief discussion with students about what qualities make a good presidential candidate and why certain people are better qualified than others to run for the presidency. Then ask them to imagine that they have an opportunity to nominate a candidate and must write a nominating speech.

- **Discuss Parts of Speech** Several vocabulary words are closely related, such as *nominate/nomination/nominator*, so this is a good opportunity to help students distinguish among them. Point out that one way to distinguish these words is by part of speech. *Nominate* is a verb. *Nomination* and *nominator* are nouns. Ask volunteers to use these words in sentences to show their understanding.

Learn Words in Context

Materials Needed
- Student Workbook, p. 114
- Transparency 1

Getting Started

Mystery Word of the Week Clue 3
The twenty-dollar bill is the _____ usually given by ATMs.

⭐ **Review and Share** Invite volunteers to give their presidential speeches for the **Give a Speech** activity on page 113 in their workbooks. As speeches are given, ask the class to pay attention to which vocabulary words are used and if they are used in the correct context.

Model/Teach

- Have students turn to page 114 in their workbooks.
- Tell students that you are going to read a story that includes vocabulary words they are now learning. Ask them to follow along silently as you read the story aloud.
- Tell students you are going to reread the passage. You will stop at each boldface word so that they can determine its meaning.
- Before rereading the passage, do the **Think Aloud**.
- Place the transparency on the overhead projector. Reread the passage aloud, stopping at each vocabulary word. Remind students to use the Word Learning Tip and the Vocabulary Building Strategy. Record their thinking on the transparency.
- After you have finished reading the passage a second time, review the meaning of the vocabulary words.

Independent Activity

⭐ **Create Acronyms** Take a few minutes to review the definition of *acronym*. Then invite pairs to make up the name of an organization using an *acronym*. When students are finished, give them an opportunity to share their *acronyms* with the class. You might also have them hunt for *acronyms* in magazines and newspapers.

Think Aloud

I want to show you what I do when I come across an unfamiliar word that contains *name*, *nomen/nomin*, or *onym*. Read the first sentence silently as I read it aloud: "The convention is meeting to **nominate** a candidate for president." If I didn't know what the word *nominate* means, the first thing I would notice is the root *nomin*. I know that this root means "name." I think that *nominate* is a verb, since it tells me what the convention is meeting to do and it has the verb ending *-ate*. It probably is a verb that means "name." Now I am going to replace *nominate* with *name* in the sentence to see if it fits: "The convention is meeting to name a candidate for president." That makes sense, so now I am sure that *nominate* is a synonym for *name*.

Answer Key
See page 214 for definitions.

LESSON 15
Word Families (*name, nomen/nomin, onym*)

Use Words in Context

Materials Needed
- Student Workbook, p. 115

Getting Started

Mystery Word of the Week Clue 4

Dictators of countries sometimes put their picture on every _____ of the country's money.

★ **Review and Share** Invite invite students to share their **acronyms** from the activity on page 123 in the teacher's edition. Create a bulletin board display of acronyms.

Model/Teach
- Have students turn to page 115 in their workbooks.
- Before students start, do the **Think Aloud**.
- Have students complete the activity on their own and share their responses.

Think Aloud

The first sentence reads, "My fellow Americans, it is with great pride that I accept your _____ for President of the United States." I know that the speaker has just been *nominated* because he's giving an acceptance speech. I've noticed that the vocabulary words that are about politics all have the root *nomen/nomin* in them, so I'm pretty sure that the word that fits in the blank is in the *nomen/nomin* family. I eliminate *nominal* and *denomination* because they just don't fit the context of politics. Next I try *nominate*, but *nominate* is a verb, and I am looking for a noun. I try *nominator*, but this is the person who is named. Then I try *nomination*. That's the correct word. Someone would accept a *nomination*.

Independent Activities

★ **Design a Campaign Slogan** Spend a few minutes talking about the purpose of campaign slogans and posters in elections for public offices. Then invite students to work on their own to create campaign slogans and posters for Brent Brentson. Remind them to use at least three vocabulary words.

- **Make a Nametag** Invite students to make a *nametag* for themselves on which they write their given name. Then ask them to *rename* themselves. Ask: If you could give yourself another name, what name would it be? Have them write their new name underneath their given name. Then have them write about why they chose this name.

Answer Key
1. nomination 2. nominator
3. nominate 4. acronym
5. anonymous *or* nameless
6. nametag 7. namesake
8. denominator 9. synonym
10. antonym

Review and Extend

Materials Needed
- Student Workbook, p. 116

Getting Started

Mystery Word of the Week Clue 5

"Mr. McIntyre," said the bank manager to the teller, "please arrange the cash neatly according to _____."

⭐ **Review and Share** Invite students to display their **posters** and **slogans** from the **Design a Campaign Slogan** activity on page 115 in their workbooks. Give them an opportunity to look at and discuss them among themselves. Then lead a class discussion having students point out the variety of ways they used the vocabulary words.

Model/Teach
- Have students turn to page 116 in their workbooks.
- Before students begin, use the **Think Aloud**.
- Read the directions for the second activity aloud, and have students complete both activities. Invite students to share their responses for both activities.

English Language Learners
- Many English language learners will pronounce the word part *-onym* as if the *-y* were long. Tell them that the *-y* in *-onym* is pronounced like a short *i*. Invite them to say aloud after you the following words: *antonym*, *synonym*, *acronym*, *pseudonym*, and *anonymous*.

Independent Activity

⭐ **Interview a Candidate** Brainstorm with students issues that affect them in their communities and which they feel a presidential or senatorial candidate should address. Write their ideas on the chalkboard. Then challenge them to write two questions to ask one of these candidates. Remind them to use at least three vocabulary words.

Think Aloud

Let me model for you how I would respond to the first item. The question is: "You want to become a famous actor, and you decide your name is too ordinary. You want a more memorable name. What can you do?" Hmm, what would I do? It's pretty obvious that I would give myself a new name. Now I need to choose a vocabulary word that describes giving myself a new name. I look at the vocabulary words to see which one I would use. I see the word *rename*. That's definitely the word I want to use in my sentence. Now I can write my sentence: "If I wanted a new name, I would <u>rename</u> myself."

Answer Key

Mystery Word of the Week: denomination
Accept other words that fit the context, too.

Students' responses will vary. See page 222 for sample sentences.

Lesson 15 • Word Families

LESSON 15

Word Families
(*name, nomen/nomin, onym*)

Check Your Mastery

Materials Needed
- Student Workbook, p. 117

Student Self-Assessment

Journal Writing Have students grade themselves on their understanding of each word. Use whatever grading system you normally use in the classroom. Invite students to explain their grades in journal entries, and to suggest ways they could improve their grades by using word parts more effectively to learn new words.

Give the Test
- Have students turn to page 117 in their workbooks.
- Read the directions aloud: "Circle the letter of the correct answer." Explain to students that there are four word choices and their job is to choose the best word.
- Model how to circle the letter of the correct answer by writing the following on the chalkboard:

   Someone who is nominated for an office is a _____.

   A. president   **B.** nominee   **C.** speaker   **D.** official

- Ask a volunteer what is the best word to complete the sentence. Then ask the student to explain his or her response.
- Have students complete the Check Your Mastery activity. Tell students to read over their answers after they have finished. Point out that if they want to change an answer, they need to erase the old answer completely.
- Review the Check Your Mastery activity orally with the students.
- Tally students' correct responses.

Answer Key
1. B 2. C 3. D 4. A 5. C 6. A
7. D 8. D 9. A 10. B

LESSON 16

Word Families (graph)

Be a Word Architect

Getting Started

Mystery Word of the Week Clue 1

In the Old West, the _____ operator was often the first person in a town to learn important news.

- See page 14 for routines for using the Mystery Word of the Week Clue. The mystery word of the week is *telegraph*.

Model/Teach

- Have students turn to page 118 in their workbooks.
- Ask a student volunteer to read the Word Learning Tip aloud. Explain that many words are built from *graph*. Tell them that prefixes, suffixes, roots, and other words can be added to *graph* to form new words. Ask students to suggest words that contain this word part and are members of the *graph* word family.
- Have a student volunteer read the Vocabulary Building Strategy. Explain that whenever they see *graph* in an unfamiliar word, they know that that word has something to do with writing, drawing, or communications. By adding the meanings of other word parts in a specific word to this meaning, they can learn a lot of new words in the *graph* or other word families.
- Ask a student to read the directions for the activity aloud. Doing this activity will help students understand the many different ways that words can be formed using *graph* as the base.
- Do the **Think Aloud** on page 128 to model how to do the activity.
- To reinforce the Think Aloud, write the following on the chalkboard: _____ + graph = autograph
- Have students fill in the blank with the missing word part and explain how they can use the word parts to find the meaning of *autograph*.
- Ask students to complete the activity on their own. Check answers orally. If you wish, write the words on the chalkboard and show their divisions into word parts.

Materials Needed
- Student Workbook, p. 118

Vocabulary Words
autobiographical
autobiography
autograph
biographical
biography
graphic
graphics
graphite
monograph
oceanography
paragraph
phonograph
photograph
photographic
photography

LESSON 16 Word Families (*graph*)

Think Aloud

Let's look at the third word on the vocabulary list: *autograph*. First I'm going to locate *graph* in this word. I see that there is one prefix before it: *auto*. So *autograph* is formed by adding a prefix in front of *graph*. Now that I understand how the word is formed, I write it on the branch of the tree that is labeled "Prefix + Graph," and I circle the word part *graph*. Adding these word-part meanings together helps me to determine that *autograph* means "your own name or signature that you write on something."

- As students tell you where each word belongs on the tree, invite them to try to determine the meaning by putting together the meaning of the word parts. Explain that some words will be easy to understand, such as *biography*. Others will be more difficult. Give the correct meaning of each word, but at this point do not mark students' responses as right or wrong. The purpose of this activity is to build proficiency in using the Word Learning Tip and Vocabulary Building Strategy to determine the meaning of words.

- After students have completed this activity, allow time for them to work in small groups to use flashcards to reinforce word meanings.

English Language Learners

- The letter combination *ph* may pose trouble for English language learners for various reasons in addition to the fact that they need to remember it is pronounced /f/. For example, in Spanish, the letter *h* is silent and final consonant blends are uncommon. In some languages of India, the *p* and the *h* would be pronounced separately as part of separate syllables. For speakers of Chinese, Japanese, or Urdu, /f/ is a problematic sound. If applicable, encourage your English language learners to practice the sounds separately as well as in the vocabulary words. Have them read aloud all the words with *graph* in this lesson so that these words can more quickly become automatic sight words.

Independent Activity

Collect Autographs Before students start writing, have them work in small groups to create a list of autographs to collect. Then ask them to work individually to write their paragraphs.

Answer Key

Prefix + graph
auto(graph)   para(graph)
mono(graph)

One or More Prefixes + graph + Suffix
autobio(graph)y   bio(graph)y
autobio(graph)ical   bio(graph)ical

Root + graph
photo(graph)   phono(graph)

Graph + suffix
(graph)ic   (graph)ite
(graph)ics

Word or Root + graph + Suffix
ocean(ograph)y   photo(graph)ic
photo(graph)y

See page 215 for definitions.

Chapter 2 • Words and Their Parts

Connect Words and Meanings

Getting Started

Mystery Word of the Week Clue 2

_____ messages today are sent by satellite as well as through wires and cables.

⭐ **Review and Share** Have students share the paragraphs they wrote for the activity on page 118 in their workbooks. Add the "graph" words to the word wall.

Model/Teach

- Ask students turn to page 120 in their workbooks.
- Do the **Think Aloud**.
- After students complete the activity, have them share their responses and explain the thinking they did to complete each sentence.

Independent Activities

⭐ **Have a Biographical Chat** Give students time to discuss different types of biographical material they have read. Walk around the classroom while they have their chats so that you can suggest different biographies and autobiographies. Then ask students to write their paragraphs.

- **Make a Science Connection** Have interested students search for other scientific words using *graph*. Some of these words might be the names of devices, such as **seismograph**, a machine that records earthquakes, or **polygraph**, a lie detector. Invite students to discuss briefly the meanings of their words.

Materials Needed
- Student Workbook, pp. 120–121

Think Aloud

Let's read the definition for *oceanography* together: "the science dealing with oceans and the plants and animals that live in them." I see the word *ocean* in *oceanography* and the suffix *-y*, which sometimes indicates an activity. I guess that when you engage in the activity of studying the ocean, you read just about everything that was written about it. That's the connection with *graph*—writing. Now that I understand the word, I'm going to complete the sentence: "In a book on oceanography, I would find information about creatures that live in the sea."

Answer Key
Students' responses will vary. See page 222 for sample sentences.

Lesson 16 • Word Families

LESSON 16 Word Families (*graph*)

Learn Words in Context

Materials Needed
- Student Workbook, p. 122
- Transparency 1

Getting Started

Mystery Word of the Week Clue 3

The first _____ cable across the Atlantic Ocean was laid down in 1866.

⭐ **Review and Share** Have students share the paragraphs they wrote after their **biographical chats** from the activity on page 121. Post a list on the bulletin board of classroom favorites.

Model/Teach
- Have students turn to page 122 in their workbooks.
- Read the passage aloud as students follow along silently.
- Before rereading the passage, do the **Think Aloud**.
- Place the transparency on the overhead projector. Read the passage aloud a second time, stopping at each vocabulary word so that students can determine the word's meaning. Remind them to use the Word Learning Tip and the Vocabulary Building Strategy. Record their responses on the transparency.
- After you have reread the passage and discussed all the vocabulary words, review all of the meanings of the vocabulary words again.

English Language Learners
- Help English language learners learn how suffixes can indicate the part of speech of a word. The *-y* suffix indicates a noun. The *-ic(al)* suffix indicates an adjective, but *-ics* is once again a noun suffix. Build additional words by changing the endings of the vocabulary words: for example, *oceanographic*, *photographic*. Show how the different variants function grammatically. For example: *The oceanographer studies oceanography at the oceanographic center.*

Independent Activity
- **Continue the Interview** Ask students to jot down other questions they would like to ask Dr. Luce. Then, using the format of "Interview with a Writer," have them continue the interview.

Think Aloud

I want to model for you the way I go about understanding a word with *graph* in it. The writer being interviewed, Dr. Luce, says, "So far, I have written twelve **biographies** of famous people. . . ." I know that *graph* usually has to do with writing or drawing, and the phrase "I have written" tells me I'm right about that. A biography is something that is written. But what kind of writing, specifically? Well, she says "biographies of famous people." So I guess a *biography* is a piece of writing about a famous person. If I looked in the dictionary, I would find out that that's a very close guess. It's not the exact definition, but it's close.

Answer Key
See page 215 for definitions.

Use Words in Context

Materials Needed
- Student Workbook, p. 123

Getting Started

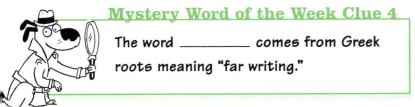

Mystery Word of the Week Clue 4
The word _____ comes from Greek roots meaning "far writing."

⭐ **Review and Share** Allow pairs of students time to act out their **interviews** from the activity on page 122, with one student playing the role of Dr. Luce and the other the role of the interviewer.

Model/Teach

- Have students turn to page 123 in their workbooks.
- Tell students that the comic strip on this page shows the writer who was interviewed on the previous page, Dr. Lucille Luce. Dr. Luce is in her study.
- Before students start, do the **Think Aloud**.
- Ask students to complete the activity independently. Then ask volunteers to read the comic frames aloud.

Independent Activities

⭐ **Extend the Comic Strip** Invite students to draw their comic-strip frames either in class or at home. Encourage them to use their imaginations in thinking up what might happen to Dr. Luce.

- **Review Word Meaning With a Board Game** Divide the class into small groups. Distribute heavy stock paper or have the students use a single sheet of regular paper to draw a path. Ask them to mark fifteen spaces along the path and write a vocabulary word in each space. Provide coins, bottle caps, or other items as counters. Each student places his or her counter at the starting line. One by one students take turns rolling the dice and moving the spaces indicated. As he or she lands on a space, the student must tell the meaning of the word or else go back that number of spaces.

Think Aloud

Let me model for you how I would complete this activity. I need to use the clues from what Dr. Luce says to fill in what she doesn't say. I know that all of the blanks will be filled with *graph* words, so I have to keep in mind the meanings of those words to comprehend what she's talking about. In the first frame, she says, "It's so exciting to write about myself! I'm just starting to write my _____. . . ." Well, if she's writing about herself, what kind of writing is she doing? I remember that an *autobiography* is a person's own story, but is the word that fits *autobiography* or *autobiographical*? To determine this, I'll reread the sentence and see which word fits grammatically. "I'm just starting to write my *autobiographical*?" No, I need a noun here, not an adjective. "I'm just starting to write my *autobiography*?" Yes, that's it.

Answer Key
1. autobiography 2. biography
3. paragraph 4. photography
5. phonograph 6. oceanography
7. monograph 8. graphics
9. autograph 10. photograph

Lesson 16 • Word Families   **131**

LESSON 16 Word Families (*graph*)

Review and Extend

Materials Needed
- Student Workbook, p. 124

Think Aloud

Let's read the first item together. "A person who takes pictures with a camera is a(n)_____." I see the clue "takes pictures." I remember that a *photograph* is a picture taken with a camera. So I add the ending *-er* to *photograph* to create the word *photographer*, which means "a person who takes photographs." If I had started with the word *photography*, I would have dropped the suffix *-y* before adding *-er* to form *photographer*.

Answer Key
Mystery Word of the Week:
telegraph
Accept other words that fit the context, too.

1. photographer 2. oceanographer
3. biographer 4. monographer

Students' responses to 5–8 will vary. See page 222 for sample sentences.

Getting Started

Mystery Word of the Week Clue 5
The _____ was invented by Samuel F. B. Morse.

⭐ **Review and Share** Invite students to display the comic-strip frames they created for the **Extend the Comic Strip** activity on page 123 in their workbooks. Have them read the texts aloud and describe the drawings.

Model/Teach
- Ask students to turn to page 124 in their workbooks.
- Use the **Think Aloud** to model how to complete the first activity.
- Have students complete the activity on their own. Then ask them to complete the second activity and check their answers.

English Language Learners
- Many Spanish-speaking students will be familiar with words in their native language that contain *graf*. Provide time for students to work in small groups to generate a list of these words and then share them with the class. See how many English/Spanish cognates they can come up with. For example, *biography-biografía*.

Independent Activity

⭐ **Write About It** Allow students to talk about their preferred "graph" goals in pairs or groups of three. To share this activity, you might take a poll of students' preferred goals, and have students discuss the reasons behind their choices.

132 Chapter 2 • Words and Their Parts

Check Your Mastery

Materials Needed
- Student Workbook, p. 125

Give the Test
- Have students turn to page 125 in their workbooks.
- Read the directions aloud. "Read each item below. Write the word in the blank that best completes each sentence." Explain that students will select the correct word to fit in the sentence by choosing from the three words in parentheses. Instruct them to write their choices in the blanks.
- Model answering a question by writing the following on the chalkboard.

    A machine that measures shock waves in the earth is a _____ (*stenographer*, *graph*, *seismograph*).

- Ask students why *seismograph* is the correct choice.
- Have students do the Check Your Mastery activity independently.
- Remind them to check their answers when they are finished.
- Review the answers orally as a group.
- Ask students to discuss how the Word Learning Tip and the Vocabulary Building Strategy helped them find correct responses to these ten items.
- Tally students' correct responses.

Student Self-Assessment

Journal Writing Ask students, "If you were to read a different unfamiliar word containing *graph*, how well do you think you would be able to guess the word's meaning before looking it up?" Have them respond to this question in their journals.

Answer Key
1. biography 2. autobiography
3. photographic 4. photography
5. graphics 6. phonograph
7. oceanography 8. graphite
9. monograph 10. graphic

CHAPTER 3

Content Words

Lesson 17 Words About Problem Solving **136**

Lesson 18 Words About the
Circulatory System **143**

Lesson 19 Words About the Water Cycle **150**

Lesson 20 Words About Great Leaders **157**

Lesson 21 Words About Research **164**

Lesson 22 Test-Taking Words **171**

Research Base

- **Word Learning Tip** Academic content-area words are words that describe something about the specific subject about which you are reading. You can determine that a new word is a content word because it is usually the longest and most difficult word in the sentence and does not appear in books about other subjects.

- **Vocabulary Building Strategy** You can learn the meaning of content words by thinking about how they relate to the main subject of the material you are reading.

- **Research-Based Lists** Chapter 3 includes content words that may be assessed on standardized and state achievement criterion tests. They are derived from state and national standards and frameworks of what is taught at each grade level in that content area, from textbooks dealing with those content areas, as well as from the McRel lists. These words are not only conceptually rich, but important because they are frequently used in the content areas beginning at this grade level and continuing into subsequent grades.

LESSON 17

Words About Problem Solving

Learn Words About a New Subject

Materials Needed
- Student Workbook, pp. 128–129
- Transparency 2

Vocabulary Words
approximate
calculate
certain
estimation
probability

Getting Started

Mystery Word of the Week Clue 1

The _____ that an event will happen sometimes has to be estimated.

- See page 14 for routines for using the Mystery Word of the Week Clue. The mystery word of the week is *likelihood*.

Model/Teach

- Ask the class to turn to page 128 in their workbooks.

- Invite a volunteer to read the Word Learning Tip aloud. Discuss with students that the content words may be words with which they are not familiar. Explain that these words are often used in a specific content area; they are not used as often in books that are not about that subject or in everyday speech and writing.

- Read the Vocabulary Building Strategy to the class as they follow along in their books. Point out that content words may seem difficult, but students can learn their meaning when they remember that these content words all relate to the big idea of problem solving. Have students talk about what they already know about problem solving.

- Direct students to read the directions and look at the story in their workbook. Read the text aloud.

- Before you read the text a second time, do the **Think Aloud** on page 137 to model how to find the meaning of the content words.

- After you have modeled how to find the meaning of the word *probability* by associating the word with the topic, read each scene aloud again. This time, pause at each boldface word to give students time to think about the word's definition.

Chapter 3 • Content Words

- Place the transparency on the overhead projector. Have the class add the big idea of the lesson to the top of the transparency.

- Reread the page, again pausing at each word in boldface. Direct the class to think about how each boldface word is linked to the idea of problem solving or to one of the other words. Explain that you also want them to tell you what each word means. For example, probability is connected to the idea of problem solving because it is how likely something is to happen. Be sure they tell you their thinking as they determine each word's meaning.

- As students discuss a word, record their thinking and the definition of the word on the transparency.

- After students have discussed each word, allow them to work in small groups. Give them an opportunity to use flashcards to reinforce word meanings

Independent Activities

- **Discuss the Outcome** Spend a few minutes having the class discuss what they think the outcome will be when Jamal picks a marble from the jar. Do they think the marble will be black or white? Why? Give all students an opportunity to predict the outcome by taking a vote and recording the results on the chalkboard. Encourage students to use vocabulary words in their predictions.

- **Solve a Visual Problem** Arrange students in groups of four to create a visual math problem similar to the problem in the story. If possible, have available tiles, marbles, or small squares of paper on which they can color or write numbers. Ask groups to exchange problems with another group and solve. Encourage them to use new vocabulary words in their discussions. Add any new content words to the word wall.

Think Aloud

Before I share my thinking about how to understand the meaning of these content words, I need to have an idea of what the author's big topic is. I know all of the content words will describe something about that big idea. I ask myself: How are all of these words connected? I look at the words in boldface. They all seem to have to do with problem solving. I read the dialogue between Jamal and Brittany. Jamal says: "Look at this huge jar. It looks like there are more than 300 black and white marbles in it." Brittany asks: "What is the **probability** that you can close your eyes, put your hand in the jar, and choose a black marble?" If I didn't know the word *probability*, I could understand from the dialogue that it probably means: "how likely it is that something will happen." When you want to know the *probability* of something happening, it's important to use problem-solving skills to help you determine outcomes. That's the big idea!

Answer Key
See page 215 for definitions.

LESSON 17
Words About Problem Solving

Connect Words and Meanings

Materials Needed
- Student Workbook, p. 130
- Umbrella Chart Graphic Organizer, p. 228

Think Aloud

Here's what I would do to complete this activity. First I would read the definition to see which vocabulary word fits in the blank. Here's the definition: "an answer that you believe is close to the exact answer; the act of coming up with an answer that is close to the exact answer." I notice the words "close to the exact answer." I know from my math experience that when I want an answer that is close to the exact answer I estimate, and since *estimation* is one of the words, I think that's the correct word. So I write *estimation* in the blank.

Answer Key
1. estimation 2. approximate
3. probability 4. certain
5. calculate 6. estimation
7. certain 8. calculate
9. approximate 10. probability

Getting Started

Mystery Word of the Week Clue 2

The weatherperson said that the _____ of snow was about 75 percent.

★ **Review and Share** Continue the discussion about the possible **outcomes** for the activity on page 137 in the teacher's edition. To extend the activity, change the ratio of white marbles to black marbles to 3 times as many black marbles as white marbles. Encourage students to use vocabulary words in their discussion. Have them discuss how the Word Learning Tip and Vocabulary Building Strategy helped them learn new content words.

Model/Teach
- Ask the class to open their workbooks to page 130.
- Use the **Think Aloud** to model how you would complete this activity.
- Have students finish the rest of the page on their own. Then ask students to share their responses.

Independent Activities

★ **Review of Chapter 2: Word Parts and Content Words** Remind students that a *suffix* is a letter or group of letters added to the end of a word or root to change its meaning. If necessary, help students generate a list of suffixes, such as *-ing*, *-ed*, and *-or*. Have students work on their own or in pairs to see how many new words they can make from the vocabulary words by changing their suffixes. Ask students to check their work in a dictionary.

- **Create an Umbrella Chart** Arrange students in five groups to create an umbrella chart for *calculate*, *probability*, or *estimation*. For *probability*, for example, students might suggest *more likely*, *less likely*, *possibly*, *sometimes*, or *unlikely* and write these words on the spokes of the umbrella.

Use Content Words

Materials Needed
- Student Workbook, p. 131

Getting Started

Mystery Word of the Week Clue 3

In all _____, you'll choose a blue marble because there are twice as many blue marbles as green marbles.

⭐ **Review and Share** Invite students to share the **new words** they used in the activity on page 130. Possibilities include *approximately, approximated, calculated, calculating, calculator, estimator, estimate, estimated,* or *probable*. Add these words to the chart.

Model/Teach
- Have students open their workbooks to page 131.
- Before students begin, use the **Think Aloud**.
- After you have modeled how to complete the first tip, have students complete the rest of the page on their own. Then ask students to work in pairs to share their responses.

English Language Learners
- Pair more fluent English language learners with those in early speech emergence. Give each pair a handful of small objects, such as coins. Challenge pairs to estimate how many objects there are. Depending on students' fluency they can either write the estimates or say it aloud: "My *estimation* is 25 coins."

Independent Activity

⭐ **Research a Famous Problem Solver** Provide students with reference materials—such as encyclopedias, mathematics textbooks, and computers with Internet access—to research their reports. Remind them to use at least three vocabulary words, along with two new words that relate to problem solving.

Think Aloud

I'd like to share with you how I'd complete this activity. I notice right away that there are ten mathematical tips. That's interesting. The first tip is "When all the tiles in a jar are the same color, you can be _____ that you will choose a tile that is that color." Actually, this is pretty easy because the word that I thought of immediately was "sure," which also means *certain*. I know that "sure" is not a vocabulary word, but *certain* is, and in the context of problem solving, *certain* means that "something will definitely happen." I also know that *certain* deals with *probability* outcomes, so that reinforces that I've chosen the correct word. I write *certain* in the blank.

Answer Key
1. certain 2. calculate
3. probability 4. approximate
5. estimation 6. probability
7. calculate 8. certain
9. estimation 10. approximate

Lesson 17 • Words About Problem Solving

LESSON 17
Words About Problem Solving

Put Words Into Action

Materials Needed
- Student Workbook, p. 132

Think Aloud

Let's take a look at the first problem. "Jesse has to be at work at 9:00 A.M. It takes him 15 minutes to get dressed, 20 minutes to eat, and 35 minutes to walk to work. What time should he get up? How can you _____ exactly when Jesse has to get up?" Well, I notice that I don't have to solve the problem! I just have to decide which vocabulary word makes sense in the question. Since there are different times mentioned, I think that I probably have to do some mathematical calculations. I look at the vocabulary list and see the word *calculate* so I try it in the question. "How can you calculate exactly when Jesse has to get up?" It makes sense, so I write *calculate* in the blank.

Answer Key
1. calculate 2. approximate
3. estimation 4. certain
5. probability 6. approximate
7. calculate 8. probability

Getting Started

Mystery Word of the Week Clue 4

What is the _____ that you will choose a yellow tile?

★ **Review and Share** Invite volunteers to read their **research** reports to the class. After all the reports have been read, take a class vote to decide which problem solver made the most significant contribution to mathematics and why.

Model/Teach
- Direct the class to open their workbooks to page 132.
- Before students start, do the **Think Aloud**.
- After you have modeled how to complete this page, ask students to finish the rest of the items on their own and then share their answers.

English Language Learners
- Group more fluent students with those in intermediate and early speech emergence to play "Guess My Word." Invite individual students to choose a vocabulary word without telling it. One person can ask word questions, such as "What do you mean?" "How are you used?" and "Who are your friends?" to determine the word. Challenge other students in the group to guess the word.

Independent Activity

★ **Write a Probability Problem** Before students begin this activity, briefly share a typical word problem, such as "The weather bureau says there is a one in four chance that it will rain on Monday. They also say that there is a 50 percent chance that it will rain on Tuesday. On which day is the *probability* greater that it will rain?" Then arrange students in small groups to write their word problems, using the vocabulary words.

140 Chapter 3 • Content Words

Review and Extend

Materials Needed
- Student Workbook, p. 133

Getting Started

Mystery Word of the Week Clue 5

The word _____ means that something has a greater probability of occurring than of not occurring.

⭐ **Review and Share** Have volunteers read their **probability problems**. If problems can be easily worked out in the classroom, give students an opportunity to work them out. Lead a discussion about new words students may have used in their problems that relate to probability. Add them to the Word Wall.

Model/Teach

- Direct the class to turn to page 133 in their workbooks.
- Tell students that they will learn three more problem-solving words as well as review the words they've already learned.
- Share the **Think Aloud** to model how to complete this page.
- After you have modeled how to fill in the blanks, have students complete the activity on their own. Then ask them to share their responses.

Independent Activities

⭐ **Search for More Words About Probability** Challenge students to make a list of words that they associate with *probability*. Words and phrases such as *almost always, always, likely, most likely, often, possibly, possible outcome, sometimes, never,* or *unlikely* are all words that can be associated with *probability*.

- **Create Ads** Assign each student one of the vocabulary or bonus words to advertise. The ads should explain the word's advantages by highlighting the big idea, explaining how the word is used, and giving examples of the word in context. Group students who have the same word so they can work together to present their ads to the class.

Think Aloud

I'd like you to follow along as I model how I would complete this page. From the directions, I know that I have to fill in each blank with a problem-solving word that fits. Let's read the first sentence: "The word problem required only a(n) _____ answer, but the students had to make sure that it was _____ and made sense." I see that there are two words to fill in for this sentence. For now, we'll focus on the first blank and then you can do the second blank on your own. Well, even though there are two words that might work here: *estimation* and *approximate*, I can rule out *estimation* immediately because it is a noun and it doesn't make sense in the sentence. The word that makes sense is the adjective *approximate* so I write that in the blank. "The word problem required only an approximate answer...."

Answer Key

Mystery Word of the Week: likelihood
Accept other words that fit the context, too.

1. approximate, reasonable
2. probability, likelihood, certain
3. estimation, calculate
4. strategy
5. probability, likelihood

LESSON 17 — Words About Problem Solving

Check Your Mastery

Materials Needed
- Student Workbook, p. 134

Student Self-Assessment

Journal Writing Have students explain in their journals some techniques for learning new content words they will encounter. Also ask them to rephrase the Word Learning Tip and the Vocabulary Building Strategy as a song, jingle, or rhyme to make it easier to remember.

Answer Key
1. C 2. B 3. B 4. A 5. A
6. probability 7. calculate
8. approximate 9. estimation
10. certain

Give the Test
- Direct the class to open their workbooks to page 134.
- Explain that that this Check Your Mastery activity has two parts.
- Read the directions for the first part to the class: "Read each item below. Then write the vocabulary word that best completes each sentence." Students should pick the vocabulary word that best fits the context and write it in the blank.
- Model how to answer a question by writing the following item on the chalkboard and reading it aloud:

    We _____ the exact batting averages after each inning.
    A. probability   **B.** calculate   **C.** estimation

- Ask students to choose the vocabulary word that best completes the sentence (B). Guide them to explain their choice by discussing the context clue they used.
- Read the directions for the second part of the activity: "Read the passage below. Then select the vocabulary words that best fit the context. Write the words in the blanks. Use each vocabulary word only once." Tell students that they will choose one of three vocabulary words to fill in each blank.
- Model how to fill in the blank by writing the following item on the chalkboard and reading it aloud:

    There is only a 5 percent _____ (*certain, estimation, probability*) of rain today, so it's likely to be another sunny day!

- Ask students to choose the word that best completes the sentence (*probability*). Have them explain how they used the context clues to determine the missing word.
- Remind students to check their work after they finish this activity.
- Review the Check Your Mastery activity with the class.
- Have students explain how they used the Word Learning Tip and Vocabulary Building Strategy to help them find the correct answers.

LESSON 18
Words About the Circulatory System

Learn Words About a New Subject

Getting Started

Mystery Word of the Week Clue 1

Blood cells are suspended in a yellowish liquid called _____.

- See page 14 for routines for using the Mystery Word of the Week Clues. The mystery word of the week is *plasma*.

Model/Teach

- Ask the class to turn to page 135 in their workbooks.

- Invite a student to read the Word Learning Tip to the class. As a class, talk about how understanding the connections among content words will make them easier to remember.

- Have a volunteer read the Vocabulary Building Strategy aloud. Discuss with students how they can often define these unfamiliar words by linking them to the big idea of what they are reading. Point out the title of this lesson and emphasize that all the new words relate to this big idea of how blood circulates or travels around the body.

- Ask students to read the directions and look at the diagrams in their workbook. Read the text to the class as they study the diagrams.

- Model how to determine the meaning of content words by using the **Think Aloud** on page 147.

- As you read the page again, point out the words in boldface. Pause to allow students time to focus on each word.

- Place the transparency on the overhead projector. Guide students to complete the title by adding the big idea (the circulatory system). Have the class explain how each word in boldface is connected to the big idea and define it. For example, aorta is connected to the idea of the circulatory system because it names the main tube that carries blood from the heart.

Materials Needed
- Student Workbook, pp. 135–136
- Transparency 2

Vocabulary Words
aorta
artery
atrium
capillary
vein

LESSON 18: Words About the Circulatory System

Think Aloud

I start by making sure that I understand the big idea, because all the new words relate to it. I do this by looking at these pictures. The large one shows the human body, and there are also two smaller pictures on page 136. One, I think, shows the heart but I'm not sure what the other shows. The title of the illustration is "The Circulatory System." Now I know that the big idea is how blood flows through the whole body, and because of the title, I know that this process is called the "circulatory system." Let's read the beginning labeled 1. "The action starts in the heart. The heart pumps blood through the **aorta**. The **aorta** is the main tube for all of the **arteries**." I know that an *aorta* is something that blood is pumped through, so it must be a tube of some kind. The illustration supports this guess. I also notice that the text defines *aorta* as "the main tube for all of the arteries." This happens a lot in content material: the writer defines the important words in order to make sure the reader understands them.

Answer Key
See page 215 for definitions.

- Help students share their thinking and explain how they determined the meaning of each word.
- After students have discussed the meaning of each word, divide the class into pairs. Distribute flashcards and invite pairs to use them to reinforce word meaning.

English Language Learners
- *Aorta*, *artery*, and *atrium* look and sound alike, so they are apt to prove difficult for English language learners. Write each word on the chalkboard, dividing into syllables. Say each word slowly and have students repeat after you. Then have them write the words on a piece of paper and draw an outline around them. This will help them to visualize the placement of the *t* in each word. Last, ask them to write a sentence they create that uses all three words so that they can remember the meaning of each word.

Independent Activity
- **Understand Cause and Effect** Explain to students that understanding science is in part based on understanding causes and effects. Ask them to think about what would happen if their arteries get blocked up with a fatty substance called cholesterol. Then have them create a cause-and-effect chart explaining their answer.

Connect Words and Meanings

Getting Started

Mystery Word of the Week Clue 2
When all blood cells are removed from blood, _____ is the clear liquid that is left.

★ **Review and Share** Ask students to share the **cause-and-effect** charts they created for the activity on page 144 of the teacher's edition. Next, create a word wall of circulatory system words. Add all of the vocabulary words to the Word Wall.

Model/Teach

- Have students turn to page 137 in their workbooks.
- Do the **Think Aloud** to show the class how you would complete this activity.
- Guide students to finish the rest of the page on their own. Go over their answers as a class. Ask students to explain their thinking.

Independent Activities

★ **Diagram the Heart** Divide the class into small groups for this activity. You may wish to have students access the American Red Cross web site (www.redcross.org) to find some statistics on blood donation. Be sure that students use at least three of the vocabulary words and two new content words about the big idea that they learned using the Word Learning Tip and Vocabulary Building Strategy.

- **Learn More Words About the Circulatory System** Explain that the study of blood is called *hematology*. The prefix *hema-/hemo-* relates to blood. Challenge students to see how many other words on the big idea they can find with this prefix, such as *hemoglobin* (a protein in blood), *hemorrhage* (to bleed), *hemostasis* (stoppage of blood flow), and *hemophobic* (fear of blood.) Add the new words to the word wall.

Materials Needed
- Student Workbook, p. 137

Think Aloud
Let's look at the first definition together: "a blood vessel that carries blood away from the heart, but not the main tube." I think about the main subject: the circulatory system." This helps me to understand that there are three types of blood vessels: arteries, veins, and capillaries. I see the word *away* in the definition, which helps me determine that this blood vessel takes blood away from the heart, so *artery* is the correct word choice. I write it in the blank. Now I double-check my answer by reading the sentence and inserting the word *artery*: "You can remember that an *artery* carries blood *away* from the heart because both words start with *a*."

Answer Key
1. artery 2. artery 3. aorta
4. aorta 5. atrium 6. atrium
7. capillary 8. capillary
9. vein 10. vein

LESSON 18: Words About the Circulatory System

Use Content Words

Materials Needed
- Student Workbook, p. 138

Getting Started

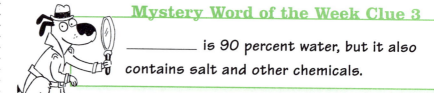

Mystery Word of the Week Clue 3

_____ is 90 percent water, but it also contains salt and other chemicals.

Think Aloud

Let's do the first item together: "The heart has four chambers or rooms. One of its two upper chambers is called a(n) _____." The word choices are *atrium*, *capillary*, and *vein*. These sentences are telling me about the four chambers in the heart. Since all my vocabulary words are content words that tell something about the big idea of how blood travels around the body—the circulatory system—I think about how the meaning of the unknown word ties in to this process. I remember that blood leaves the heart through the aorta and travels through arteries to various parts of the body. The capillaries link the arteries to the veins, which bring the blood back to the heart. The room or part of the heart that this blood comes to is called the right atrium, which is in the upper part of the heart. So *atrium* is the word that fits in the blank, since it names one of these two chambers.

Answer Key
1. atrium 2. aorta 3. artery
4. capillary 5. aorta 6. capillary
7. vein 8. artery 9. vein
10. atrium

Review and Share Display all the **diagrams** that students created for the activity on page 137 in their workbooks. Invite volunteers from each group to point out the new words they used. Then write these words on index cards and add them to the word wall.

Model/Teach
- Have students open their workbooks to page 138.
- Do the **Think Aloud** to model how to complete the activity.
- Have students complete the rest of the page on their own. Then arrange them in pairs to share their responses.

English Language Learners
- This lesson provides a good springboard for having English language learners generate lists of health words. First point to various parts of your body and ask student volunteers to name it. Write the words on the chalkboard. Then have students make flashcards for each word with the word and a picture on the front of the card and a definition on the back.

Independent Activity

Ask Questions About the Circulatory System Allow students to work in small groups to generate questions. Then have them use the group questions as a springboard for generating their own questions. Challenge them to use as many vocabulary words and other words about the circulatory system as they can learn by using the Word Learning Tip and Vocabulary Building Strategy.

Put Words Into Action

Materials Needed
- Student Workbook, p. 139

Getting Started

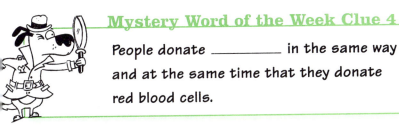

Mystery Word of the Week Clue 4

People donate _____ in the same way and at the same time that they donate red blood cells.

Think Aloud

Read the first sentence with me as I read it aloud: "I carry blood back to the heart. What am I?" I can think of only one answer for this question because I began by thinking about how the sentence connected to the big idea of the circulatory system. The sentence tells me that this word carries blood so it must be one of the blood vessels. It carries blood toward the heart. The answer must be a vein. I know this because I have learned that a vein takes blood back to the heart. I write *vein* in the blank.

⭐ **Review and Share** Invite volunteers to enact an **interview** with a panel of doctors from the activity on page 138. One student should ask the questions while three or four other students play the doctors and try to answer them. When the interviews are completed, lead a class discussion about which questions and answers were the most interesting and thoughtful. Prior to this activity, have the "doctors" complete research about the circulatory system so they have new knowledge to share.

Model/Teach
- Ask students to open their workbooks to page 139.
- Before students begin the activity, use the **Think Aloud** to model your thinking.
- Invite students to work independently to complete this page. Then partner students to compare answers and their thinking.

Independent Activities

⭐ **Stage a Heart Show** Divide the class into three or four equal groups, depending on the number of students. Then guide the groups to assign the tasks fairly so that everyone participates fully. Allow students sufficient time for them to prepare and rehearse.

- **Compile a List of Sources** Ask students to imagine that they are writing a research paper on the circulatory system. Have them work with a partner to compile a list of print and electronic resources they could use.

Answer Key
1. vein 2. artery 3. aorta
4. capillary 5. atrium 6. artery
7. aorta 8. vein 9. capillary
10. atrium

LESSON 18 Words About the Circulatory System

Review and Extend

Materials Needed
- Student Workbook, p. 140
- Idea Web Graphic Organizer, p. 229

Getting Started

Mystery Word of the Week Clue 5
The mystery word _____ is on the same page in the dictionary as *plane* and *plastic*.

★ **Review and Share** Have volunteer groups perform the **Stage a Heart Show** activity from page 139. After each performance, lead a class discussion about interesting aspects of the show.

Model/Teach
- Have students turn to page 140 in their workbooks.
- Tell students that they will learn three new terms related to the circulatory system and review their vocabulary words.
- Use the **Think Aloud** to model how to complete this page.
- When you have shared your thinking, have students complete the activity on their own. After everyone finishes, invite volunteers to write the answers.

Think Aloud

Here's how I would complete this page. I see that I have to look at the three bonus words as well as the five vocabulary words before I decide which word to use. Read the first sentence with me: "A ___ can be so small that blood cells have to pass through one at a time, in a straight line." I see the words "small" and "one at a time" so I know that I'm looking for the word for the smallest blood vessel. That's a *capillary*, so I'll write *capillary* in the blank.

Independent Activities

★ **Keep Your Heart Healthy** Pass out copies of the Idea Web Graphic Organizer. Tell students to write "healthy heart" in the center circle. To prepare students for sharing their answers, have them work with a partner to fill out this chart with new content words that they learned by using the Word Learning Tip and Vocabulary Building Strategy.

- **Search for More Words About the Heart** Ask students to use science books, dictionaries, and other books that contain information about the circulatory system. Encourage them to find as many new words as they can that have to do with the heart and the circulatory system. Ask students to write each word and a description of how they learned the meaning of that word on a note card, and then place the cards on the word wall.

Answer Key
Mystery Word of the Week: plasma Accept other words that fit the context, too.

1. capillary 2. chamber 3. aorta
4. circulate 5. blood vessel

For sample bonus sentence, see page 223.

Chapter 3 • Content Words

Check Your Mastery

Materials Needed
- Student Workbook, p. 141

Give the Test

- Ask students to turn to page 141 in their workbooks.
- Read the directions to the class: "Read each item below. Then circle the letter of the vocabulary word that best completes each sentence." Be sure students understand that they must circle the letter in front of their choice.
- Model how to answer the questions by writing the following item on the chalkboard and reading it aloud:

    Under a microscope, we could see the smallest blood vessel, a _____.

    A. vein   **B.** capillary   **C.** atrium

- Ask students to choose the vocabulary word that best completes the sentence. Ask them to explain their choice (B. *capillary*).
- Tell students to go over their answers before they hand in their papers.
- When everyone is finished, review the Check Your Mastery activity with the class.
- Arrange students in small groups to isolate the items they answered incorrectly. Have them write each word and its definition.
- Ask students to describe how they used the Word Learning Tip and Vocabulary Building Strategy to help them find the correct answers.
- Tally students' correct responses.

Student Self-Assessment

Journal Writing In their journals, have students write a paragraph to explain how they will use the Word Learning Tip and Vocabulary Building Strategy from this lesson to learn new content words in the future. Ask them to also rewrite the Word Learning Tip and the Vocabulary Building Strategy in their own words by giving an example using the digestive system as the big idea.

Answer Key
1. B **2.** C **3.** C **4.** A **5.** B
6. A **7.** A **8.** C **9.** B **10.** A

Lesson 18 • Words About the Circulatory System

LESSON 19 Words About the Water Cycle

Learn Words About a New Subject

Materials Needed
- Student Workbook, pp. 142–143
- Transparency 2

Vocabulary Words
condensation
droplet
evaporation
precipitation
water vapor

Getting Started

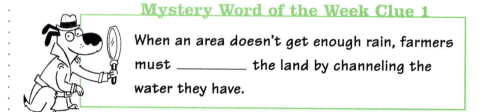

Mystery Word of the Week Clue 1

When an area doesn't get enough rain, farmers must _____ the land by channeling the water they have.

- See page 14 for routines for using the Mystery Word of the Week Clue. The mystery word of the week is *irrigate*.

Model/Teach

- Have students open their workbooks to page 142.

- Ask students to read the Word Learning Tip silently to themselves. Remind them what they have learned thus far about content words. Discuss how these words are often the most challenging to learn because they are long and not used in everyday speech.

- Have students read the Vocabulary Building Strategy silently to themselves. Invite volunteers to rephrase the strategy for the class. Guide the class to discuss how they can often define content words by relating them to the specialized subject area or the big idea. Elicit from students the subject of this lesson—the water cycle.

- Direct the class to read the directions and look at the diagram in their workbook. Read the text aloud.

- Before you read the text a second time, do the **Think Aloud** on page 153 to model your thinking.

- Read the page again, pausing at each word in boldface.

- Place the transparency on the overhead projector. Ask students to fill in the big idea (the water cycle). Explain that you want them to try to tell you what each word means. For example, water vapor is connected to the idea of the water cycle because it names the gas that water changes into. Guide students to describe how each boldface word relates to the big idea. Write their responses on the transparency.

Chapter 3 • Content Words

- Arrange students in small groups to talk about the water cycle, using these vocabulary words in their dialogues.
- Distribute flashcards. Have students work with a partner to reinforce the meaning of the vocabulary words.

English Language Learners

- Pronounce each content word for students and have them repeat it. Then have students write the pronunciation to help them remember it. For example, for *condensation* they might write "con-den-SAY-shun." Partner students to compare pronunciation guides and use the words in sentences. Correct pronunciation and usage as necessary.

Independent Activity

- **Learn Content Words** Ask students to find information about pollution in lakes. They can use books, magazine articles, or the Internet. Tell them to read about how it could lead to polluted drinking water. Have them refer to the diagram. In their personal word journals, have students explain how the Word Learning Tip and Vocabulary Building Strategy can help them learn more content words when they read further about pollution in a lake.

Think Aloud

Let me demonstrate the thinking that I do to determine the meaning of these words about the water cycle. First I review the topic, since I know that all five content words describe part of it. I ask myself, "How are all these words linked? What idea connects them?" All of these words are connected because they're about the process of water changing to a gas and then back to water again. That's the water cycle. Now let's look at the text at the top of the diagram: "Heat from the sun causes water to change into a gas called **water vapor**." Even if I didn't know what *water vapor* meant, I would know that it tells me about the water cycle. I see the words *change* and *gas*. They help me understand that *water vapor* is the gas that water changes into as part of the water cycle.

Answer Key
See page 215 for definitions.

LESSON 19 Words About the Water Cycle

Connect Words and Meanings

Materials Needed
- Student Workbook, p. 144

Think Aloud

Let's look at item 2 under Across, so I can model for you how to complete this puzzle. The clue is "the act or process by which a liquid becomes a gas." I remember that in the water cycle, the sun heats up water and turns this liquid into water vapor. The process is called *evaporation*. I've seen evaporation at work. For example, if I leave water in the tea kettle overnight, some of it evaporates. Now I'm going to see if *evaporation* fits in the puzzle. I find 2 Across and count eleven boxes. *Evaporation* has eleven letters, so it fits and I write it in the boxes.

Answer Key
Across
2. evaporation 4. condensation
5. vapor 7. water 8. droplets
Down
1. droplet 3. precipitation 6. dry

Getting Started

Mystery Word of the Week Clue 2

Farmers _____ the land through a series of ditches, pipes, and canals that carry the water.

⭐ **Review and Share** Allow time for students to share their thoughts about **pollution** and how they learned new content words from the activity on page 151 in the teacher's edition. Post their new content words on the word wall.

Model/Teach
- Ask students to turn to page 144 in their workbooks.
- Complete the **Think Aloud** to model your thinking.
- Have students finish the rest of the puzzle on their own.

Independent Activities

⭐ **Find Related Words** Before students start, model how to find the word *vapor* in *evaporation*. Then explain that *evaporate* is a verb. When you turn it into a noun, you drop the *e* and add *-ation*. The meanings of both *vapor* and *evaporate* are connected to the topic of the water cycle. Ask student to use the Word Learning Tip and Vocabulary Building Strategy to tell you the meaning of these words.

- **Create a Fact File** Have students create a Fact File about the water cycle by writing one fact per index card or slip of paper. Each fact should use one vocabulary word or a new content word that they learned this week. Encourage them to use three new content words. When everyone is finished writing, have each student contribute two fact cards to a class Fact File. Tape or staple the cards together to show the water cycle. Display the cards in the front of the classroom. Add new content words to the word wall.

152 Chapter 3 • Content Words

Use Content Words

Materials Needed
- Student Workbook, p. 145
- Transparency 2
- Transparency 2 Blackline Master, p. 226

Getting Started

Mystery Word of the Week Clue 3

Farmers _____ the desert so they have enough water to grow dates, oranges, and tomatoes.

Think Aloud

Let's look at the first item together: "In the early morning, you can see tiny _____(s) of water on flowers. This is called *dew*." I've seen this in the morning, and I bet you have too. The water is in liquid form, and it is in very small drops. The word for very small drops is *droplets*, so I write *droplets* in the blank.

- ⭐ **Review and Share** Invite volunteers to share the words they found for the **Find Related Words** activity on page 144. Add the words they learned to the word wall. As a class, discuss how the Word Learning Tip and Vocabulary Building Strategy can help them learn new content words every time they read in the future.

Model/Teach
- Ask students to turn to page 145 in their workbooks.
- Use the **Think Aloud** to show students how to complete this page.
- After you model how to fill in a sentence, have students finish the activity on their own.

Independent Activities

- ⭐ **Write an Editorial** Distribute copies of the blackline master of Transparency 2. Before students begin this activity, arrange them in groups to read about specific reasons why people must work to protect Earth's water from pollution. Then have students write their editorials in their personal word journals using three vocabulary words and two additional content words they learned by using the Word Learning Tip and Vocabulary Building Strategy. Ask them to fill out the blackline master for each new word.

- **Deliver Weather Reports** Arrange students in small groups to write weather reports based on the actual weather or on their favorite climate conditions. Each report should include at least three vocabulary words. After students write their scripts, invite them to read them to the class in a simulated television weather report. If possible, videotape the "broadcasts" for students to watch in their free time.

Answer Key
1. droplets 2. water vapor
3. evaporation 4. precipitation
5. condensation 6. precipitation
7. droplets 8. condensation
9. evaporation 10. water vapor

LESSON 19: Words About the Water Cycle

Put Words Into Action

Materials Needed
- Student Workbook, p. 146

Think Aloud

I want to show you the thinking I do when I complete this activity. Let's read the first part together. "Notice the sun shining brightly. It heats up the water in the lake. This begins the process of _____." I know that the missing word tells me about the water cycle. It names the stage when liquid water is heating up and turns to something else. I remember that the list of vocabulary words includes words for two processes: *evaporation* and *condensation*. *Evaporation* is when water is turned into a gas, and *condensation* is when the gas in turned back into water. The process I'm looking for is called *evaporation*, so I right *evaporation* in the blank.

Answer Key
1. evaporation 2. water vapor
3. droplets 4. condensation
5. water vapor 6. droplets
7. precipitation 8. precipitation
9. evaporation 10. condensation

Getting Started

Mystery Word of the Week Clue 4
Because settlers _____ the land with water, crops grow and many new people move in.

Review and Share Have students share their **editorials** from the activity on page 145. As each student reads, jot down on the chalkboard the reasons they give. Put a checkmark next to each new content word they use. Ask students which reasons they think were the most persuasive. Why? Encourage students to submit their editorials to the school newspaper, if they wish.

Model/Teach
- Have students turn to page 146 in their workbooks.
- Use the **Think Aloud** to get started.
- When you have finished modeling your thinking, ask students to work on their own to complete this page. Invite volunteers to share their responses.

English Language Learners
- Explain to students that a *compound word* is made up of two or more smaller words. Point out that there are three types of compound words in English: combined compounds (*lakefront*), hyphenated compounds (*mother-in-law*), and open compounds (*water vapor*). Have students sort the following compound words into the appropriate categories: *groundwater*, *ice caps*, *overflow*, *take-off*, *water cycle*, *mix-up*, *runoff*.

Independent Activity

Make a Cartoon Before students begin, briefly discuss the different types of cartoons they can create, such as political cartoons, humorous cartoons, cartoons that tell a serious story, flip-book "animated" cartoons, single-panel cartoons, and so forth. Tell students to make sure their cartoons contain their vocabulary words and two new content words.

154 Chapter 3 • Content Words

Review and Extend

Materials Needed
- Student Workbook, p. 147

Getting Started

Mystery Word of the Week Clue 5
This mystery word _____ is on the same page in the dictionary as *irregular* and *island*.

⭐ **Review and Share** Have students display their **cartoons** from the activity on page 146 and share them with the class. Ask them to discuss the vocabulary words they used and the new content words. Add new content words to the word wall. Then bind the pages into a booklet. Place this in the classroom library.

Model/Teach

- Instruct students to open their workbooks to page 147.
- Read the two bonus words and explain that they relate to the same topic as the five vocabulary words.
- Do the **Think Aloud** to show students how to complete this activity.
- After you complete the modeling, allow students sufficient time to answer the remaining questions and share their answers with the class.

Independent Activities

⭐ **Search for New Words About Weather** Provide time and resources for students to conduct their word searches. Ask them to share their new words and sentences. Add the new words to the word wall.

- **Learn About Clouds** Partner students to identify at least three more types of clouds, such as *cirrus*, *stratus*, and *cirrocumulus*, or three words about another water cycle topic. Tell them to use the Word Learning Tip and Vocabulary Building Strategy as they read a text or use the Internet. Students can draw each cloud on a piece of 8 1/2" x 11" paper and label it with the name of the cloud and its characteristics. Then they can write paragraphs comparing and contrasting the characteristics of the clouds.

Think Aloud

Read the first question with me as I read it aloud: "I am often called the 'fair weather clouds' because I form in warm air on sunny days. What am I?" I see the words *fair weather clouds*. This tells me that I need a word or phrase that has to do with clouds. The only phrase that includes "clouds" is *cumulus clouds*, so I know that has to be the correct answer. I'll write it in the blank.

Answer Key
1. cumulus clouds 2. evaporation
3. precipitation 4. dew point
5. droplet

LESSON 19
Words About the Water Cycle

Check Your Mastery

Materials Needed
- Student Workbook, p. 148

Student Self-Assessment

Journal Writing Have students jot notes in their journals telling how they will use the Word Learning Tip and the Vocabulary Building Strategy as they learn more content words

Give the Test
- Tell students to open their workbooks to page 148.
- Explain to the class that that this Check Your Mastery activity has two parts.
- Read the directions for the first five items: "Circle the letter of the correct answer to each statement below."
- Model how to answer the item by writing the following on the chalkboard and reading it aloud:

   Precipitation can take all of the following forms BUT _____.
   A. rain   **C.** hail   **B.** snow   **D.** clouds

- Ask students to choose the word that best completes the sentence. Guide them to explain their choice (D. *clouds*) by identifying *precipitation* as "rain, snow, or other moisture that falls from the sky."
- Read the directions to questions 6–10 to the class: "Read each item below. Then circle the letter of the vocabulary word that best completes each sentence."
- Explain to students that they will choose between three vocabulary words to fill in each blank.
- Model how to answer the question by writing the following item on the chalkboard and reading it aloud:

   A small, round _____ of water dripped into the lake.
   A. condensation   **B.** evaporation   **C.** droplet

- Have students select the content word that correctly completes the sentence. Ask them to explain their choice by telling how they used context clues to determine the missing word (C. *droplet*). They should isolate the words *small*, *round*, and *water*.
- Remind students to check and double-check their work.
- Go over the Check Your Mastery activity with the class.
- Tally students' correct responses.

Answer Key
1. A 2. C 3. D 4. B 5. A 6. C
7. C 8. B 9. A 10. B

156 Chapter 3 • Content Words

LESSON 20

Words About Great Leaders

Learn Words About a New Subject

Getting Started

Mystery Word of the Week Clue 1

A leader is expected to be a person of _____ who earns our respect.

- See page 14 for routines for using the Mystery Word of the Week Clue. The mystery word of the week is *integrity*.

Model/Teach

- Ask students to open their workbooks to page 149.

- Read the Word Learning Tip to the class as students follow along. Ask students why they need to know content words. Guide them to see that these words are often crucial to understanding the texts they read.

- Have students read the Vocabulary Building Strategy silently to themselves. As a class, paraphrase the strategy and write the paraphrase on the chalkboard. Underline the key points: relating new words to familiar words and to the big idea or subject.

- Have the class read the directions and skim the passage.

- Do the **Think Aloud** on page 158 to model how to learn the meaning of a content word.

- Read the passage again, this time pausing at each boldface word.

- Place the transparency on the overhead projector. Ask students for the big idea (great leaders). Explain that as you stop at each boldface word, students should explain how it is linked to the big idea. You also want them to try to define the word. For example, *persistence* is connected to the idea of great leaders because it names a quality great leaders should have—refusing to give up in spite of difficulties. Guide students to explain their reasoning.

- After students discuss each content word, record their thinking on the transparency.

Materials Needed
- Student Workbook, pp. 149–150
- Transparency 3

Vocabulary Words
compassion
cooperation
persistence
self-discipline
trustworthy

LESSON 20 Words About Great Leaders

Think Aloud

I want to share my method for learning the meaning of long content words. As I understand from the Word Learning Tip and Vocabulary Building Strategy, knowing the subject that's being discussed will help me to see how all the words are related. All of the words in this lesson are connected to the topic of great leaders. The title of this passage supports this: Martin Luther King, Jr.: A Great Leader. Now listen while I read the first paragraph: "Martin Luther King, Jr., is honored as a great leader of the American Civil Rights movement. He was a champion for equal justice under the law. Through his years of **persistence**, Dr. King used peaceful protest to gain equal rights under the law for all people." By considering these sentences and focusing on the word *years*, I can tell that *persistence* must mean "refusing to give up."

- When you have filled in the transparency, have each student in turn provide a sentence about a great leader that uses one of these content words.
- Divide the class into small groups. Have them use flashcards to reinforce word meaning.

English Language Learners
- Knowing a content word's part of speech can help students use it correctly. Explain that *compassion*, *cooperation*, *persistence*, and *self-discipline* are all nouns; *trustworthy* is an adjective. Remind students that nouns name people, places, things, or ideas; while adjectives describe nouns or pronouns. Then ask each student to use each content word correctly in a sentence. Have students label the noun or pronoun that *trustworthy* modifies and then share their sentences.

Independent Activity
- **You Are There! Headlines** Tell students to choose a leader whom they admire. Explain that the leader can be famous around the world, in the United States, or simply in their community. Ask them to write three headlines about this leader's great actions. Before students begin writing, read some newspaper headlines to the class. Emphasize that headlines are brief and direct. Distribute the newspapers and encourage students to use the headlines as models as they write. Remind students to make sure that their headlines contain at least three vocabulary words.

Answer Key
See page 216 for definitions.

Connect Words and Meanings

Getting Started

Mystery Word of the Week Clue 2

We tend to follow people of _____ because they impress us with their honesty.

★ **Review and Share** Cut pieces of 8 1/2" x 11" paper in half lengthwise and give one strip to each student. Have each student choose the **headline** they like best from the activity on page 158 in the teacher's edition, write it on their strip of paper, and circle the vocabulary word. Display the headlines around the classroom.

Model/Teach
- Ask students to turn to page 151 in their workbooks.
- Use the **Think Aloud** as an effective way to model the activity.
- Have students work independently to fill in the rest of the puzzle.
- Invite volunteers to share their answers.

Independent Activities

★ **Understand Famous Sayings** Write additional models on the chalkboard, such as "Freedom is the recognition that no single person, no single authority or government, has a monopoly on truth" (Ronald Reagan) and "Some men see things as they are and say, 'Why?' I dream of things that never were and say, 'Why not?'" (Robert F. Kennedy). Ask students to discuss how they can use the Word Learning Tip and Vocabulary Building Strategy to learn any content word in these quotations that they do not know.

- **Celebrate Great Leaders** Group students and have them look through newspapers to choose a modern-day leader. Have them cut out his or her picture, and glue it to a sheet of paper. Ask each member of the group to write a sentence explaining what traits make the leader admirable. The sentence should contain a new content word the student learned by using the Word Learning Tip and Vocabulary Building Strategy. Together, make a "Guide to Good Leadership."

Materials Needed
- Student Workbook, p. 151

Think Aloud

I see that this is a crossword puzzle, so I know I have to write the words in the boxes, one letter per box. I start with the Across column. Read the clue with me: "If you have **self-discipline**, you can ____ your behavior, even when you are angry." I know that the missing word helps me understand the meaning of *self-discipline*. Then I count the number of spaces: seven. This tells me that I am looking for a seven-letter word to fit in the blank. Well, I know that another word for *self-discipline* is *self-control*. If I have *self-discipline*, I can control myself or my behavior. I think *control*, which has seven letters, is the word that fits in the blank, so I write it in the puzzle.

Answer Key
Across
1. control 2. cooperation
3. self-discipline 4. depend
7. persistence 9. trustworthy
Down
1. compassion 5. easily 6. well
8. other

Lesson 20 • **Words About Great Leaders**

LESSON 20 Words About Great Leaders

Use Content Words

Materials Needed
- Student Workbook, p. 152
- Transparency 2 Blackline Master, p. 226

Getting Started

Mystery Word of the Week Clue 3
The citizens know that the leaders have _____ because they act with decency.

⭐ **Review and Share** After students write their **sayings** from the activity on page 151, have them choose the two they like the best and write them on construction paper. Display these around the classroom. Read all the sentences aloud and have the class decide which ones are the most memorable.

Model/Teach

- Have the class to open to page 152 in their workbooks.
- Before students begin the page, use the **Think Aloud**.
- Direct the class to complete the page on their own.

Independent Activities

⭐ **Understand Leadership Words** Write the three words *self-assurance*, *self-confidence*, and *self-control* on the chalkboard. Discuss their meaning and ask students to tell how each word connects to the idea of good leaders. Ask them to list other "self" words that also connect to this idea; for example, *self-reliance*, *self-knowledge*. Distribute copies of the blackline master for Transparency 2 and have students complete it for each "self" word.

- **Make a Synonym/Antonym Chart** Partner students to make a synonym/antonym chart using the content words. Challenge students to include as many words as they can. For example:

Content Word	Synonym	Antonym
compassion	pity, mercy	indifference, disgust
cooperation	teamwork	separateness

Think Aloud

Here's how I would approach this activity. Read the first sentence with me: "In World War II, Winston Churchill, Franklin Roosevelt, and Joseph Stalin showed ____ and **worked together** to defeat the Nazis." The words "worked together" tell me that I need a word that means "teamwork." That's *cooperation*, so I'll write it in the blank. Now I am going to think about how this fits in with the idea of good leaders. Good leaders have to be able to act on their own, but they also must be able to show cooperation and work with others.

Answer Key
1. cooperation 2. trustworthy
3. self-discipline 4. persistence
5. compassion 6. cooperation
7. trustworthy 8. persistence

Chapter 3 • Content Words

Put Words Into Action

Materials Needed
- Student Workbook, p. 153

Getting Started

Mystery Word of the Week Clue 4
Abraham Lincoln was known for his _____, as shown by his nickname, "Honest Abe."

★ **Review and Share** Divide students into groups to share their **leadership words** from page 152. Have one student in each group record the *self-* words with a positive connotation and another student record the *self-* words with a negative connotation. Have each group contribute their words to a class list. Display this prominently in the classroom.

Model/Teach
- Have students open their workbooks to page 153.
- Model the activity with the **Think Aloud**.
- Have students finish the page on their own, using your modeling as a guide.
- Partner students to share their answers and model their thinking, as you did.

English Language Learners
- Arrange students in groups of three. Give each group a story starter that uses one of the content words, such as "The great leader showed *compassion*, when …" Have students in turn continue the story by providing sentences that each use one of the content words. Allow students to continue the stories as long as they can. If time permits, give additional story starters and repeat the activity.

Independent Activity

★ **Write a Letter of Application** Before students begin writing their letters, discuss with the class the leadership traits that make people good company presidents. Guide students to use the vocabulary words as well as new words such as *honesty*, *courtesy*, *determination*, and *vision*.

Think Aloud

Follow along as I read the second sentence for the ad: "The person chosen must be ____ and reliable." The word that I am looking for will tell me something about the person selected, a great leader. Now I know that great leaders can be the president of a country, a general in the army, a doctor leading a team of health professionals, and even the head of a company. Whatever their roles, they have certain traits in common. What is the most important trait that a great leader must have? In the sentence from this want ad, it must be a word that matches *reliable*. The closest word is *trustworthy*, because we trust someone who is reliable. I write *trustworthy* in the blank.

Answer Key
1. trustworthy 2. cooperation
3. self-discipline 4. persistence
5. compassion 6. self-discipline
7. trustworthy 8. cooperation
9. compassion 10. persistence

Lesson 20 • Words About Great Leaders

LESSON 20 Words About Great Leaders

Review and Extend

Materials Needed
- Student Workbook, p. 154

Getting Started

Mystery Word of the Week Clue 5
The mystery word is on the same page in the dictionary as *insurance* and *intelligence*.

⭐ **Review and Share** Invite volunteers to read their **letters of application** for the activity on page 153 to the class. Have class members raise their hands when they hear one of the vocabulary words. As a class, briefly discuss what traits make someone a great leader and why.

Model/Teach
- Direct students to turn to page 154 in their workbooks.
- Read the information in the box. Be sure that students understand that the two bonus words are about the same big idea as the content words: great leaders.
- Use the **Think Aloud** to model your thinking.
- Have students complete the page on their own and then share their responses.

Think Aloud
Read the first sentence aloud with me to see how I would complete this page: "These leaders have the ability to put themselves in the other person's place and feel mercy and pity for them. What trait do these leaders have?" I have to fill in the blank with a content word or bonus word that describes the trait great leaders have when they feel mercy and pity for others. The word that fits here is *compassion*, since *compassion* means "mercy" or "pity." I'll write *compassion* in the blank.

Independent Activities

⭐ **Give a Leadership Award** To brainstorm a list of famous leaders, have students read about one and learn three new content words that describe and relate to leadership as demonstrated by that leader. After students write their speeches that use these three words, provide time for students to read their speeches aloud. Vote for the top three words that best relate to leadership.

- **Write Sentence Parts** Have students complete five pairs of sentences following this pattern: A great leader is _____ because _____. A great leader is not _____ because _____. Tell them to use content words they learned this week by using the Word Learning Tip and Vocabulary Building Strategy.

Answer Key
Mystery Word of the Week: integrity
Accept other words that fit the context, too.

1. compassion 2. loyalty
3. persistence 4. adaptable
5. cooperation

Students' responses to the bonus activity will vary. See page 223 for a sample sentence.

162 Chapter 3 • Content Words

Check Your Mastery

Materials Needed
- Student Workbook, p. 155

Give the Test

- Have everyone open their workbooks to page 155.
- Explain that this Check Your Mastery activity has two parts.
- Read aloud the directions to the first part of the activity: "Read each item below. Circle the letter of the vocabulary word that best completes each sentence. Use each vocabulary word only once."
- Model how you would answer the question by writing the following sentence on the chalkboard and reading it aloud:

  Leaders who understand the importance of _____ work well in committees and other groups.

  A. persistence **B.** cooperation **C.** compassion

- Ask students to choose the vocabulary word that best completes the sentence. Elicit their reasons for choosing B (*cooperation*). Be sure they picked up on the context clue "work well in committees and other groups."
- Next, read aloud the directions to items 6–10: "Read the passage below. Then select the vocabulary word that best fits the context. Write the word in the blank. Use each vocabulary word only once."
- Model how you would fill in each blank by writing this sample sentence on the chalkboard and reading it aloud:

  Clara Barton never gave up her goals: she had great _____ (*compassion, persistence, cooperation*) and determination.

- Have the class complete the sentence. Guide them to explain how they used the context clues "never gave up her goals" and "determination" to determine that the missing word is *persistence*.
- Tell students to check their answers when they have finished.
- Review the Check Your Mastery activity with the class.
- Partner students to discuss techniques for completing sentences, especially by using the Word Learning Tip and Vocabulary Building Strategy.
- Tally students' correct responses.

Student Self-Assessment

Journal Writing In their journals, have students describe the strategies they learned in this lesson. How will they apply these skills when they learn new content words? How did the Word Learning Tip and the Vocabulary Building Strategy help them define and use new words?

Answer Key
1. A 2. C 3. B 4. B 5. C
6. compassion 7. self-discipline
8. persistence 9. cooperation
10. trustworthy

LESSON 21
Words About Research

Learn Words About a New Subject

Materials Needed
- Student Workbook, pp. 156–157
- Transparency 2

Vocabulary Words
- bibliography
- citation
- data
- paraphrase
- valid

Getting Started

Mystery Word of the Week Clue 1

You can avoid _____ in your research papers by giving credit to your sources.

- See page 14 for routines for using the Mystery Word of the Week Clue. The mystery word of the week is *plagiarism*.

Model/Teach

- Have the class turn to page 156 in their workbooks.

- Invite a student to read the Word Learning Tip aloud. Remind the class that content words are very important because they convey the meaning of a passage. Discuss with the class the importance of focusing on the big idea of a passage as they determine the meaning of unfamiliar content words. Then tell students that all of the words in this lesson are about research. Explain that research is the study and investigation of a subject. Have them tell you what they have done when they have researched a subject.

- Read the Vocabulary Building Strategy to the class. Remind students that content words may look difficult because they are long and new. However, all of the words relate to the topic, which is a valuable clue to their meaning. Next, have a volunteer read the directions.

- Allow students time to skim the comic strip. Then read it aloud.

- Model learning the meaning of a content word with the **Think Aloud** on page 165.

- After you have modeled how to learn the meaning of *data* by linking it with the big idea, read the dialogue again. This time, pause at each word in boldface.

164 Chapter 3 • Content Words

- Place the transparency on the overhead projector. Guide the class to complete the title phrase "The Author's Big Idea or Subject Is . . ." with the word "Research." Tell the class that as you pause at each boldface word, you want them to explain how it is linked to the big idea. You also want them to try to tell you its meaning. For example, *data* connects to the big idea of research because it means information or facts. Guide students to explain their thinking.

- As the class talks about each content word, record their thinking on the transparency.

- After the transparency is filled in, distribute flashcards. Allow students to work in small groups to reinforce the meaning of the vocabulary words with the flashcards.

English Language Learners

- The idea of research may be unfamiliar to some non-native speakers. Explain the concept by dividing the word into parts: the prefix "re" and the root word "search." Tell students that when they *research*, they "search again" through material that other people have written to find the facts they need. Have students brainstorm instances when they have to research in life and school.

Independent Activity

- **Write About a Time When You Did Research** In their personal word journals, have students write about a time when they researched a topic and wrote a paper based on their findings. Instruct them to list the steps that they followed in order, using the vocabulary words in their descriptions.

Think Aloud

Let me explain how I learn what new content words mean. I start by understanding the subject of the passage. This is what the passage is mostly about. I can usually find it in the title. Read the title with me: "Writing a Research Report." This tells me that all the words will be about research. Now I look at the first item. Follow along as I read it. One student says, "I am writing a research report on whales." The other student says, "I'm looking for **data** on the North Pole." Relating the big idea from the title and the clues "research report" and "North Pole" together, I can tell that *data* means "information, facts."

Answer Key
See page 216 for definitions.

LESSON

21 Words About Research

Connect Words and Meanings

Materials Needed
- Student Workbook, p. 158
- Transparency 2 blackline master, p. 226

Think Aloud

Let's look at the first definition together: "to restate a text or passage in your own words." I remember that when you write a research report, you read many sources. Sometimes, you use a quotation from one of the sources, and you put quotation marks around the author's exact words. Sometimes, you put the author's words into your own words. To make the author's statements easier to understand, you put them in your own words, or you *paraphrase* them. So *paraphrase* is the vocabulary word I am looking for, and I write it in the blank. Now I am going to try *paraphrase* in the sentence to see if it fits: "Mia wanted to paraphrase the author's words before she included them in her report." This fits, so I write *paraphrase* in the blank in the sentence.

Answer Key
1. paraphrase 2. paraphrase
3. data 4. data 5. valid
6. valid 7. citation 8. citation
9. bibliography 10. bibliography

Getting Started

Mystery Word of the Week Clue 2

_____ takes place when a writer puts a quotation in a paper and does not tell where it came from.

 Review and Share Provide time for students to read aloud the passages they wrote in their journals about **research** from the activity on page 165 in the teacher's edition. Add the vocabulary words to the word wall as well as other "research" words they use.

Model/Teach

- Have students open their workbooks to page 158.
- Before students begin the page, use the **Think Aloud**.
- After you have modeled how to complete this activity, ask students to share it on their own. Then request that they share their answers. Be sure they explain their thinking, as you did.

Independent Activities

Be Prepared When You Go to the Library Remind students to explain why each item is important as they write in their journals.

- **Learn More Words About Research** Distribute copies of the blackline master of Transparency 2. Suggest that students use this organizer to learn new content words. Have students work in groups of three to skim through nonfiction books to find as many words as they can about research. Spark the activity with the following words: *glossary, abstract, editorial*. Then have students arrange the words on a flow chart to show where they fit in the research process: the beginning, middle, or end.

Use Content Words

Materials Needed
- Student Workbook, p. 159
- Idea Web Graphic Organizer, p. 229

Getting Started

Mystery Word of the Week Clue 3
_____ also takes place when a writer copies someone else's ideas and claims them as his or her own.

★ **Review and Share** Provide time for students to share their list of **library items** and the reasons for choosing those items from the activity on page 158. Add any new "research" words they use to the word wall.

Model/Teach

- Ask students to open their workbooks to page 159.
- Use the **Think Aloud** to model how to complete the activity.
- After you have modeled how to complete the chart, have students complete the page independently.

English Language Learners

- Ask students to choose a partner. Then have them role-play to practice asking and answering questions. Tell students to imagine they are having trouble finding information in the library. One student should play the role of the librarian, while the other student should play the role of a student. The "student" should prepare five questions and ask the librarian these questions, for example: "Where are the computers with Internet access?" Then the "librarian" should try to answer each question, for example: "The computers are in the center of the room."

Independent Activity

★ **Create a Research Web** Distribute copies of the Idea Web Graphic Organizer. Before students start working with a partner to complete the web, ask the class to generate at least two new words that relate to research.

Think Aloud

I see that this is a chart that traces the steps in the research process. First one thing happens, then a second thing, and so on until the last step. Let's look at the first item together: "Search through books, magazines, and newspapers, and use the Internet to finds lots of _____ about your topic." I think about the topic—research. What would I find in books, magazines, and newspapers and on the Internet that would help me write a research report? Well, I would find a lot of information. Another word for information is *data*, and that is one of my vocabulary words, so I write *data* in the blank.

Answer Key
1. data 2. valid 3. paraphrase
4. bibliography 5. data 6. citation
7. bibliography 8. valid
9. citation 10. paraphrase

Lesson 21 • Words About Research

LESSON 21 Words About Research

Put Words Into Action

Materials Needed
- Student Workbook, p. 160

Think Aloud

Let's do the first item together so that I can share my thinking with you. "Please include a _____. You need to have a listing at the end of your paper of all the sources for information you used." This is a teacher's comment telling about something that is missing that belongs at the end of a research paper. It is a list of all of the sources that the writer consulted. I remember that the name for this list is a *bibliography*, so I write *bibliography* in the blank.

Answer Key
1. bibliography 2. valid 3. data
4. paraphrase 5. citation
6. bibliography 7. data
8. Paraphrase 9. valid 10. citation

Getting Started

Mystery Word of the Week Clue 4
Taking someone else's original work and passing it off as your own is called _____.

⭐ **Review and Share** Ask partners to share their **research webs** from the activity on page 159 by reading them to the class. After everyone has read the words on their webs, compile a class web of research words.

Model/Teach
- Tell students to turn to page 160 in their workbooks.
- Use the **Think Aloud** to demonstrate your thinking.
- After you have modeled how to choose the word that best fits in the blank, have students complete the rest of the items on their own. Then ask them to share their responses.

Independent Activities

⭐ **Write About Research on the Internet** Before students start, you might want to demonstrate for them, or have student volunteers demonstrate, how to use the Internet for research. Write on the chalkboard new "research" words that come up during your demonstration, such as *search engine*, *link*, and *home page*. Add these new words to the word wall.

- **Write Research Questions** Have each student write research questions, such as "Why is the sky blue?" "Why did the dinosaurs become extinct?" and "Who was Wilma Rudolph?" Have students exchange papers and write sentences explaining how they can find the answers to their questions. Each answer should use one or more of the vocabulary words. Then ask students to research to find the answer to one question. They should use the Word Learning Tip and Vocabulary Building Strategy to learn three new content words about that subject.

Review and Extend

Getting Started

Mystery Word of the Week Clue 5

The mystery word _____ is on the same page in the dictionary as *place* and *plan*.

Review and Share Invite students to share their papers about doing **research** on the Internet. Based on the information, ask the class to create a chart showing the benefits and drawbacks of Internet research.

Model/Teach

- Have students open their workbooks to page 161. Read the boxed information aloud and talk about the two bonus words.

- Use the **Think Aloud** to demonstrate how to complete this page.

- After you have modeled your thinking, ask students to finish the activity independently and then share their responses.

Independent Activities

Find "Library" Words Before students begin creating their lists of new words, you might have them visit the school library. Compile a class list of "library" words after they have completed and shared their individual lists. Post the class list on the bulletin board.

- **Create Trivia Questions** Have students work in groups to create a Research Trivia Game after they agree on a subject to research. Have groups write five research questions on the front of index cards and the answers on the back, one question and answer per card. Each question should use at least one content word, one bonus word, or one new content word they learned from the material that everyone read to get ready for the game. Collect the cards, divide the class into two teams, and play Research Trivia with the cards.

Materials Needed
- Student Workbook, p. 161

Think Aloud

The first sentence says: "A(n) _____ at the end of a book or report may contain charts, lists, tables, graphs or other materials." I'll turn the statement into a question: "What do I find at the end of a book or report that may contain charts, lists, tables, graphs or other materials?" The word I'm looking for is part of a research report or book. A *bibliography* and an *appendix* both fit because they name part of a report that comes at the end. I know that a *bibliography* is a list of books and writings. An *appendix* is an extra section that gives more information about the topic. "Extra information" can be charts, lists, tables, graphs or other material, so the answer is *appendix*.

Answer Key
Mystery Word of the Week:
plagiarism
Accept other words that fit the context, too.

1. appendix 2. paraphrase
3. citation 4. relevant
5. bibliography

Lesson 21 • Words About Research

LESSON 21 Words About Research

Check Your Mastery

Materials Needed
- Student Workbook, p. 162

Student Self-Assessment

Journal Writing Have students explain in their journals what methods they learned for learning and remembering new content words. Ask them to tell how the Word Learning Tip and the Vocabulary Building Strategy helped them determine the meaning of unfamiliar content words.

Give the Test
- Ask students to turn to page 162 in their workbooks.
- Read the directions aloud: "Read each item below. Then write the vocabulary word that best completes each sentence. Use each vocabulary word twice."
- Model how to answer the questions by writing the following sentence on the chalkboard and reading it aloud:

  At the end of her research report, Marci put a _____ that listed all the books she used.

  A. valid   **B.** bibliography   **C.** data

- Have the class select the vocabulary word that best completes the sentence. Elicit their reasons for choosing B (*bibliography*).
- Remind the class to double-check their answers when they have filled in each sentence. They should also check that they have used each vocabulary word twice.
- Review the Check Your Mastery activity with the class.
- Have students work in groups of three to share successful methods for completing sentences. They should refer to the Word Learning Tip and Vocabulary Building Strategy.
- Tally students' correct responses.

Answer Key
1. A 2. A 3. B 4. B 5. C
6. A 7. A 8. B 9. C 10. C

LESSON 22

Test-Taking Words

Learn Words About a New Subject

Getting Started

Mystery Word of the Week Clue 1
The author leaves the ending of this chapter uncertain. Make a _____ about what will happen next.

- See page 14 for routines for using the Mystery Word of the Week Clue. The mystery word of the week is *prediction*.

Model/Teach
- Ask students to open their workbooks to page 163.
- Read the Word Learning Tip to the class. Call on volunteers to explain how they can learn new content words. Guide them to see that they can link these new words to the main idea or "big idea" of a passage. All of the words in this lesson are connected to the big idea of test-taking. They are words students encounter in test questions and directions.
- Have a volunteer read the Vocabulary Building Strategy aloud. Remind students that content words are often long and unfamiliar, but they are all about the same big idea.
- Ask students to read the directions silently to themselves. Have them read the test items and text on pages 163 and 164 as well. When everyone is finished, read the pages to the class.
- Use the **Think Aloud** on page 172 to demonstrate your thinking.
- When you finish modeling, read the five test items and text again. This time, pause at each word in boldface.

Materials Needed
- Student Workbook, pp. 163–164
- Transparency 2

Vocabulary Words
classify
elaborate
evidence
judgment
revise

LESSON 22 Test-Taking Words

Think Aloud

Now I'll share my method for defining new content words. First, I focus on the topic of the passage. What big idea connects all the words? I see the title, "Sample Test Questions." I also see five sample test questions and text that explains what the boldface words mean. There are questions about social studies, English, and science. Now I know that all the words will be on the subject of taking tests. Read the first item along with me: "In your **judgment**, should the president be able to serve more than two terms? Why or why not?" The text says, "The key word **judgment** tells you to give your reasoned opinion." This tells me that a *judgment* must be a specific type of test-taking thought. When I think this way, I make a reasoned opinion. So to answer this test item, I have to give a reasoned thought or opinion.

- Place the transparency on the overhead projector. Ask students what word best completes the phrase "The Author's Big Idea or Subject Is . . ." Guide them to supply the word *test-taking*. Explain that as you pause at each boldface word, you want students to tell you how it relates to the big idea. You also want them to tell you what each word means. For example, judgment is connected to the idea of taking tests because it is an informed opinion you might be asked to make. Students should explain how they determine what each word means. Record their thinking on the transparency.

- After students have defined and discussed each content word, partner students to answer the test questions on this page, using the content words as they work.

English Language Learners
- Remind students that English words are classified into eight parts of speech. Two very important parts of speech are nouns and verbs. A noun is a word that names a person, place, or thing, while a verb is a word that shows action or a state of being. Partner students to classify each of the content words according to its part of speech. When everyone is finished, go over the answers: *classify*, *elaborate*, and *revise* are verbs: *evidence* and *judgment* are nouns. Have students work in groups to use these words in sentences.

Independent Activity
- **Write Test Items** Ask students to write five more test items, each using one of the vocabulary words. Tell them that their test items can be about any subject. Walk around the room as they work to check that they are using each word correctly.

Answer Key
See page 216 for definitions.

Connect Words and Meanings

Getting Started

Mystery Word of the Week Clue 2

The conflict, or struggle, in this story has now come to a head. Make a _____ about who will win.

★ **Review and Share** Have partners trade papers and take each other's "tests" from the activity on page 161 in the teacher's edition. Then as a class talk about what each content word means as it is used on the test. How did knowing the precise meaning of the content words make it easier to answer the test items?

Model/Teach

- Ask the class to turn to page 165 in their workbooks.
- Use the **Think Aloud** to model your thinking.
- When you have finished modeling how to complete the activity, direct students to work independently to finish the page. Ask them to share their answers, and be sure they explain their thinking.

Independent Activities

★ **Paraphrase Definitions** Putting definitions in their own words will ensure that students understand them and remember them. Remind students to use the actual vocabulary word in each of their sentences.

- **Create Word Posters** Arrange students in small groups and assign one vocabulary word to each group. Distribute crayons, markers, and sheets of unlined 8 1/2" x 11" paper for groups to use as they make a poster for their word. Posters should feature the word, its definition, sentences, and pictures to illustrate how the word relates to the big idea of this lesson.

Materials Needed
- Student Workbook, p. 165

Think Aloud

Read the first definition along with me: "proof; details, facts, and examples that help you prove something or convince others that it is true." Now I know that some test items ask you to supply proof in order to support your position or opinion. I think the word that is used on tests is *evidence*. Let me see if *evidence* fits in the sentence. "Remember to provide evidence to back up your ideas." *Evidence* fits, so I write it in the blank by the definition and in the blank in the sentence.

Answer Key
1. evidence 2. evidence 3. revise
4. revise 5. elaborate 6. elaborate
7. judgment 8. judgment
9. classify 10. classify

LESSON 22 Test-Taking Words

Use Content Words

Materials Needed
- Student Workbook, p.166

Getting Started

Mystery Word of the Week Clue 3

This type of story is called a cliff-hanger, because each episode leaves you hanging. Make a _____. Will Armando survive the fall from the roof?

Think Aloud

For this activity, I have to use a vocabulary word to tell what each item asks me to do. Read the first item with me: "Reread your response. Then make any changes necessary to make your ideas clearer." The vocabulary word closest in meaning is *revise*. When I *revise* my writing, I try to improve it. So *revise* is the word I write in the blank.

⭐ **Review and Share** Give students an opportunity to work with a partner to share how they **paraphrased** each definition from the activity on page 165. Ask the partners to revise each other's sentences. Tell students to write the revised versions of their own sentences on separate pieces of paper or sentence strips. Create a bulletin board display of students' sentences.

Model/Teach

- Have students open to page 166 in their workbooks.
- Before students begin the page, read the **Think Aloud**.
- After you have modeled how to choose the word that fits the task, direct the class to finish the page on their own. Then have them share their responses.

Independent Activities

⭐ **Write Test-Taking Tips** Spark discussion by modeling some test-taking tips that you would use, such as "Always leave time to *revise* your work before you hand it in," "Be sure to *elaborate* on your ideas with specific evidence," and "Use your best *judgment* if you need to guess." Then form student groups to complete the activity.

- **Create Concept Maps** Group students to map the vocabulary words in ways that show their relationships. For example, students might link *evidence* and *judgment* because they are both nouns and you make a judgment about what evidence to include in a report. Invite each group to share its explanation of the relationships among the words.

Answer Key
1. revise 2. elaborate 3. classify
4. evidence 5. judgment
6. elaborate 7. judgment
8. classify

Put Words Into Action

Materials Needed
- Student Workbook, p. 167

Getting Started

Mystery Word of the Week Clue 4

After the pirates reach the island, they discover that someone has stolen half of their treasure map. Make a _____. Will they discover who has taken it and then retrieve the treasure?

⭐ **Review and Share** Have each group choose their top three **test-taking tips** to share with the class from the activity on page 166. Invite a member from each group to write these tips on chart paper. Tell the class to use the content words as they discuss why these tips are helpful. Then display the chart for students to use as they take tests.

Model/Teach

- Ask students to open their workbooks to page 167.
- Read the **Think Aloud** to show students how to complete the activity.
- Have students complete the remaining items independently and share their responses.

English Language Learners

- Students are likely to find these words challenging because they have many syllables. Say each word and ask students to repeat it several times. Then have students sort the words according to the number of syllables they have. Allow students to check their answers in a dictionary.

Independent Activity

⭐ **Write a Test with a Partner** Before students start their independent work, have the class generate a few questions. For example: "Do children need more sleep than adults? Support your answer with **evidence** from the article you just read?" or "Do you think music education should be part of the school curriculum? Include facts and details to support your **judgment**."

Think Aloud

These are comments that a teacher might make about your work on a test. Let's look at the first comment together: "You have not supported your _____ or opinion. Please back it up with facts." Well, this happens a lot on the writing part of tests. A student just gives an opinion, but doesn't back it up or support it. I know that another word for opinion, especially one that is backed up by facts, is *judgment*. This is a word that often appears in test directions Let me show you how it fits in the sentence: "You have not supported your judgment or opinion. Please back it up with facts." Now that sounds like something I might write.

Answer Key
1. judgment 2. elaborate (also accept revise) 3. revise
4. evidence 5. Classify 6. revise
7. evidence 8. Elaborate
9. judgment 10. classify

LESSON 22 Test-Taking Words

Review and Extend

Materials Needed
- Student Workbook, p. 168

Think Aloud

Read the first item to yourself as I read it aloud: "Make sure you use quotation marks when you ____ a person's exact words." I see the words "quotation marks" and "exact words." I know that a test item sometimes asks that you give a person's exact words. The vocabulary word that means "to give someone's exact words" is *quote*, so *quote* is the word I write in the blank. Now I read the sentence over to check that *quote* fits: "Make sure you use quotation marks when you quote someone's exact words." That's correct, so I am sure of my answer.

Answer Key
Mystery Word of the Week: prediction
Accept other words that fit the context, too.

1. quote 2. revise 3. classify
4. observation 5. evidence
6. elaborate

Getting Started

Mystery Word of the Week Clue 5
Harry receives a letter that tells him his family's secret history. Make a _____. How will he react to this news?

★ **Review and Share** Provide time for students to share their **test-taking questions**, with one student asking the questions and the other answering them. After one student has asked all of his or her questions, have students switch roles.

Model/Teach

- Ask students to turn to page 168 in their workbooks. Have a volunteer read the boxed information aloud. Then discuss the two bonus words, linking them to the big idea of test-taking.
- Read the **Think Aloud** to model your thinking.
- When you have modeled how to complete each sentence, have students fill out the page on their own. Have them share their responses as a class.

Independent Activities

★ **Find More Test-Taking Words** This activity is especially well-suited for a homework assignment. Students can share their words and definitions by posting them on the class web page under the heading "Test-Taking Words."

- **Write a Commercial** Divide the class into seven equal groups and assign one of the content words or bonus words to each group. Then have each group write a commercial that uses their word to sell a product. After each group performs its commercial, have the class vote to decide which word was most useful and why.

Check Your Mastery

Materials Needed
- Student Workbook, p. 169

Give the Test

- Direct the class to open their workbooks to page 169.
- Read the directions aloud: "Read each item below. Then write the vocabulary word that best completes each sentence. Use each vocabulary word twice."
- Demonstrate how to complete this activity by writing the following item on the chalkboard and reading it aloud:

  You would _____ a cheetah, lion, and tiger together as "mammals."

  A. evidence   **B.** revise   **C.** classify

- Ask students to choose the vocabulary word that best fits the blank. Have them explain their reasons for choosing C (classify).
- Tell students to check over their answers by rereading the sentences and their choices.
- Review the Check Your Mastery activity with the class.
- Partner students to discuss the answers they missed. Guide them to review the Word Learning Tip and Vocabulary Building Strategy as they analyze their answers.
- Tally students' correct responses.

Student Self-Assessment

Journal Writing Direct students to write in their journals telling how they can learn new content words. Have them explain how they used the Word Learning Tip and the Vocabulary Building Strategy to make these new words part of their vocabulary.

Answer Key
1. A 2. B 3. C 4. B 5. A
6. C 7. C 8. A 9. C 10. B

CHAPTER 4

Words and Their Histories

Lesson 23	Words From Other Languages	**180**
Lesson 24	Homophones	**187**
Lesson 25	Easily Confused Words	**194**
Lesson 26	Idioms and Other Common Expressions	**201**

Research Base

- **Word Learning Tip** Some words have interesting histories or other letter sound clues that help you understand their meaning.

- **Vocabulary Building Strategy** Use knowledge of word origins, derivations, and unusual spelling patterns to determine word meaning.

- **Research-Based Lists** Chapter 4 focuses on words that have interesting histories or sounds. This chapter includes words from other languages, homophones, commonly confused words, and idioms.

LESSON 23 — Words From Other Languages

Materials Needed
- Student Workbook, p. 172
- Transparency 3
- Idea Web Graphic Organizer, p. 229

Vocabulary Words
admiral
butte
cashmere
eureka
gourmet
kangaroo
menu
mesa
moustache
pajamas
parka
patio
safari
sherbet
tortilla

Read Words in Context

Getting Started

Mystery Word of the Week Clue 1

The _____ is the principal female singer in an opera or concert company.

- See page 14 for routines for using the Mystery Word of the Week Clue. The mystery word of the week is *prima donna*.

Model/Teach

- Ask students to turn to page 172 in their workbooks.

- Have students read the Word Learning Tip. Discuss with students the fact that some words have fascinating pasts. English is rich in words that have entered the language from other languages. Sum up by explaining how knowing a word's history can help us understand what the word means and how to use it.

- Have a volunteer read the Vocabulary Building Strategy. Explain to the class that because some words come from other languages, they may look, sound, or be spelled differently from what the students expect. Knowing the history of a word can help students learn its meaning.

- Read the complete story aloud once, directing students to follow along in their books.

- Explain to the class that you are going to read the story a second time. This time you want them to think about the words in boldface type and to try to determine what they mean.

- Do the **Think Aloud** on page 181.

- After you have modeled how to determine the meaning of *patio*, read the story again. This time, pause at each boldface word.

180   Chapter 4 • Words and Their Histories

- Put Transparency 3 on the overhead projector. Tell students that as you pause at each boldface word, you want them to tell you what is special about the word. In other words, what language does it come from? What do they know about the country of origin? How does the word look different? Then you will ask students to tell you how they will remember the word and what it means.

- Read the story a second time. As students discuss each word, add their responses to the transparency.

- Divide the class into small groups. Distribute flashcards and ask students to work with them to reinforce the meanings of the vocabulary words.

English Language Learners

- Ask students to take turns pointing to a vocabulary word as you pronounce it and they repeat the word after you. Then have students write the pronunciation to help them remember it. For example, for *eureka* they might write "yoo-REE-kah." Group students to compare pronunciation guides and practice using them to say the words.

Independent Activity

Create Idea Webs Distribute copies of the Idea Web Graphic Organizer. Have students create individual idea webs to show how some of their vocabulary words are related. For instance, they might link *pajamas*, *cashmere*, and *parka* because they relate to clothing, and *sherbet* and *tortilla* because they are both foods.

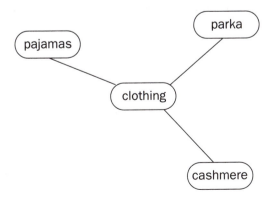

Think Aloud

Here's what I would think about if I saw an unusual-sounding or unusual-looking word that I did not know. Suppose I did not know what *patio* means. I know that some words that end in *o* come from Spanish, and I think that *patio* may come from this language, too. It seems to have something to do with the house. I also see the word *deck*, so I think that *patio* may be a type of deck. Now I know that some Spanish and Mexican houses have large outdoor areas where people sit and eat and rest. When I add together all that I know about how Spanish words are spelled and what the Spanish culture is like, I think that *patio* must be an outdoor area like a deck where people sit and eat.

Answer Key
See page 216 for definitions.

Lesson 23 • Words From Other Languages

LESSON 23 Words From Other Languages

Connect Words and Meanings

Materials Needed
- Student Workbook, pp. 173–174

Getting Started

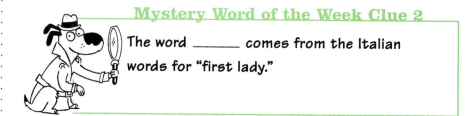

Mystery Word of the Week Clue 2

The word _____ comes from the Italian words for "first lady."

⭐ **Review and Share** Invite students to display the **idea webs** they created for the activity on page 181 in the teacher's edition. Have the rest of the class explain the relationships they see among the words. Highlight any relationships based on the word's origins and derivations. Display the webs in the classroom.

Model/Teach

- Have students turn to page 170 in their workbooks.
- Before students begin the activity, do the **Think Aloud**.
- After you have modeled finding the word and writing the answer, have students complete the rest of the crossword puzzle on their own. Then tell students to do the second activity.
- Have students share their responses. Make sure they explain their thinking, as you did with the Think Aloud.

Independent Activities

⭐ **Understand More Words From Spanish** Tell students to complete the activity in groups. Provide groups with dictionaries or allow them to use the Internet to look up each word in an online dictionary. As necessary, help students pronounce each word.

- **Story Starters** Arrange students in groups. Give each group a story starter that uses one of the vocabulary words, such as "It was so exciting on the *safari* when . . ." Have students continue the story by taking turns providing sentences that use one of the vocabulary words. Students should use all the vocabulary words, repeating words if they need to. Have one student write down the stories.

Think Aloud

I see that this is a crossword puzzle, so I know that I have to write the vocabulary words in the boxes, one letter per box. Let's look at 3 Across together. Read the clue with me: "An ancient Greek word that means 'upper lip.'" It came into English from French and Italian. Like the French and Italians, we use the word to refer to the hair that grows above the upper lip." Then I count the spaces: nine. This tells me that I am looking for a nine-letter word. I study the word list and see that there is one word with nine letters, *moustache*. I know that a *moustache* is the hair above the upper lip. I've always wondered why this word doesn't look the way it sounds and now I know why: It's because it comes from other languages.

Answer Key
Across 3. moustache 4. safari
7. tortilla 9. patio
Down 1. butte 2. gourmet
5. parka 6. pajamas 8. menu

1. admiral 2. admiral 3. eureka
4. Eureka 5. sherbet 6. sherbet
7. cashmere 8. cashmere
9. kangaroo 10. kangaroo

Use Words in Context

Getting Started

Mystery Word of the Week Clue 3
The word _____ is also used to refer to someone who likes to be in the spotlight.

⭐ **Review and Share** Guide students to discuss the other **words from Spanish** they learned from the activity on page 174. Which words had the most interesting histories? How did knowing a word's origin make it easier to learn it? Ask students to explain what they learned about building their vocabulary. Add the new words to the word wall.

Model/Teach

- Have students turn to page 175 in their workbooks.
- Before students begin the activity, share the **Think Aloud** with the class.
- After you have modeled how to chose the correct word to complete each sentence, have students work on their own to complete the rest of the items.
- Ask students to share their responses and guide them to explain their thinking.

English Language Learners

- Arrange English language learners in small groups to read the sentences and substitute a word that makes sense for each missing word. As students generate synonyms, have them look at the list of vocabulary words to find the word that matches best.

Independent Activity

⭐ **Dress for (Word) Success!** Before students begin creating their ads, be sure they can correctly use each word in context. Point out that all five new words are nouns, but some of the vocabulary words function as other parts of speech as well. *Eureka*, for example, is an interjection and *gourmet* is an adjective as well as a noun. Students may wish to illustrate their ads.

Materials Needed
- Student Workbook, p. 175

Think Aloud

Listen closely while I model my thinking. Read the first sentence to yourself as I read it aloud: "We are selling soft 1._____ (*gourmet, sherbet, cashmere*) sweaters." The context clues "soft wool" and "sweaters" tell me that I need a word that describes sweaters. I can eliminate *gourmet* and *sherbet* because they describe food, not sweaters. The only word that makes sense is *cashmere*. I'll check my answer by using the word in the sentence: "We are selling soft wool *cashmere* sweaters." That fits.

Answer Key
1. cashmere 2. parka 3. kangaroo
4. moustache 5. Eureka 6. gourmet
7. tortilla 8. sherbet 9. menu
10. patio

Lesson 23 • Words From Other Languages

LESSON 23: Words From Other Languages

Put Words Into Action

Getting Started

Mystery Word of the Week Clue 4
A _____ may find it difficult to work as part of a team because she likes to be in the spotlight all the time.

Materials Needed
- Student Workbook, p. 176

Think Aloud

I have to do two things: first, sort the words according to the language they come from and second, define each word. The first word on the list is *admiral*. I know that admiral comes from an Arabic word which means "commander of the sea." The actual Arabic word was *'amīr al-'ālī*, but when the word moved into English, the spelling changed. I'll write the word in the column headed "Words from Arabic." Under the definition column, I'll write "commander of ships."

 Review and Share Invite volunteers to share the **ads** they made for the activity on page 175. Have the rest of the class write down the vocabulary words they see in the ads. Display the ads around the room and add the new words to the word wall.

Model/Teach

- Have students turn to page 176 of their workbooks.
- Use the **Think Aloud** to introduce the activity.
- After you have modeled how to complete the activity, have students complete it on their own. Partner students to compare their charts.

Independent Activities

Name That Word's History Tell students to write and number their clues, starting with the most general clue first.

- **Make a Word Map** Arrange students in small groups and provide each group with a blank map of the world. Have students write the vocabulary words on the map in their countries of origin. Then have students add as many more words as they can to the map, to show their origins. You can provide these words to get them started: *silhouette, cuisine, bouillon* (French); *adobe, canyon, sierra* (Spanish); *bravo, quartet, soprano* (Italian); *garble, zero* (Arabic, Indian); *bungalow, shampoo* (India).

Answer Key
1. patio–porch 2. mesa–tableland
3. tortilla–flat bread
4. eureka–exclamation of surprise
5. moustache–hair under nose
6. kangaroo–large, hopping animal
7. admiral–commander of ships
8. safari–trip to see animals
9. sherbet–frozen fruit dessert
10. gourmet–person who knows good food
11. menu–list of a restaurant's foods
12. butte–a small mesa or tableland
13. parka–heavy coat
14. cashmere–soft wool
15. pajamas–clothes for sleeping

Also accept *moustache* listed under French or Spanish.

184 Chapter 4 • Words and Their Histories

Review and Extend

Materials Needed
- Student Workbook, p. 177

Getting Started

Mystery Word of the Week Clue 5

This word is on the same page in the dictionary as the words *pride* and *prime*.

⭐ **Review and Share** Have students share the **word clues** they wrote for the activity on page 176. Caution students not to name the word as they read their clues! At the end of each clue, have the class guess the word.

Model/Teach

- Direct students to turn to page 177 of their workbooks. Read the boxed information to the class and discuss the histories and meanings of the five new words.
- Use the **Think Aloud**.
- After you have modeled completing an item, have students finish the rest of the activity on their own. Have students share their responses with the entire class or in small groups.

Independent Activities

⭐ **Play a Word Game** If necessary, provide students with index cards or slips of paper to write on. Then allow them sufficient time to play the game until everyone gets all of the words right.

- **Thereby Lies a Tale** Divide the class into ten equal groups and have each group find the history and meaning of one of these words: *boycott, gerrymander, quixotic, silhouette, denim, jeans, tuxedo, thespian, zeppelin, mocha*. Then have each group share its findings with the class. Add these words to the word wall.

Think Aloud

Please read the first question silently to yourself as I read it aloud: "Why might a **gourmet** chef send his **resumé** to a new restaurant?" I notice the two boldface words, *gourmet* and *resumé*, which is one of my bonus words. I know that both of these words come from French. They sound a little alike, but they don't sound like they are spelled. You don't pronounce the final *t* in *gourmet* and *resumé* has three syllables instead of two. Most English words don't have accent marks, but the accent mark over the final *e* in *resumé* tells me to pronounce *me* as a syllable. Also, the *e* at the end sounds like an *a*. These pronunciation differences happen a lot with words from French. Now that I have thought about that, I will try to answer the question. A gourmet chef would be someone who cooks fine food and dishes. A *resumé* is a list of jobs. So a gourmet chef might send his resumé to a new restaurant to get a job cooking at a better place.

Answer Key
Mystery Word of the Week:
prima donna
Accept other words that fit the context, too.

Students' answer will vary. See page 223 for sample sentences.

LESSON 23 Words From Other Languages

Check Your Mastery

Materials Needed
- Student Workbook, p. 178

Student Self-Assessment

Journal Writing In their journals, have students write about how in the future they can learn the pronunciation and meaning of unusual-looking or unusual-sounding new words by thinking about a word's history and origin. Ask them to give examples of words from this lesson that they can define by using the Word Learning Tip and Vocabulary Building Strategy.

Give the Test
- Tell students to open their workbooks to page 178.
- Explain that this Check Your Mastery activity has only one part.
- Read the directions: "Circle the letter of the correct answer to each question below." Explain to students that their task is to choose the item that best answers each question.
- Model how to answer a question by writing the following sentence and choices on the board. Then read the sentence and choices to students.

   What are **pajamas** most likely made of?

   A. wood   **B.** plastic   **C.** metal   **D.** soft fabric

- Ask students to choose the word that best answers the question. Have them justify their choices by explaining what word origin they used. Guide students to understand that the correct answer is D (soft fabric).
- Direct students to reread their answers and check their work after they finish this activity.
- Review the Check Your Mastery activity with students.
- Arrange students in pairs to discuss the questions they did not answer correctly. Have them write new sentences using the correct vocabulary word for each item they missed.
- Guide students to discuss how the Word Learning Tip and the Vocabulary Building Strategy helped them choose the correct response.
- Tally students' correct responses.

Answer Key
1. C 2. B 3. D 4. A 5. A
6. C 7. D 8. A 9. B 10. D

Read Words in Context

LESSON 24 — Homophones

Getting Started

Mystery Word of the Week Clue 1

Many people are working together for world _____.

- See page 14 for routines for using the Mystery Word of the Week Clue. The mystery words of the week are the homophones *peace/piece*.

Model/Teach

- Have students open their workbooks to page 179.
- Ask a volunteer to read the Word Learning Tip to the class. Be sure students understand that homophones can often be distinguished if we know their histories. Use this example: *deer* and *dear* sound alike. However, *deer* comes from an Old English word for "beast." Knowing the history of "deer" helps us remember that the word refers to the animal, not a beloved person.
- Read the Vocabulary Building Strategy to the class. Discuss with students that clues in surrounding words and phrases can help them determine which one of a pair of homophones is meant.
- Read the story aloud.
- Do the **Think Aloud** on page 188 to model how to differentiate between two homophones.
- After you have modeled how to determine the meaning of *barren*, read the story aloud again. Pause at each boldface word to give students the opportunity to define the words, using the technique that you modeled. For each word, make sure they identify the other word in the homophone pair.

Materials Needed
- Student Workbook, p. 179
- Transparency 3

Vocabulary Words
aid/aide
baron/barren
chord/cord
coarse/course
colonel/kernel

LESSON 24 Homophones

Think Aloud

Follow along silently as I read aloud: "Have you ever considered traveling to the **barren** planet Mars at some point in the future?" I know the sound of the word *barren* can have two different meanings: It can mean "empty; not fertile" or "a nobleman." Words like this that sound alike but have different meanings are called homophones. I have to learn the spelling of these words to know the meanings. The words *barren* and *baron* are homophones. *Barren*, spelled b-a-r-r-e-n, means "empty; not fertile." *Baron*, spelled b-a-r-o-n, means "a nobleman." In the story, *barren* describes the planet Mars, so it means "empty, not fertile." This meaning is spelled b-a-r-r-e-n. Later in the story, we will see how the writer used *baron*, spelled b-a-r-o-n.

Answer Key
See page 217 for definitions.

- Place the transparency on the overhead projector. Tell the class that you are going to write down the words and the clues that they created to determine the meaning of each boldface word. As the class talks about each word, enter that word as an entry on the transparency and complete each column relative to it.

- When the chart is complete, divide the class into small groups to work with flashcards to reinforce the meaning of each word.

Independent Activities

- **Make a Word Chain** Partner students to write the vocabulary words and their definitions on strips of paper, one set of homophones and their definitions per strip. Encourage students to read the homophones and definitions to each other as they work. Provide dictionaries as necessary.

- **Play a Word Game** Arrange students in groups of four and give each player a number, 1 to 4. Give each group a vocabulary word and tell the students to work together to define the word. Then call a number between 1 and 4, and have that student from each group provide the answer. Continue playing until all of the vocabulary words have been used and each player has had multiple turns.

188 Chapter 4 • Words and Their Histories

Connect Words and Meanings

Getting Started

Mystery Word of the Week Clue 2

The problem of world hunger is one _____ of the larger issue of poverty.

⭐ **Review and Share** Invite students to display the **word strips** they created for the activity on page 188 in the teacher's edition. Then staple the paper strips together to create a chain. Tape the word chain around the room, where it is easily visible.

Model/Teach

- Ask students to open their workbooks to page 180.
- Start the activity with the **Think Aloud**.
- When you are done modeling how to use word histories and context clues to understand word meanings, direct students to finish the rest of the page independently.
- Allow students time to compare answers and explain their thinking.

Independent Activities

⭐ **Understand Multiple Meanings** This is an ideal activity for early finishers or for students to complete on their own for homework. Remind them to use a print or online dictionary as they work.

- **Become Experts** Arrange students in groups of five. Assign each student one pair of homophones. Next, have students work on their own to become experts on the histories and meanings of their word pair. Last, have students come together to teach their words to the rest of the group.

Materials Needed
- Student Workbook, p. 180

Think Aloud

Read the first item along with me: "The noun **colonel** comes from the Old French word *coronel*. The French adapted an Italian word that meant 'commander of a column of soldiers.'" The word looks like it has three syllables but we pronounce only two. I can eliminate *small seed* because it has nothing to do with a commander. In fact, it defines the homophone *kernel*. *Statue* is not the right word, but I can see how someone might pick this answer, since *statue* and *column* are somewhat connected. The correct choice is *officer in the U.S. Military*. This meaning relates to the original meaning. I've always wondered why the *l* in *colonel* is pronounced /r/; now I see that this is a carry over from the French word.

Answer Key
1. officer in the U.S. Military
2. three or more tones
3. grain or seed 4. string
5. not fertile soil 6. path
7. assistant 8. nobleman
9. not smooth 10. assist

Lesson 24 • Homophones **189**

LESSON 24 Homophones

Use Words in Context

Materials Needed
- Student Workbook, p. 181

Think Aloud

I start by reading the question: "Don't write a news story without a **kernel** of truth. Why not?" I know that a kernel is a seed or a grain, so if a story doesn't have a grain of truth, it is completely inaccurate. So here is my answer: "You shouldn't write a news story without a *kernel* of truth because it is important to be accurate when you report the news."

Answer Key
Students' responses will vary. See page 223 for sample sentences.

Getting Started

Mystery Word of the Week Clue 3

The word _____ comes from an Old French word spelled "pais" and the Latin word *pax*, which meant "absence of war."

★ **Review and Share** Give students the opportunity to share the **different meanings** they found for the homophones in the activity on page 180. Make a chart with each word and its different meanings. As you work, talk about how knowing a word's origin helps us define its meaning and distinguish it from its homophone. Display the chart in a prominent place in the classroom.

Model/Teach
- Ask the class to open their workbooks to page 181.
- Use the **Think Aloud** to model how to complete the activity.
- When you complete the modeling, arrange students in pairs to finish the page.
- Allow students time to compare answers and explain their thinking.

English Language Learners
- Arrange English language learners in small groups to complete this activity together. Have each student in turn write a sentence as paper and pencil are passed around the table. This encourages students to compare answers and self-correct as they work. Then have the entire group write their final answers to the questions.

Independent Activity

★ **More Homophones About People** Explain to students that only one word in each pair refers to people. Divide the class into groups of three. Make sure that each student in the group chooses a different homophone pair. Provide dictionaries for them to use or allow them to work online.

Chapter 4 • Words and Their Histories

Put Words Into Action

Materials Needed
- Student Workbook, p. 182

Getting Started

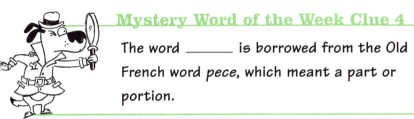

Mystery Word of the Week Clue 4

The word _____ is borrowed from the Old French word *pece*, which meant a part or portion.

⭐ **Review and Share** Invite groups to share their **homophones about people** from the activity on page 181. Add the new homophones and their histories to the word wall.

Think Aloud

From the directions, I see that I have to write an answer to each question. The first question is, "What route should we take to get to Mars?" The answer has to contain the vocabulary word in parentheses, *course*. I remember that the noun *course* comes from a Latin word for "run." Then I add the context clue "route." This tells me that I have to write a sentence that describes the path to take. I'll write this sentence: "We should take the most direct **course** past the Moon."

Model/Teach
- Ask students to open their workbooks to page 182.
- Before students begin the activity, use the **Think Aloud**.
- When you have completed the modeling, ask students to finish the page independently. Arrange students in pairs to discuss their answers. Have one student read the question and another read the answer. Then have partners alternate tasks.

Independent Activities

⭐ **Write a Martian Weather Report** Before students begin this activity, divide the class into small groups. Ask each group to share what they know about the weather on Mars, based on what they have read. Then have students work in pairs or small groups to write their weather reports.

- **Sing a Song** Create groups to set these homophones, their histories, and their meanings to music. Encourage students to use a familiar tune, such as "Twinkle, Twinkle, Little Star," "On Top of Old Smoky," or the alphabet song. When each group is finished, have them share their song with the class. Discuss how these songs help us remember homophones.

Answer Key
Students' responses will vary. See page 223 for sample sentences.

LESSON 24 Homophones

Review and Extend

Materials Needed
- Student Workbook, p. 183

Getting Started

Mystery Word of the Week Clue 5
The letters *ea* in _____ and *ie* in _____ spell the same sound.

⭐ **Review and Share** Allow students time to deliver the **Martian weather reports** they wrote for the activity on page 182. If possible, videotape the presentations so students can watch the tapes during their free time and review the words.

Model/Teach
- Ask students to open their workbooks to page 183. Have a volunteer read the boxed information aloud. As a class, talk about the histories and meanings of the new pairs of homophones.
- Use the **Think Aloud** to model your thinking for students.
- When you finish modeling your thinking, direct students to finish the rest of the activity on their own. Ask them to share responses and their thinking, based on the model you provided.

English Language Learners
- Explain to students that in English the same sound can be spelled different ways. Write the words *weather* and *whether* on the chalkboard and say these words aloud. Explain that in the first word, the sound /w/ is spelled *w* and in the second word, the same sound is spelled *wh*. Ask students to list five words in which /w/ is spelled *w* and five words in which it is spelled *wh*. Then explain that the short sound /e/ can be spelled *e* or *ea*. Repeat the process for listing new words.

Independent Activity

⭐ **Put on a Skit** Before students begin the activity, arrange them in groups. Assign one student to be the Recorder who writes the script as the other members suggest lines. You may also want to appoint a Facilitator to help groups stay focused on the task. After the scripts are complete, allow students the opportunity to rehearse their skits.

Think Aloud

The first sentence talks about the climate on Mars. Since *climate* is in boldface, I know that it is my context clue. This tells me that I need to find a word that means "climate." I know that *weather* means "climate," but I'm not sure if it is spelled "weather" or "whether." Those two words are homophones, so they are easy to confuse. I'll look back at the two words *weather/whether* in the box to check which word is correct here. *Weather* is the homophone that means "climate" so I will write *weather* in the blank.

Answer Key
Mystery Word of the Week:
peace/piece

1. weather 2. whether 3. write
4. right 5. coarse 6. aid 7. barren
8. course

192 Chapter 4 • Words and Their Histories

Check Your Mastery

Give the Test

- Ask students to turn to page 184 in their workbooks.
- Explain that this Check Your Mastery activity has one part.
- Read the directions: "Read each item below. Then write the vocabulary word that best completes each sentence. Use each vocabulary word only once."
- Model how to answer a question by writing the following sentence and choices on the chalkboard. Then read the sentence and choices to students.

  The musicians sang a _____ in perfect harmony.

  cord   chord   coarse

- Have students choose the word that best completes the sentence. Guide them to explain their answers by telling what word origin and context clues they used. Help students understand that the correct answer is *chord*. The context clues are "musicians," "sang," and "harmony."
- Be sure that students check their work after they finish.
- When everyone is finished working, go over the Check Your Mastery activity with students.
- Have students work with a classmate to identify the questions they did not answer correctly. Ask them to write new sentences using the correct vocabulary word for each item they missed.
- Encourage students to explain how the Word Learning Tip and the Vocabulary Building Strategy helped them choose the correct response.
- Tally students' correct responses.

Materials Needed
- Student Workbook, p. 184

Student Self-Assessment

Journal Writing Have students write in their journals explaining how they distinguish between homophones by using the word's history and clues in the word's spelling. Have them rewrite the Word Learning Tip and Vocabulary Building Strategy in their own words.

Answer Key
1. chord 2. barren 3. course
4. aide 5. kernel 6. coarse
7. colonel 8. aid 9. cord
10. baron

Lesson 24 • Homophones

LESSON 25
Easily Confused Words

Read Words in Context

Materials Needed
- Student Workbook, p. 185
- Transparency 3

Vocabulary Words
accent/ascent/assent
bazaar/bizarre
canvas/canvass
carton/cartoon
convince/persuade

Getting Started

Mystery Word of the Week Clue 1
After the team lost the game, the coach gave them a pep talk to boost their _____.

- See page 14 for routines for using the Mystery Word of the Week Clue. The mystery words of the week are the commonly confused words *moral* and *morale*.

Model/Teach

- Ask students to open their workbooks to page 185.
- Have a student read the Word Learning Tip to the class as students follow along in their books. Be sure students realize that words can be confused because they sound alike or have similar spellings. Explain that the words *convince* and *persuade* don't sound at all alike, but because they deal with the same general idea, people mix them up.
- Read the Vocabulary Building Strategy aloud. Explain to students that listening carefully to how a word sounds, paying attention to its spelling, and creating clues to remind them of the differences between the words can help them determine which word and which meaning are meant.
- Read the story to the class. Guide students to look at the words in boldface type and use sound and context clues to define them.
- Before you read the story a second time, use the **Think Aloud** on page 195.
- After you have shared your thinking with the class, read the story to students again. Now, pause at each boldface word.

- Place the transparency on the overhead projector. Point out the heading "What's Special About This Word," and ask students to give the word with which it is commonly confused. Remind them to think about the Word Learning Tip and the Vocabulary Building Strategy as they define each word. Have students share their thinking as they tell how they will remember the word and what it means. Record their thinking on the transparency.
- When the transparency is completed, arrange students in pairs and have them work with flashcards to reinforce word meaning.

English Language Learners
- The key to distinguishing between many of these words is pronunciation. For example, the accent is on the second syllable of *cartoon* but on the first syllable of *carton*. Pronounce each word for students and have them repeat the words after you. Then have students make their own personal pronunciation guides on index cards. Partner students and ask them to use the cards to practice saying the words correctly.

Independent Activity
- **Make Word Mobiles** Arrange students in small groups to write one vocabulary word on the front of an index card and its definition and a sentence containing it on the back. Students can staple the cards to pieces of yarn and hang them from a wire coat hanger, arranging all of the easily confused word pairs or triads together.

Think Aloud

Let's read the first two sentences together: "You don't have to **persuade** true explorers to set sail, soar into space, or plunge into the ocean's depths. You don't have to give them reasons to **convince** them that travel is rewarding." I see the words *persuade* and *convince* in boldface, and I know that these words are often confused. I'm going to try to clarify their meaning by seeing how they are used in the sentences. *Persuade* is used with the words "to set sail, soar into space, or plunge into the ocean's depths." These are all actions or things people do. So *persuade* must mean "to get people to do something." *Convince* is used with the words "that travel is rewarding." This isn't an action but a belief or idea. *Convince* must mean "to get people to believe something." So it seems that you *persuade* people to do something, and you *convince* them that something is true. I see why these words are so easily confused. I'm going to try to remember the distinction by linking *persuade* with *to* and *convince* with *that*. So you *persuade to* and you *convince that*.

Answer Key
See page 217 for definitions.

LESSON

25 Easily Confused Words

Connect Words and Meanings

Materials Needed
- Student Workbook, p. 186

Getting Started

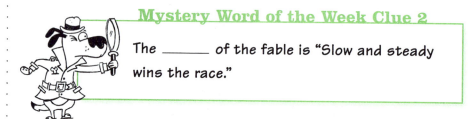

Mystery Word of the Week Clue 2

The _____ of the fable is "Slow and steady wins the race."

Think Aloud

Let's look at the first word together: *carton*. I know that *carton* and *cartoon* are sometimes confused because their spelling is so similar. I know that *cartoon* with two o's means a comic strip or drawing. I remember this because comic strip characters are sometimes called "toons." *Carton* with one *o* means a box or container. The trick that helps me remember which meaning to attach to *carton* is that a carton usually has six faces or surfaces—the four sides and the top and bottom—and the word *carton* has six letters. Now I look down the right-hand column for a definition that matches *carton*. It is "C—a box or container usually made of cardboard of plastic; from the Italian word *cartone*, meaning 'pasteboard' because boxes were made of pasteboard."

★ **Review and Share** Have students share their **mobiles** and use the words in sentences, providing context clues to reinforce meaning. Then display the mobiles around the room to help students remember these words, their definitions, and ways they are confused.

Model/Teach

- Ask students to open their workbooks to page 186.
- Use the **Think Aloud** to model your thinking.
- After you finish modeling how to use definitions, word histories, and context clues to complete each sentence, ask students to finish the page on their own. Have them work in small groups to go over their answers.

Independent Activities

★ **Understand *Persuade* vs. *Convince*** Create a two-column chart on the chalkboard. Label one column "Persuade" and the other "Convince." For each word, have the class generate a list of items that could fit in that column. For example, *to go for a swim* could fit under "Persuade," while *that swimming is fun* could fit under "Convince." Once you are sure that students understand the distinction between the two words, allow them to work individually to write sentences.

- **Write a Paragraph** Have students write a paragraph about a place they would like to explore. It might be a real place, such as the Arctic, or a make-believe place such as Never-Never Land. Ask students to name the place and explain why it interests them. They can also describe the equipment they would bring, how they would explore, and who might come with them on their expedition. Have students use at least five vocabulary words in their paragraphs.

Answer Key
1. C 2. F 3. D 4. B 5. I 6. K
7. H 8. G 9. E 10. A 11. J

Use Words in Context

Materials Needed
- Student Workbook, p. 187

Getting Started

Mystery Word of the Week Clue 3

After the hare lost the race, his _____ or spirit was very low.

 Review and Share Invite students to read the sentences they wrote for the **Understand Persuade vs. Convince** activity on page 186. Check that the two words are used correctly in each sentence. Then post the sentences on the bulletin board.

Model/Teach

- Ask the class to open their workbooks to page 187.
- Use the **Think Aloud** to model your thinking.
- After you model how to fill in the blank to complete the sentence, direct students to work on their own to complete the other items. Then have students trade papers and correct each other's answers.

English Language Learners

- Many English language learners may have difficulty differentiating between the sound spelled by *s* and by *z*. Write the word *canvas* on the chalkboard and isolate the sound spelled by the letter *s*. Say it three times and have students repeat it three times after you. Then repeat the process by the word *bizarre* and the sound spelled by the letter *z*. Last, arrange students in small groups to use these words and sounds in a dialogue.

Independent Activity

 Write a Journal Entry Suggest that students consult an almanac, encyclopedia, or their community's web page to gather information about their home town. They can date their "discovery" of the town in the distant past or much more recently, even when they moved into the area. Remind them to proofread their writing to make sure they have not confused words.

Think Aloud

Here's how I would fill in the missing word in each sentence. The first sentence says, "Be sure to bring along a _____ to carry your supplies." The article *a* tells me that I need a noun to fill in the blank. The context tells me that the missing word must be a container of some sort. It might be a box, a bag, or a suitcase. Looking at the vocabulary words in the parentheses, I see *carton*. That's the right word because it is a noun that names a container. I won't confuse it with *cartoon*. When I see these two words, I sometimes get them mixed up because they sound very much alike. However, when I pronounce them carefully, I immediately know the difference. A *cartoon* with a long -u sound is a drawing or an animated comic strip, like the animated shows kids watch on television.

Answer Key
1. carton 2. canvas 3. ascent
4. accent 5. persuade 6. convince
7. bazaar 8. assent 9. bizarre
10. cartoon

Lesson 25 • Easily Confused Words

LESSON 25: Easily Confused Words

Put Words Into Action

Materials Needed
- Student Workbook, p. 188

Think Aloud

Let's read the first item together: "On July 16, 1969, Mike Collins, Neil A. Armstrong, and Edwin E. Aldrin, Jr., began their _____ (accent, ascent, assent) into space." The first thing I am going to do is say the three words in parentheses carefully. *Accent*—a-c-c-e-n-t—is pronounced with a stress on the first syllable. Now that I hear the word *accent*, I know that it means "stress" or "the way you say something." *Ascent*—a-s-c-e-n-t—is pronounced with a stress or accent on the second syllable, and *assent*—a-s-s-e-n-t—is pronounced the same way. In the sentence, I see the words "into space." This tells me that the word I am looking for tells about "rising up" into space. I eliminate *accent*. I think the word is *ascent*—a-s-c-e-n-t—because it is spelled like its opposite, *descent*—d-e-s-c-e-n-t.

Answer Key
1. ascent 2. canvass 3. carton
4. canvas 5. accent 6. bizarre
7. persuade 8. bazaar 9. convince
10. cartoon

Getting Started

Mystery Word of the Week Clue 4
Perhaps someone should have told him this _____: "If at first you don't succeed, try, try, again."

Review and Share Have students read their **journal entries** from the activity on page 187 to their classmates, working in small groups. Then have each group select one journal entry to read to the class. Discuss how knowing the history of these vocabulary words helped students use them correctly. Display the journal entries on the class bulletin board.

Model/Teach
- Ask the class to open their workbooks to page 188.
- Use the **Think Aloud**.
- When you are finished modeling your thinking, tell students to complete the rest of the items independently. Then ask students to share their answers and to explain how they understood which word to use.

Independent Activities

Create a Mnemonic Device Explain to students that mnemonic devices are little strategies or tricks that will help them remember words. Some mnemonic devices pick up on similarities or connections between things. Some use rhyme and rhythm to create memorable sentences. If students have difficulty coming up with mnemonic devices, you may ask them to work with a partner so that they can stimulate each other's thinking and creativity.

- **Make a Cartoon** Have students make a cartoon about an explorer's adventures. The cartoon can have several panels and tell a story or contain one picture with dialogue. Regardless of the method, each cartoon should contain at least five vocabulary words—including *cartoon*!

198 Chapter 4 • Words and Their Histories

Review and Extend

Materials Needed
- Student Workbook, p. 189

Getting Started

Mystery Word of the Week Clue 5
A _____ is a lesson at the end of a fable, while _____ refers to your spirit.

⭐ **Review and Share** Have students read the **mnemonic devices** they created for the activity on page 188. Create a class booklet of these memory tricks, grouping them according to the sets of easily confused words.

Model/Teach

- Ask students to open their workbooks to page 189. Read the boxed copy aloud to the class. Discuss the histories and meanings of the new pair of easily confused words.

- Use the **Think Aloud**.

- Have the class complete the rest of the activity on their own and then share their responses and their thinking.

Independent Activities

⭐ **Write About Two Words That Confuse You** Before students begin this activity, make sure that they understand the distinction between the words *except* and *accept*. Have them brainstorm ideas that will help them to remember the difference between *except/accept*, then have them write their paragraphs. Provide time for students to share their writing.

- **Think About Word Histories** Remind students that the words *carton* and *cartoon* both come from an Italian word meaning "pasteboard." Ask them to write in their journals about how pasteboard or cardboard might be connected to both words. What does this history tell them about how two different words may originally come from the same word?

Think Aloud

Let's read the first item together: "If you **lend** a book to someone, you expect _____." *Lend* is one of the new bonus words. It means "to let someone have something temporarily." I know it's commonly confused with *borrow*. I've heard people ask, "Can I *lend* that book?" when they should ask, "Can I *borrow* that book?" *Lend* means that you *give* something temporarily; *borrow* means that you *take* something temporarily. Now that I am sure that I understand these two words, I am going to complete the sentence: "If you **lend** a book to someone, you expect that person to return it."

Answer Key
Mystery Word of the Week: moral, morale

Students' responses will vary. See page 223 for sample sentences.

Lesson 25 • Easily Confused Words

LESSON 25 Easily Confused Words

Check Your Mastery

Materials Needed
- Student Workbook, p. 190

Student Self-Assessment

Journal Writing Direct the class to explain in their journals how they can distinguish between easily confused words. Have students rewrite the Word Learning Tip and Vocabulary Building Strategy in their own words.

Give the Test
- Have the class open to page 190 in their workbooks.
- Explain that this Check Your Mastery activity has two parts.
- Read the directions for the first part: "Circle the letter of the correct answer to each question below."
- Model your method for answering these questions by writing the following question and answer choices on the chalkboard. Then read the question and choices to students.

  For what would you be most likely to use **canvas**?

  A. to make sails **C.** to get a political candidate elected

  B. for a spice **D.** to climb a mountain

- Ask students to choose the phrase that best answers the question. Request that they explain why A (to make sails) is the best choice.
- Read the directions for the second part of the activity: "Choose the correct word to fit in each blank below. Write it on the line."
- Model how to answer this type of item by writing the following on the board:

  On their trip west, they bought a postcard with a picture of a _____ (*bazaar, bizarre*) creature: a jackalope.

- Have students choose the correct answer and explain their thinking.
- Remind the class to check their work after they finish the items on this page.
- Review the Check Your Mastery activity with students.
- Arrange students in small groups to isolate any wrong answers and review their thinking. Have students define any missed words and review their histories to help them remember how to use these words correctly.
- Have students explain how using the Word Learning Tip and the Vocabulary Building Strategy helped them answer these questions.
- Tally students' correct responses.

Answer Key
1. A 2. D 3. D 4. A 5. C
6. carton 7. persuade 8. ascent
9. accent 10. convince

200 Chapter 4 • Words and Their Histories

LESSON 26

Idioms and Other Common Expressions

Read Words in Context

Getting Started

Mystery Word of the Week Clue 1

The idiom _____ comes from sailing ships passing at sea. The ships would fly their brightly-colored flags if they wanted to be identified.

- See page 14 for routines for using the Mystery Word of the Week Clue. The mystery word of the week is the idiom *passed with flying colors*.

Model/Teach

- Ask students to turn to page 191 in their workbooks.

- Have a student read the Word Learning Tip to the class. Be sure they understand that idioms have an imaginative or figurative meaning that is different from what the words seem to say. Idioms are unique to a culture. They can be as brief as a word or two, as in "blue moon." They can also be longer proverbs such as "Don't look a gift horse in the mouth."

- Read the Vocabulary Building Strategy to the class as students follow along in their books. Explain that idioms are easier to define if you focus on the overall picture the individual words make. Illustrate the point with the idiom "blue moon." Describe how taken word-by-word, it doesn't make sense. Then write this sentence on the board: "It is so dry in the desert that it rains only once in a blue moon." Challenge students to define what "blue moon" means (a rare occurrence) from this sentence.

- Have students follow along in their books as you read the passage aloud.

- Before you read the passage again, share the **Think Aloud** on page 202 to model how to define idioms through context.

Materials Needed
- Student Workbook, p. 191
- Transparency 3

Vocabulary Words
a fly in the ointment
a leg to stand on
as plain as the nose on your face
badger someone
bark up the wrong tree
be an eager beaver
catch forty winks
get a second wind
get the upper hand
not by a long shot

LESSON 26
Idioms and Other Common Expressions

Think Aloud

In this passage, an American girl, Charlene, is corresponding with her friend Serena in Italy. Charlene uses a lot of idioms, which Serena translates literally. Let's look at the beginning of Charlene's e-mail message to Serena: "I've been to the school office three times today to find out if I passed the audition for the talent show. I kept asking if there was something I could do just so I could stay around. Mrs. Long said, 'Go **badger someone** else. I'm busy.'" Let me tell you something about this idiom *badger someone*. I know these two words together don't make sense, so this is a clue that the words make up an idiom. I know that idioms have meanings that were created a long time ago. Some people used to do a cruel thing. They put a badger in a deep tub and set dogs on it. They let the dogs tease the badger until it jumped out of the tub. For some reason, they found this funny. Today, this idea of teasing or pestering has stuck with the words *badger someone*. So if Charlene is badgering Mrs. Long, she is pestering and annoying her.

- After you have demonstrated how to determine the meaning of *badger someone*, read the story aloud again, pausing at each boldface phrase.
- Place Transparency 3 on the overhead projector. Tell students that as you pause at each boldface phrase, you want them to tell you what is special about each idiom. Then they should tell you what picture they see in their minds, what the idiom means, and how they will remember it.
- As students talk about each idiom, record their responses on the transparency.
- After students have defined each idiom, arrange them in pairs to create dialogues using the idioms. Guide students to discuss common experiences to make the idioms easy to learn.
- Divide the class into small groups. Have the groups work with flashcards to reinforce the meaning of each idiom.

English Language Learners
- Idioms are especially challenging for non-native speakers because their meanings cannot be deduced from the individual words. Encourage English language learners to share some idioms from their native languages, such as "sacre bleu" from French. Then discuss each idiom with students, using the phrases in context. Finally, have students make personal dictionaries to help them remember each idiom and its meaning.

Independent Activity

Create a Chart Have students draw a two-column chart in their personal word journal. Direct them to label the left column "Idiom" and the right column "Meaning." Ask students to complete the charts by writing the idioms in the left column and their meanings in the right column. Encourage students to make the meanings as easy to remember as the idioms.

Answer Key
See page 217 for definitions.

Connect Words and Meanings

Getting Started

Mystery Word of the Week Clue 2

Rick _____ and got an A in the class!

Materials Needed
- Student Workbook, p. 192

Review and Share Copy the basic **two-column chart** on chart paper. Then have volunteers come to the easel and complete the chart, one entry at a time. The first student writes the idiom, the second the definition, and so on until the chart is complete. Post the chart in a prominent place in the classroom. Add the idioms to the word wall.

Model/Teach
- Have students turn to page 192 in their workbooks.
- Use the **Think Aloud**.
- After you have modeled matching an idiom to its meaning, direct students to complete the page independently. Then tell students to share their answers. Encourage them to share their thinking as well.

English Language Learners
- Ask students to choose an idiom and make an idiom cube (at right). On one face, they should write the idiom and its meaning. On another, they should write a similar phrase from their own language. On the third, they should write a sentence using the idiom.

Independent Activity

Idioms About Legs Have students work in pairs or small groups to find the meaning of these idioms. Provide them with Internet access to word history sites and standard reference texts. If these resources are not available, explain the meanings yourself. Have students write their sentences in their personal word journals.

Think Aloud

The first idiom is "be an eager beaver." Let me tell you something about the history of this phrase. It comes from the Canadian Army and is a World War II expression used to describe a soldier who volunteered for jobs on every possible occasion. This soldier was too enthusiastic or too eager. Today we use the idiom to describe not just soldiers but anyone who is very enthusiastic and perhaps a little annoying because of it. Now I am going to look down the right-hand column to find a meaning that fits these ideas. It's "C—have a lot of enthusiasm; be too enthusiastic," so I write C in the blank next to item 1.

Idiom Cube

(Idiom and Its Meaning / Sentence / Similar Idiom)

Answer Key
1. C 2. G 3. A 4. B 5. E
6. H 7. F 8. I 9. J 10. D

Lesson 26 • Idioms and Other Common Expressions

LESSON 26   Idioms and Other Common Expressions

Use Words in Context

Materials Needed
- Student Workbook, p. 193

Think Aloud

I see that each sentence has a vocabulary idiom in boldface type. My task is to answer each question in a full sentence. The first sentence asks, "Why do you need to **get a second wind** when you are rehearsing late for a talent show?" I'll start by defining the idiom so I know what the sentence is asking. I know that the idiom *get a second wind* means "get new energy" or "get a burst of energy." Now I can answer the sentence: "You need a burst of energy to keep on going when you are tired."

Getting Started

Mystery Word of the Week Clue 3

The idiom _____ means "to do better than expected."

Review and Share Have partners or groups share one **idiom about legs** that they learned from the activity on page 192. Then ask students to write one of the idioms and its meaning on a strip of paper. Staple these together to create a word garland. Display this in the front of the classroom.

Model/Teach

- Have students turn to page 193 in their workbooks.
- Use the **Think Aloud** to introduce this page.
- When you have shown students how to approach this page, have them work independently to complete the activity. Allow students to work in small groups to share their answers.

Independent Activities

- **Learn More "Nose" Idioms** Explain to students that the word *nose* appears in many idioms. Ask them to name idioms they know that contain this word (*nose around, be nosey, win by a nose,* etc.). Then explain the meaning of the idiom *have a nose for* and ask students to try to explain how its meaning came about.
- **Write Bumper Stickers** Have students choose three idioms from this lesson and write bumper stickers with them. The bumper stickers should teach lessons about life, such as "The truth is usually as plain as the nose on your face." Display the bumper stickers in the classroom.

Answer Key
Students' responses will vary. See page 224 for sample sentences.

Chapter 4 • Words and Their Histories

Put Words Into Action

Materials Needed
- Student Workbook, p. 194
- Idea Web Graphic Organizer, p. 229

Getting Started

Mystery Word of the Week Clue 4

Michael tried out for the team and _____.

Think Aloud

Let's look at the first item together: "If a detective keeps questioning the wrong suspect, he is _____." I see that the detective is looking in the wrong place for the answers. He should be questioning another suspect. I think the idiom that fits is *barking up the wrong tree*. This idiom comes from hunting. Dogs were supposed to mark the tree where a raccoon was hiding and bark until the hunter came. But even trained dogs sometimes made a mistake and barked up the wrong tree. Today, we use this idiom to describe any situation where someone is searching for answers or a solution in the wrong place.

★ **Review and Share** Invite volunteers to read their explanations of the **idiom have a nose for something** to the class. If time permits, ask them to try to explain one other "nose" idiom.

Model/Teach
- Have students turn to page 193 in their workbooks.
- Before students begin the page, model the activity with the Think Aloud.
- After you have modeled completing a sentence, have students complete the rest of the page on their own. When everyone is finished working, ask them to share their responses.

Independent Activities

★ **Find Other Idioms** Distribute copies of the Idea Web Graphic Organizer. Discuss the meaning of *get the upper hand*. Ask students to describe situations in which they would use this idiom. Then have students work with partners to complete the idea web with other idioms about getting an advantage (*ahead of the game, have a leg up on, have an ace in the hole,* etc.)

- **Perform a Skit** Arrange students in small groups to put on brief skits around these idioms. Groups should incorporate at least three idioms in their skit. The skits can be humorous or serious, using the idioms in the dialogue or as the punch line. Have each group perform its skit for the class.

Answer Key
1. barking up the wrong tree
2. get a second wind
3. a leg to stand on
4. as plain as the nose on your face
5. a fly in the ointment
6. catch forty winks
7. get the upper hand
8. be an eager beaver
9. badger someone
10. not by a long shot

Lesson 26 • Idioms and Other Common Expressions

LESSON 26: Idioms and Other Common Expressions

Review and Extend

Materials Needed
- Student Workbook, p. 195

Think Aloud

Let's look at the first item together: "The judge said to the sly lawyer, 'Don't try your tricks with me. I won't let you _____.'" I see that the lawyer often tries to play tricks and deceive people. I think the bonus idiom *pull the wool over your eyes* is the one that carries this meaning. Long ago, men wore wool wigs. Pulling the wig over the man's face would temporarily blind him or prevent him from seeing something. Today we use this idiom to mean that you are preventing someone from seeing the truth or deceiving that person. I change the pronoun *your* to *my* to fit the sentence: "The judge said to the sly lawyer, 'Don't try your tricks with me. I won't let you pull the wool over my eyes.'"

Answer Key

Mystery Word of the Week:
passed with flying colors
Accept any other idiom that fits the context.

1. pull the wool over my eyes
2. catch forty winks
3. get a second wind
4. as plain as the nose on your face
5. break new ground
6. a fly in the ointment
7. badger someone
8. bark up the wrong tree

Getting Started

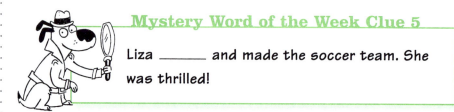

Mystery Word of the Week Clue 5
Liza _____ and made the soccer team. She was thrilled!

Review and Share Provide time for students to share the **idioms about getting the advantage** they found in doing the activity on page 194. Post their word webs on the bulletin board.

Model/Teach
- Have students turn to page 195 in their workbooks. Invite a volunteer to read the boxed information to the class. Talk about the idioms and their meanings.
- Model how to complete this activity with the **Think Aloud**.
- After you are done modeling your thinking, direct students to finish the activity independently. Have them exchange papers to check their answers.

Independent Activities

Learn Animal Idioms This is a good group activity. Some members of the group can define each idiom, while others plan the book. Encourage students to be creative in their book design: they might have a storybook, alphabet book, or nonfiction book.

- **Write a Fable** Read this fable aloud: An Ant went to the bank of a river. Carried away by the current, she was close to drowning. A Dove in a tree plucked a leaf and let it fall into the stream close to the Ant. The Ant climbed onto the leaf and floated safely to the bank. Later, a bird catcher set a trap for the Dove. The Ant, seeing the trap, stung the bird catcher in the foot. In pain, the bird catcher threw down the trap, and the noise made the Dove take wing. *The moral*: One good turn deserves another. Have students choose one of the idioms they learned in this lesson and write a fable to illustrate it.

Check Your Mastery

Materials Needed
- Student Workbook, p. 196

Give the Test

- Direct the class to turn to page 196 in their workbooks.
- Tell students that this Check Your Mastery activity has one part.
- Read the directions: "Circle the letter of the correct answer to each question below."
- Share your technique for answering an item by writing the following sample item on the chalkboard. Then read the sentence and choices to students.

> Why do people want to **get the upper hand** in a situation?
>
> **A.** to get exercise **C.** to catch forty winks
>
> **B.** to bark up the wrong tree **D.** to have an advantage

- Guide the class to choose the phrase that best answers the question. Have them justify their choice by isolating the phrase "so they are ahead of their opponent."
- When they finish this activity, have students check their answers.
- Go over the Check Your Mastery activity orally with the class.
- Students can work with a partner to talk about the questions they answered incorrectly. Ask students to write new sentences with the idioms they did not understand.
- Discuss with the class how the Word Learning Tip and the Vocabulary Building Strategy helped them choose the correct responses.
- Tally students' correct responses.

Student Self-Assessment

Journal Writing Have students write in their journals about how they can learn idioms by using the idiom's history and context clues. Also ask them to rewrite the Word Learning Tip and Vocabulary Building Strategy to make sure they remember them.

Answer Key

1. A 2. C 3. D 4. D 5. A
6. A 7. C 8. D 9. A 10. A

DEFINITIONS

The words in this program were chosen for their importance and to illustrate specific Word Learning Principles and Vocabulary Building Strategies. Therefore, for example, challenge is used in the lesson on nouns to illustrate how syntax and context can help you understand the meaning of a word.

The definitions of the words as they are used in the lessons are given below.

Lesson 1

advantage (ad-**van**-tij) *noun*: something that helps you or is useful to you or gives you a better chance

agent (**ay**-juhnt) *noun*: **1.** a person who arranges things for other people; **2.** a person who represents other people

challenge (**chal**-uhnj) *noun*: something difficult that requires extra effort or work

foundation (foun-**day**-shuhn) *noun*: **1.** base; **2.** the basis on which something stands

genius (**jee**-nee-uhss *or* **jeen**-yuhss) *noun*: an unusually smart or intelligent person

mainland (**main**-luhnd) *noun*: the largest mass of land of a country or continent

mechanic (muh-**kan**-ik) *noun*: person skilled at repairing machinery

nuisance (**noo**-suhnss) *noun*: a bother or annoyance

obstacle (**ob**-stuh-kuhl) *noun*: barrier

precaution (pri-**kaw**-shuhn) *noun*: action taken ahead of time to prevent something dangerous from happening

pursuit (pur-**soot**) *noun*: the act or instance of chasing someone or something

rival (**rye**-vuhl) *noun*: someone or something that is an opponent or competitor

scheme (**skeem**) *noun*: a plan or plot to do something

target (**tar**-git) *noun*: **1.** a goal; **2.** something that is aimed at

vehicle (**vee**-uh-kuhl) *noun*: something used to carry people or objects over land or sea or through the air

Lesson 2

apologize (uh-**pol**-uh-jize) *verb*: to say you are sorry about something

assemble (uh-**sem**-buhl) *verb*: **1.** to put together; **2.** to gather in groups

boost (**boost**) *verb*: **1.** to lift; **2.** to increase

coax (**kohks**) *verb*: **1.** to persuade someone by asking in a pleasant and easy way; **2.** to urge

concentrate (**kon**-suhn-trate) *verb*: to focus on something

consult (kuhn-**suhlt**) *verb*: to go to another person or resource for information and advice

devote (di-**voht**) *verb*: to give time and effort to some purpose

irritate (**ihr**-uh-tate) *verb*: to annoy or bother

manage (**man**-ij) *verb*: to control or direct

refer (ri-**fur**) *verb*: to tell someone to go to a certain person or place for help or information

reject (ri-**jekt**) *verb*: to refuse to accept something

reveal (ri-**veel**) *verb*: **1.** to show or make known; **2.** to uncover

topple (**top**-uhl) *verb*: **1.** to fall over; **2.** to make something fall over

transport (transs-**port**) *verb*: to move someone or something from one place to another

weaken (**week**-in) *verb*: to lose strength

Lesson 3

approve (uh-**proov**) *verb*: to check over something and give a good rating

associate (uh-**soh**-see-ayte) *verb*: to connect with something

attempt (uh-**tempt**) *verb*: to try to do something

broadcast (**brawd**-kast) *verb*: **1.** to send out a program over radio or television; **2.** to announce widely

There are no symbols used in this pronunciation system (*Scholastic Children's Dictionary*, copyright © 2002, 1996 Scholastic Inc.). Instead letters and letter combinations are used to stand for different sounds.

conquer (**kong**-kur) *verb*: to defeat and take control

dedicate (**ded**-uh-kate) *verb*: to devote a lot of time and energy to something

emerge (i-**murj**) *verb*: to come out into the open

flourish (**flur**-ish) *verb*: to grow and do well

organize (**or**-guh-nize) *verb*: to put in a certain order

overwhelm (oh-vur-**welm**) *verb*: to overpower or overcome completely

pursue (pur-**soo**) *verb*: to chase after

resemble (ri-**zem**-buhl) *verb*: to be or look like someone or something

restore (ri-**stor**) *verb*: to bring back to its original condition

surrender (suh-**ren**-dur) *verb*: **1.** to give up; **2.** to give something or yourself to someone else

withdraw (wiTH-**draw** *or* with-**draw**) *verb*: **1.** to drop out; **2.** to remove or take away something

Lesson 4

adventurous (ad-**ven**-chur-uhss) *adjective*: **1.** liking excitement and adventure; **2.** daring

assorted (uh-**sort**-ed) *adjective*: various kinds of

beloved (bi-**luhv**-id) *adjective*: adored; loved deeply

confident (**kon**-fuh-duhnt) *adjective*: self-assured and secure

distinguished (diss-**ting**-gwishd) *adjective*: **1.** known for important things; **2.** dignified

easygoing (**ee**-zee-goh-ing) *adjective*: calm and relaxed

fragile (**fraj**-il) *adjective*: **1.** delicate; **2.** easily broken

fragrant (**fray**-gruhnt) *adjective*: sweet-smelling

heroic (hi-**roh**-ik) *adjective*: very brave or daring

massive (**mass**-iv) *adjective*: very large

mature (muh-**chur** or muh-**tyur**) *adjective*: grown-up

mischievous (**miss**-chuh-vuhss) *adjective*: gets into trouble

outstanding (out-**stand**-ing) *adjective*: extremely good

peculiar (pi-**kyoo**-lyur) *adjective*: strange or odd

shrewd (**shrood**) *adjective*: clever; sharp

Lesson 5

annual (**an**-yoo-uhl) *adjective*: yearly

billowy (**bil**-oh-wee) *adjective*: swelling, as in waves

breathtaking (**breth**-tay-king) *adjective*: exciting; thrilling; very beautiful; takes your breath away

convenient (kuhn-**vee**-ny-uhnt) *adjective*: **1.** easy to reach or use; **2.** useful

dense (**denss**) *adjective*: thick; crowded

distant (**diss**-tuhnt) *adjective*: far away; removed

ebony (**eb**-uh-nee) *adjective*: deep black; made of a hard black wood

genuine (jen-**yoo**-uhn) *adjective*: **1.** real, not fake; **2.** honest

luminous (**loo**-muh-nuhss) *adjective*: **1.** shining; **2.** glowing in the dark

perilous (**per**-uhl-uhss) *adjective*: dangerous

sincere (sin-**sihr**) *adjective*: **1.** honest; truthful; **2.** heart-felt

spectacular (spek-**tak**-yuh-lur) *adjective*: **1.** remarkable; **2.** dramatic; exciting

spotless (**spot**-liss) *adjective*: perfectly clean

unique (yoo-**neek**) *adjective*: one of a kind

wondrous (**wuhn**-druhss) *adjective*: marvelous; fills you with wonder and amazement

Lesson 6

clearly (**klihr**-lee) *adverb*: in a way that is easy to understand or picture

earlier (**ur**-lee-ur) *adjective*: **1.** before the expected or arranged time; **2.** before the present time

eventually (i-**ven**-choo-uh-lee) *adverb*: **1.** at some time after a series of events; **2.** at last

everywhere (**ev**-ree-wair) *adverb*: in all places

firmly (**furm**-lee) *adverb*: **1.** not moving; **2.** not bending; **3.** not giving way easily under pressure; **4.** solidly

frequently (**free**-kwent) *adverb*: very often

immediately (i-**mee**-dee-it-lee) *adverb*: **1.** without delay; **2.** at once

largely (**larj**-lee) *adverb*: mainly; mostly

mostly (**mohst**-lee) *adverb*: almost entirely; largely

naturally (**nach**-ur-uhl-ee) *adverb*: **1.** as might be expected; **2.** without a doubt

outside (*out*-**side**) *adverb*: in the open air; not inside

practically (**prak**-tik-lee) *adverb*: **1.** very nearly but not quite; **2.** in a practical manner

precisely (pri-**sisse**-lee) *adverb*: exactly

rapidly (**rap**-id-lee) *adverb*: moving very quickly

widely (**wide**-lee) *adverb*: **1.** by a large number of people; **2.** over a great distance

Lesson 7

bridge (**brij**) *noun*: **1.** a structure built over a river or other body of water so that people can cross it; **2.** a card game for four players; *verb*: **3.** to connect

bureau (**byur**-oh) *noun*: **1.** a chest of drawers; **2.** an office that provides information or another service

cabinet (**kab**-in-it) *noun*: **1.** a piece of furniture with shelves and drawers; a cupboard; **2.** a group of advisors for the head of government

contract (**kon**-trakt) *noun*: **1.** a legal agreement, (kuhn-**trakt**) *verb*: **2.** to get

harbor (**har**-bur) *noun*: **1.** a place where ships settle or unload their cargo; *verb*: **2.** to hide someone or to take care of someone

mold (**mohld**) *noun*: **1.** a furry fungus that grows in damp places or on old food; *verb*: **2.** to model or shape something

peer (**pihr**) *noun*: **1.** a person of equal standing; *verb*: **2.** to take a careful look at something

pelt (**pelt**) *noun*: **1.** an animal skin with fur or hair still on it; *verb*: **2.** to strike or beat

range (**raynj**) *noun*: **1.** an area of open land used for a special purpose; **2.** a cooking stove

refrain (ri-**frayn**) *noun*: **1.** repeated words in a song or poem; *verb*: **2.** to stop yourself from doing something

rest (**rest**) *noun*: **1.** the others or the remaining part of something; *verb*: **2.** to relax or sleep

rung (**ruhng**) *noun*: **1.** one of the horizontal steps on a ladder; *verb*: **2.** to make a clear sound; past participle of ring

steer (**stihr**) *noun*: **1.** male cattle; *verb*: **2.** to move a vehicle in a certain direction

temper (**tem**-pur) *noun*: **1.** a tendency to get angry; *verb*: **2.** to make things less harsh or difficult

vent (**vent**) *noun*: **1.** an opening through which smoke or air can pass; *verb*: **2.** to show or let out emotion

Lesson 8

approval (uh-**proov**-uhl) *noun*: acceptance of a plan or idea; consent

bustle (**buh**-suhl) *verb*: a lot of noisy activity; commotion

civil (**siv**-il) *adjective*: courteous; well behaved; polite

commotion (kuh-**moh**-shuhn) *noun*: rush; lots of activity; bustle

consent (kuhn-**sent**) *noun*: agreement; approval

corridor (**kor**-uh-dur) *noun*: a passageway; hallway

drenched (**dren**-chud) *adjective*: completely wet; soaked

fumble (**fuhm**-buhl) *verb*: to drop or handle poorly; mishandle

glory (**glor**-ee) *noun*: great fame; honor

gnarled (**narld**) *adjective*: twisted and lumpy with age; knotty

gravity (**grav**-uh-tee) *noun*: importance; seriousness

hallway (**hawl**-*way*) *noun*: a long passageway; corridor

honor (**on**-ur) *noun*: respect and a good reputation; glory

knotty (**not**-ee) *adjective*: having many hard spots of lumps; gnarled

mishandle (miss-**han**-duhl) *verb*: to deal with poorly; to fumble

pesky (**pess**-kee) *adjective*: annoying; troublesome

polite (puh-**lite**) *adjective*: having good manners; civil

seriousness (**sirh**-ee-uhss-ness) *noun*: importance; gravity

soaked (**soh**-kuhd) *adjective*: completely wet or left in water; drenched

troublesome (**truh**-buhl-suhm) *adjective*: difficult; pesky

Lesson 9

allowed (uh-**loud**) *adjective*: **1.** given permission to do something; **2.** permitted

dismiss (diss-**miss**) *verb*: to allow to leave or to let someone go

distracted (diss-**trak**-ted) *adjective*: **1.** having your thoughts and attention on something else; **2.** not concentrating

dull (**duhl**) *adjective*: **1.** colorless, very little or no color; **2.** boring

focused (**foh**-kuhssd) *adjective*: **1.** showing great attention; **2.** concentrating on a single thing

forbidden (fur-**bid**-uhn) *adjective*: not allowed or approved

frail (**frayl**) *adjective*: weak, delicate, light

glistening (**gliss**-uhn-ing) *adjective*: shining in a sparkling way

hardy (**har**-dee) *adjective*: courageous and daring

high-priced (**hye**-prissed) *adjective*: expensive; costing a lot of money

hire (**hire**) *verb*: to employ somebody to work for you, or pay somebody to do a job for you

inexpensive (in-ik-**spen**-siv) *adjective*: not costing a lot; cheap

inferior (in-**fihr**-ee-ur) *adjective*: lower in quality or value

meaningful (**mee**-ning-fuhl) *adjective*: **1.** having meaning and purpose; **2.** significant

misery (mi-**zuhr**-ee) *noun*: **1.** something that causes great unhappiness; **2.** a condition of great unhappiness

optimist (**op**-tuh-mist) *noun*: someone who believes that things will turn out for the best

pessimist (**pess**-uh-**miss**-tik) *noun*: somebody who always expects the worst to happen in every situation

pleasure (**plezh**-ur) *noun*: a feeling of enjoyment or satisfaction

senseless (**senss**-liss) *adjective*: **1.** foolish; **2.** without purpose or meaning

superior (suh-**pihr**-ee-ur *or* soo-**pihr**-ee-ur) *adjective*: **1.** higher in rank; **2.** above average in quality

Lesson 10

casually (**kazh**-oo-uhl-lee) *adverb*: in a way that is not planned or not formal

dignity (**dig**-nuh-tee) *noun*: a quality that makes someone worthy of honor and respect

gigantic (jye-**gan**-tik) *adjective*: huge; very large; enormous

impressive (im-**press**-ive) *adjective*: having a strong or striking effect

patience (**pay**-shuhnss) *noun*: the ability to remain calm and not be hasty

perish (**per**-ish) *verb*: **1.** to spoil; **2.** to be destroyed before its time

reassure (ree-uh-**shur**) *verb*: **1.** to calm; **2.** to give confidence or courage

suitable (**soo**-tuh-buhl) *adjective*: right for a particular purpose or occasion

thrive (**thrive**) *verb*: **1.** to do well; **2.** to flourish or prosper

vividly (**viv**-id-lee) *adverb*: clearly or distinctly

Lesson 11

biannual (bye-**an**-yoo-uhl) *adjective*: **1.** happening twice a year; **2.** occurring every two years

biceps (**bye**-seps) *noun, plural*: the large set of muscles in the front of your upper arm between you shoulder and inner elbow

bifocals (**bye**-*foh*-kuhlz) *noun, plural*: eyeglasses with two different sections of each lens, one for seeing things up close and one for seeing things farther away

binoculars (buh-**nok**-yuh-lurz) *noun, plural*: a device used with both eyes to see things that are very far away

biweekly (**bye**-week-lee) *adjective*: **1.** happening twice a week; **2.** happening once every two weeks

multicolored (**muhl**-ti-kuhl-urd) *adjective*: having many colors

multimillionaire (**muhl**-ti-mil-yuhn-*air*) *noun*: a person with many millions of dollars

multitude (**muhl**-ti-tood) *noun*: a great many things or people

octagonal (ok-**tag**-uh-nuhl) *adjective*: having eight sides or angles

octopus (**ok**-tuh-puhss) *noun*: a sea animal with eight long tentacles or arms

triangular (trye-**ang**-guh-lur) *adjective*: having three sides or angles

triathlon (trye-**ath**-lon) *noun*: a long distance race that is made up of three events

tricycle (**trye**-suh-kuhl *or* **trye**-sik-uhl) *noun*: a vehicle with pedals that has three wheels, one in the front and two in the back

tripod (**trye**-pod) *noun*: a three-legged stand or stool

tristate (**trye**-state) *adjective*: involving or touching three states

Lesson 12

African (**af**-ruh-kuhn) *noun*: **1.** a person from Africa; *adjective*: **2.** having to do with Africa

announcer (uh-**noun**-sur) *noun*: a person who reports or announces information

artisan (**ar**-tuh-zuhn) *noun*: a person who makes crafts

aviator (**ay**-vee-ay-tor) *noun*: a person who flies a plane; a pilot

civilian (si-**vil**-yuhn) *noun*: a person not in the military

employee (em-**ploi**-ee *or* em-ploi-**ee**) *noun*: a person who is employed by or works for another person

janitor (**jan**-uh-tur) *noun*: a person who looks after and cleans buildings

jurist (**jur**-ist) *noun*: **1.** a person who works in the law; **2.** a lawyer or judge

laborer (**lay**-bur-ur) *noun*: a person who labors or does physical work, usually an unskilled worker

mathematician (math-uh-muh-**tish**-uhn) *noun*: someone who studies mathematics or practices it

naturalist (**nach**-u-ral-ist) *noun*: a person who studies nature

nominee (nom-uh-**nee**) *noun*: a person named to run for office; a candidate

pedestrian (puh-**dess**-tree-uhn) *noun*: someone who travels on foot

spectator (**spek**-tay-tur) *noun*: someone who watches an event

veterinarian (*vet*-ur-uh-**ner**-ee-uhn) *noun*: a doctor who takes care of animals

Lesson 13

curriculum (kuh-**rik**-yuh-luhm) *noun*: a group of courses of study that are connected

cursive (**kur**-sive) *noun*: **1.** a form of handwriting in which each letter runs into or is joined to the next letter; script; **2.** *adjective*: written in this style

excursion (ek-**skur**-zhuhn) *noun*: **1.** a trip away from home; **2.** a short journey in which you might do a lot of running around or back and forth

immortal (i-**mor**-tuhl) *adjective*: **1.** not subject to death; **2.** living or lasting forever; *noun*: **3.** one who lives forever

immortality (i-mor-**tal**-itee) *noun*: unending life or fame

kaleidoscope (kuh-**lye**-duh-skope) *noun*: **1.** a tube in which glass and mirrors create patterns of color and light; **2.** a constantly changing set of colors

microscopic (mye-kruh-**skop**-ik) *adjective*: **1.** too small to be seen by the eye alone; **2.** very small

microwave (**mye**-kroh-wave) *noun*: **1.** an electromagnetic wave that can pass through solid objects; **2.** an oven that cooks very quickly by using this type of wave

mortal (**mor**-tuhl) *adjective*: **1.** capable of causing death; **2.** not living or lasting forever; *noun* **1.** one who is subject to death

mortality (mor-**tal**-uh-tee) *noun*: the condition of being a creature that can die

occurrence (uh-**kur**-ence) *noun*: an event; something that takes place

periscope (**per**-uh-skope) *noun*: an instrument in the shape of a tube with prisms and mirrors that allows you to see someone or something that is far above you

recurring (ri-**kur**-ing) *adjective*: happening over and over

stethoscope (**steth**-uh-skope) *noun*: a medical instrument used to listen to sounds from the heart, lungs, and other areas of the body

telescopic (*tel*-uh-**skop**-ik) *adjective*: **1.** able to see at great distances; **2.** relating to a telescope—an instrument that allows you to see objects that are very far away

Lesson 14

brainstorm (**brayn**-*storm*) *noun*: **1.** a sudden powerful idea; *verb*: **2.** to think of new ideas

brainteaser (**brayn**-*teez*-uhr) *noun*: a mentally challenging puzzle or problem

brainwash (**brayn**-*washsh*) *verb*: to make someone accept or believe something by saying it over and over again

downhearted (**doun**-har-ted) *adjective*: filled with sadness

footbridge (**fut**-*brij*) *noun*: a bridge for walking across a river or other body of water on foot

foothill (**fut**-*hil*) *noun*: a low hill at the base of a mountain or mountain range

footnote (**fut**-*noht*) *noun*: information at the bottom of the page that explains something in the content on that page

headdress (**hed**-*dress*) *noun*: a decorative covering for the head

headline (**hed**-*line*) *noun*: the title of a newspaper article, which is usually set in large type

headlong (**hed**-*lawng*) *adverb*: without hesitation or thinking

headstrong (**hed**-*strong*) *adjective*: stubborn or determined to have your own way

headwaters (**hed**-*waw*-turs) *noun, plural*: the waters from which a river rises

heartbroken (**hart**-*broh*-kuhn) *adjective*: very sad or filled with sadness

heartland (**hart**-*land*) *noun*: an area or territory at the center of a country

heartwarming (**hart**-*worm*-ing) *adjective*: causing happiness and pleasure

Lesson 15

acronym (**ak**-ruh-nim) *noun*: a word formed from the first or first few letters of the words in a phrase

anonymous (uh-**non**-uh-muhss) *adjective*: written or done by a person whose name is not known or made pubic

antonym (**an**-toh-nim) *noun*: a word that means the opposite of another word

denominator (di-**nom**-uh-nay-tur) *noun*: **1.** a trait that two or more people have; **2.** the number that is below the line in a fraction that names how many equal parts the whole number can be divided into

nameless (**naym**-*less*) *adjective*: **1.** lacking a name; **2.** not able to be described or named

namely (**naym**-*lee*) *adverb*: **1.** that is to say; **2.** specifically

namesake (**naym**-*sayk*) *noun*: a person named after another person

nametag (**naym**-*tag*) *noun*: a badge telling the name of the person wearing it

nominal (**nom**-i-nuhl) *adjective*: **1.** in name only; **2.** very small or slight

nominate (**nom**-uh-nate) *verb*: to name someone as the right person to do a job, hold an office, or receive an honor

nomination (nom-uh-**na**-shuhn) *noun*: the act or instance of naming or appointing a person to office

nominator (**nom**-uh-na-tur) *noun*: a person who names another person to run for office, do a job, or win a prize

pseudonym (**sood**-uh-nim) *noun*: a false or made-up name, especially a pen name

rename (ri-**naym**) *verb*: to give a new name to someone or something

synonym (**sin**-uh-nim) *noun*: a word that means the same or nearly the same as another word

Lesson 16
autobiographical (*aw*-toh-bye-oh-**graf**-i-kuhl) *adjective*: having to do with your own life story

autobiography (aw-toh-bye-**og**-ruh-fee) *noun*: the life story of a person written by that person

autograph (**aw**-tuh-*graf*) *noun*: **1.** a person's own signature; *verb*: **2.** to write your name or signature on something

biographical (bye-*oh*-**graf**-i-kuhl) *adjective*: having to do with someone else's life

biography (bye-**og**-ruh-fee) *noun*: the life story of a person written by someone other than that person

graphic (**graf**-ik) *adjective*: **1.** having to do with art and design or handwriting; **2.** very realistic

graphics (**graf**-iks) *noun*, plural: images such as drawings, maps, and graphs, especially those made using technological devices such as computers

graphite (**graf**-ite) *noun*: a soft, black mineral used as lead in pencils and also used in paints and coatings

monograph (**mon**-uh-*graf*) *noun*: a short book or long article on a single, limited subject

oceanography (*oh*-shuh-**nog**-ruh-fee) *noun*: the science that deals with the oceans and the plants and animals that live in them

paragraph (**pa**-ruh-*graf*) *noun*: a series of sentences that develop one main idea; it begins on a new line and is usually indented

phonograph (**foh**-nuh-*graf*) *noun*: a machine that plays disk-shaped records on which sounds have been recorded in grooves

photograph (**foh**-tuh-*graf*) *noun*: a picture made by the action of light upon a surface; a picture taken by a camera

photographic (foh-tuh-**graf**-ik) *adjective*: **1.** having to do with recalling from memory the exact order in which a long list of names was read; **2.** having to do with photography

photography (foh-**tog**-ruh-fee) *noun*: the making of pictures by exposing film in a camera to light

Lesson 17
approximate (uh-**prok**-si-muht) *adjective*: **1.** more or less correct or exact; *verb*: **2.** to come up with an answer that is more or less correct

calculate (**kal**-kyuh-late) *verb*: to find the answer by using mathematics

certain (**sur**-tuhn) *adjective*: **1.** will definitely happen; **2.** sure

estimation (**ess**-ti-ma-shuhn) *noun*: **1.** an answer that you believe is close to the exact answer; **2.** the act of coming up with an answer that is close to the exact answer

probability (**prob**-uh-bil-i-tee) *noun*: how likely something is to happen

Lesson 18
aorta (ay-**or**-tuh) *noun*: the main blood vessel in the heart; the main tube that transports blood to all of the arteries

artery (**ar**-tuh-ree) *noun*: a blood vessel that carries blood away from the heart, but not the main tube

atrium (**ay**-tree-uhm) *noun*: either of the two upper chambers on both sides of the heart

capillary (**kap**-uh-ler-ee) *noun*: one of the tiny tubes that carries blood between the arteries and the veins

vein (**vayn**) *noun*: a blood vessel that carries blood to the heart

Lesson 19
condensation (**kon**-den-**say**-shuhn) *noun*: the process by which water vapor becomes a liquid

droplet (**drop**-lit) *noun*: a tiny drop or quantity of liquid

evaporation (i-**vap**-uh-ra-shuhn) *noun*: the act or process by which a liquid becomes a gas

precipitation (pri-sip-i-**tay**-shuhn) *noun*: the falling of water from the sky in the form of rain, sleet, or snow

water vapor (**waw**-tur-*vay*-pur) *noun*: water in its gaseous form, formed by condensation

Lesson 20

compassion (kuhm-**pash**-uhn) *noun*: kindness and mercy

cooperation (koh-**op**-uh-ra-shuhn) *noun*: **1.** teamwork; **2.** the quality of working well with others

persistence (pur-**sist**-enss) *noun*: the quality of refusing to give up

self-discipline (**self**-*diss*-uh-plin) *noun*: self-control

trustworthy (**truhst**-*wur*-THee) *adjective*: reliable; able to be depended on

Lesson 21

bibliography (*bib*-lee-**og**-ruh-fee) *noun*: **1.** a list of books and other writings about a specific subject; **2.** the list of sources used to write a research paper

citation (**si**-tay-shuhn) *noun*: a note that gives credit to a source

data (**day**-tuh) *noun*: information or facts

paraphrase (**pa**-ruh-*fraze*) *verb*: to restate a text or passage in your own words

valid (**val**-id) *adjective*: trustworthy; reliable; well grounded

Lesson 22

classify (**klass**-uh-fye) *verb*: to put things into groups according to their characteristics or traits

elaborate (i-**lab**-uh-rate) *verb*: to add details to make fuller or more complete

evidence (**ev**-uh-duhnss) *noun*: proof; details, facts, and examples that help you prove something or convince others that it is true

judgment (**juhj**-muhnt) *noun*: an informed opinion, evaluation, or decision

revise (ri-**vize**) *verb*: to change and correct something to improve it

Lesson 23

admiral (**ad**-muh-ruhl) *noun*: officer in the Navy

butte (**byoot**) *noun*: a large mountain with steep sides and a flat top that stands by itself

cashmere (**kash**-mihr) *noun*: a soft wool

eureka (**u**-*ree*-kuh) *noun*: an exclamation meaning "I have found it!"

gourmet (gor-**may**) *noun*: **1.** a person who knows and appreciates fine foods; *adjective*: **2.** a word describing a food store or restaurant that provides fine food

kangaroo (*kang*-guh-**roo**) *noun*: an Australian animal with short front legs and long, powerful hind legs

menu (**men**-yoo) *noun*: a detailed list of food in a restaurant

mesa (**may**-suh) *noun*: a small high plateau or tableland with steep sides

moustache (**muhss**-*tash*) *noun*: the hair that grows above the upper lip

pajamas (puh-**jahm**-uhz) *noun, plural*: clothes worn for sleeping

parka (**par**-kuh) *noun*: any hooded coat or jacket

patio (**pat**-ee-oh) *noun*: a paved area next to the house used for dining or relaxing; a courtyard

safari (suh-**fah**-ree) *noun*: a trip to see animals, especially in eastern Africa

sherbet (**shur**-buht) *noun*: frozen fruit dessert

tortilla (tor-**tee**-yuh) *noun*: a flat Spanish bread

Lesson 24

aid (**ayd**) *verb*: to assist or help

aide (**ayd**) *noun*: an assistant; a shortened form of the word *aide-de-camp*, which is a word from French that means "military officer acting as a secretary or helper"

baron (**ba**-ruhn) *noun*: a nobleman

barren (**ba**-ruhn) *adjective*: not fertile; empty

chord (**kord**) *noun*: three or more tones that create a pleasant sound or harmony

coarse (**korss**) *adjective*: not smooth; rough

colonel (**kur**-nuhl) *noun*: an officer in the U.S. Military

cord (**kord**) *noun*: string

course (**korss**) *noun*: **1.** path; **2.** a series of lessons that helps you learn a subject

kernel (**kur**-nuhl) *noun*: **1.** a grain or seed; **2.** the most important part of something

Lesson 25

accent (**ak**-sent) *noun*: **1.** the way that you pronounce things; *verb*: **2.** to stress or emphasize

ascent (uh-**sent**) *noun*: **1.** an upward slope or rise; **2.** moving or rising up

assent (uh-**sent**) *verb*: **1.** to agree to something; *noun*: **2.** agreement, approval

bazaar (buh-**zar**) *noun*: a market, especially one held outdoors

bizarre (bi-**zar**) *adjective*: strange, odd, fantastic

carton (**kar**-tuhn) *noun*: a box or container usually made of cardboard or plastic

cartoon (kar-**toon**) *noun*: a drawing or animated comic strip

canvas (**kan**-vuhss) *noun*: a strong coarse cloth

canvass (**kan**-vuhss) *verb*: **1.** to gather support; **2.** to ask people for their opinions and votes; **3.** to examine carefully

convince (kuhn-**vinss**) *verb*: to make someone see the truth or believe what you have to say

persuade (pur-**swade**) *verb*: to succeed in making someone do something

Lesson 26

a fly in the ointment: something or someone that upsets a situation or causes a problem

a leg to stand on: a supportable position

as plain as the nose on your face: easy to see

badger someone: pester or bother someone

bark up the wrong tree: search for clues or answers in the wrong place

be an eager beaver: have a lot of enthusiasm; be too enthusiastic

catch forty winks: take a short nap

get a second wind: get enough energy to become active again

get the upper hand: get in a position that makes you superior to someone else; get the advantage

not by a long shot: not at all; definitely not

Sample Sentences

LESSON 1

Use Words in Context, page 23 (TE), 9 (SE)

1. The **vehicle** I would choose is a van since it would carry my whole family and be air-conditioned.
2. A good map and planning ahead for problems would give me an **advantage** while exploring.
3. A broken leg and lack of time are two **obstacles**.
4. Bringing a buddy and carrying extra supplies are two **precautions** I would take.
5. Bugs and thorny bushes are two **nuisances** that would bother me.
6. Raising money and getting in shape are two **challenges** for me.
7. One **target** would be finding fossils and another would be hiking for five miles.
8. The **mainland** is bigger and more exciting.

LESSON 2

Put Words Into Action, page 31 (TE), 17 (SE)

1. **Coax**: The picture might show a farmer gently ushering animals such as cows, pigs, chickens, and horses into his house. The statement might read: "My dear animals, will you please join me inside?"
2. **Assemble**: The picture might show farm animals crowded into a small kitchen, with chickens roosting in cabinets and pigs sleeping under the table. The statement might read: "If only I had a chair to sit on."
3. **Irritate**: The picture might show the farmer's wife and children with angry scowls walking around the messy animals and picking feathers out of their hair. The statement might read: "How can we sleep with all this racket?"
4. **Topple**: The picture might show a bookcase or rack of dishes beginning to collapse as a horse leans into it. The statement might read: "Oh no, move away quickly!"
5. **Apologize**: The picture might show the Wise Woman sitting down and looking up at the farmer, who has a contrite look on his face. The statement might read: "I apologize for not valuing what I had and for not trusting you."
6. **Reveal**: The picture might show the Wise Woman patting the farmer on the back and talking to him. The statement might read: "Now you know my secret plan. All is at last revealed."

LESSON 3

Use Words in Context, page 37 (TE), 23 (SE)

1. I won't **pursue** a bear because it might hurt me.
2. I wouldn't **broadcast** that I always burn cookies because no one would want me to make them.
3. I won't **approve** because twelve chilies would make the salsa much too spicy.
4. No one wants to eat a cake that **resembles** mud, no matter how good it tastes.
5. I won't **overwhelm** myself, because then I couldn't finish the task.
6. No one would **organize** meat and vegetables on a counter a week before cooking because they would spoil!
7. You would hurt yourself if you **attempted** to balance a refrigerator on your head.
8. If you **associate** with people like that, you'll never have any food to eat.

Put Words Into Action, page 38 (TE), 24 (SE)

In this humorous episode from *The Pie Factory Show*, two chefs attempt to make apple pies. First, they **organize** their ingredients and equipment, but they are soon **overwhelmed** by the task. The kitchen soon **resembles** a disaster zone. However, they **restore** order and produce two beautiful pies. This episode will be **broadcast** on Sunday night at 8:00 P.M.

LESSON 4

Use Words in Context, page 44 (TE), 30 (SE)

1. A **mischievous** puppy could get in trouble by hiding my socks.
2. You might find these **assorted** animals in an animal shelter: dogs, cats, and rabbits.
3. I could explore the North Pole with an **adventurous** dog!
4. A **heroic** dog might go for help.
5. A **massive** dog could help people by pulling heavy loads of food and other necessary items.
6. The most **peculiar** dog I've ever seen had brown spots around his eyes and big ears.
7. People like **easygoing** dogs because they are relaxed and calm.

TE = Teacher's Edition; SE = Student's Edition

8. An **outstanding** reward to give to a brave dog is a big hug.
9. A **shrewd** store owner might lower prices.
10. A manufacturer might add sweet-smelling herbs to make the dog food **fragrant**.

Put Words Into Action, page 45 (TE), 31 (SE)

1. She is an **adventurous** person who lives with chimpanzees.
2. She is a **beloved** person to the chimps that she has tried to protect.
3. This **confident** person is very sure of herself and secure.
4. Her **heroic** actions have saved the lives of many chimps.
5. Her **outstanding** contributions are well-known throughout the world.

The mystery person is Jane Goodall!

LESSON 5

Put Words Into Action, page 52 (TE), 38 (SE)

2. The Chung family had a good time at their **annual** reunion.
4. Lee could see her way because the lantern was **luminous** and lit up the dark.
6. The **billowy** clouds look like waves on the ocean.
8. The family cleans up so the picnic area will be **spotless**.
10. The stars twinkled against an **ebony** sky.

LESSON 7

Put Words Into Action, page 66 (TE), 52 (SE)

5. The rainstorm washed out the **bridge** over the river.
6. Every Saturday night my parents play **bridge** with friends.
11. The raindrops **pelt** down, like drumbeats on the roof.
12. The rabbit's **pelt** is soft and furry.

LESSON 8

Use Words in Context, page 72 (TE), 58 (SE)

1. There is an old oak tree in the park that is **gnarled** and **knotty**.
2. Squirrels can be **pesky** and **troublesome** because they chatter so much.
3. I have to ask my parents' **consent** and **approval** to stay overnight at a friend's home.
4. Important conversations with friends sometimes require **gravity** and **seriousness**.
5. Street fairs and parties are filled with **bustle** and **commotion**.
6. Schools buildings are linked by a **corridor** and **hallway** so people walk through the school.
7. I admire Martin Luther King, Jr., for the **glory** and **honor** he brought to America when he won the Nobel Prize.
8. People show they are **civil** and **polite** when they say *please* and *thank you*.

LESSON 9

Put Words Into Action, page 80 (TE), 66 (SE)

1. An **optimist** would think that he or she will win the contest, while a **pessimist** would think that he or she has no chance or winning.
2. Breaking a leg could cause a pet to feel **misery**, while a hug and a pet could cause a pet to feel **pleasure**.
3. Bike riding is **forbidden** in the park and playing softball is **permitted**.
4. One dog might have a **dull** coat because of a poor diet, while another might have a **glistening** coat because of a good diet.
5. Cheap materials make one model **inferior**, while careful craftsmanship makes another model **superior**.
6. It is important to be **focused** and not **distracted** so that you understand what you are studying.
7. A good resume might make an employer **hire** someone, and tardiness might make an employer **dismiss** someone.
8. Someone who is **frail** is more likely to be in a hospital than someone who is healthy and **hardy**.

Review and Extend, page 81 (TE), 67 (SE)

Bonus: Don't think of your future as **dull**, but as shiny and **glistening**.

LESSON 10

Put Words Into Action, page 87 (TE), 73 (SE)

4. Treat all people with respect and dignity.
9. Plants thrive with water and sun.

LESSON 11

Connect Words and Meanings,
page 94 (TE), 80 (SE)

1. A race that has ten events is not a **triathlon**, since a **triathlon** has three events.
2. A newspaper that comes out on Mondays and Fridays is published **biweekly** because it comes out twice a week.
3. If a building is shaped like a square it does not have an **octagonal** shape, since it has four sides instead of eight.
4. Since the prefix *multi-* means "many," a **multicolored** tee-shirt will have many colors rather than just one color.
5. If my grandfather needs glasses only for reading, he does not need **bifocals**, since **bifocals** help us to see things both close and far and are not just for reading.
6. If someone were running for office, that person would want to speak to a **multitude** in order to reach as many people as possible.
7. Since the prefix *octo-* means "eight," I know that an **octopus** has eight tentacles, so the **octopus** would be holding eight divers.
8. I would not conclude that someone had been sitting on a **tripod**, since a **tripod** has three legs not four.
9. An anniversary occurs once a year, so it is not a **biannual** event, which occurs twice a year or every two years.
10. If I live in a **tristate** area, the state I live in would touch two other states.
11. I would flex my **biceps** to show how strong I am.
12. I'd rather be a **multimillionaire**, since a **multimillionaire** has many millions of dollars.
13. If a game board has a **triangular** shape, there would be three players since their are three corners.
14. I would be likely to use **binoculars** to watch a football game.
15. A small child would ride a **tricycle** since the three wheels would help the child balance.

LESSON 12

Connect Words and Meanings,
page 101 (TE), 88 (SE)

1. During a football game, a **spectator** might cheer loudly for her team.
2. For fun, a **naturalist** might go hiking.
3. For a special occasion, an **artisan** might give you a necklace he made.
4. A **laborer** might help build a new building by carrying its bricks.
5. During a hurricane, an **announcer** might tell people where to go for help.
6. In an office building or school building, the **janitor** is responsible for keeping the building clean.
7. A **nominee** for mayor might give a speech to persuade people to vote for him.
8. When crossing a street, a **pedestrian** should look both ways.
9. A **jurist** can help protect the rights of a person who is charged with a crime by putting up a solid defense in court.
10. An **African** exchange student might tell you about the folktales of his country.
11. A boss might give an **employee** a raise when that person gets promoted.
12. You might bring a pet to a **veterinarian** when it needs to get vaccinated.
13. A **mathematician** might work a long time to solve a problem.
14. A **civilian** might join the military when there is an emergency.
15. To become an **aviator**, a person needs to learn how to fly a plane.

Use Words in Context, page 103 (TE), 91 (SE)

1. I would give a **pedestrian** a good pair of walking shoes because a **pedestrian** walks a lot.
2. I would give a **naturalist** a painting of a lake and mountains because a **naturalist** enjoys nature.
3. I would give an **aviator** a model plane because I know **aviators** enjoy flying planes.
4. I would give an **announcer** voice lessons because an **announcer** has to speak clearly.
5. I would give a **mathematician** a calculator to help him or her solve problems.
6. I would give a **jurist** a book about famous court cases because a **jurist** is interested in legal matters.
7. I would give a **veterinarian** a book about caring for cats and dogs since a **veterinarian** treats animals.
8. A homemade quilt would be made by an **artisan** since an **artisan** usually makes things by hand.

LESSON 13

Connect Words and Meanings,
page 108 (TE), 96 (SE)

1. A poet can make a person **immortal** by writing a poem so that this person lives on in the minds of all who read the poem.
2. Doctors can study **microscopic** germs with a microscope.
3. A **recurring** dream is one that you have over and over again.
4. If a soldier receives a **mortal** wound, the soldier dies.
5. By listening to your chest with a **stethoscope**, a doctor can find out if your heart is healthy.
6. It would be fun to look through a **kaleidoscope** to see all of the bright colors and patterns.
7. People searched for the fountain of youth because they wanted **immortality** so they could live forever.
8. I would like to make an **excursion** to the Natural History Museum.
9. A **periscope** would allow a person in a submarine to see ships on the water above it.
10. I like to write in **cursive** because it is easier and takes less time.
11. History is my favorite part of the **curriculum**.
12. I would use a **telescopic** lens to take a picture of something far away.
13. The everyday **occurrence** I enjoy the most is the sunrise.
14. I would use a **microwave** if I wanted to heat up leftovers very quickly.
15. Scientists keep track of **mortality** rates so they can know how many people have died from a disease.

Use Words in Context, page 110 (TE), 99 (SE)

1. It takes a lot of work and effort to put the **microscopic** pieces back together again.
2. This museum does not have an early example of a **periscope**.
3. Artists sign their work in both **cursive** script and bold print.
4. The mummies show that the ancient Egyptians hoped for **immortality**.
5. The looting of ancient burial places is a commonplace **occurrence**.
6. The Egyptian kings had their bodies preserved because they refused to accept their **mortality**.
7. We do have some exhibits that show warriors in armor that protects them from **mortal** wounds.
8. The Egyptian exhibit would be very useful in the ancient history **curriculum**.

LESSON 14

Connect Words and Meanings,
page 115 (TE), 104 (SE)

1. If enemy agents **brainwash** a captured soldier, they might convince the soldier to act against his country.
2. In our school newspaper, the **headline** for the article about school elections read, "Jackson wins!"
3. At the **foothill** of the mountain, the hikers waited for the group leader.
4. When the runner slid **headlong** into home plate, she won the game for her team.
5. When the **headwaters** rose during the storm, the people living along the riverbank worried that their houses would be flooded.
6. A **footnote** can help you by explaining something that is unclear in a paragraph.
7. One state that is in the **heartland** of the United States is Indiana.
8. When we **brainstorm** ideas, we come up with lots of possibilities.
9. The **footbridge** crossed over the stream.
10. Marissa was so **headstrong** that she would not admit she was wrong.
11. I like to work on a **brainteaser** because it gives my brain a workout.
12. The boy was **heartbroken** when his dog ran away.
13. In the museum, I saw a **headdress** made from feathers.
14. The magazine contained a **heartwarming** story about two twins who were reunited after twenty years.
15. He felt **downhearted** after he failed the test.

Use Words in Context, page 117 (TE), 107 (SE)

1. One rainy day I had a **brainstorm** to write and put on a play.
2. When I let my friends **brainwash** me, I feel disappointed with myself.
3. You can convince a **headstrong** person to listen to you by promising to listen to him.
4. When I am **downhearted**, I listen to my favorite music.
5. When people are **heartbroken** singing songs makes them feel better.

6. I don't like **brainteasers** because they feel like work, not play.
7. If someone drives over a **footbridge**, the bridge will probably break.
8. If you want to find out what a newspaper article is about, read the **headline**.
9. If you rush **headlong** down a crowded hallway, you may bump into people.
10. You can find out who discovered the **headwaters** of the Nile River on the Internet.

LESSON 15

Connect Words and Meanings,
page 122 (TE), 112 (SE)

1. An author might use a **pseudonym** to prevent people from knowing her true identity.
2. The **acronym** for the group would be PART.
3. I would **nominate** my mother to win an award for the person whom I admire most because she is a great mother and she works hard at her job and in our home, too.
4. I would **rename** my favorite breakfast cereal PowerTreats because I get lots of energy after I eat them.
5. The **antonym** I would use is *timid*.
6. I would supply a **nametag** for each person because a lot of people would not know each other.
7. If I pay only a **nominal** fee, I pay only a little money.
8. After someone gets the **nomination**, that person might start making speeches.
9. A person might want to remain **nameless** because she is shy and does not like attention.
10. The common **denominator** is that they all like outdoor sports.
11. The **namesake** might have the nickname Joe or Joey.
12. **Namely**, I would babysit for my little brother and offer to do more chores around the house.
13. I might use the **synonym** *sleepy*.
14. The artist might be **anonymous** because he or she never signed the artwork.
15. The **nominator** might say, "I nominate Catherine O'Malley for president."

Review and Extend, page 125 (TE), 116 (SE)

1. If I wanted a new name, I would **rename** myself.
2. I would use a thesaurus or dictionary because it would help me find **synonyms**.
3. I would use a **pseudonym**.
4. I don't think the **acronym** FOE is a good name because it suggests enemies, not friends.
5. My feelings are so vague and confused that they are **unnameable**.
6. Let's **renominate** Roger even though he lost the last election.
7. I don't mean to **namedrop**, but I am a close personal friend of the mayor.
8. Jasmine liked the **nameplate** that Enrico designed for the store.

LESSON 16

Connect Words and Meanings,
page 129 (TE), 120 (SE)

1. creatures that live in the sea
2. all the players of my favorite baseball team
3. they present information in a visual way
4. CD players
5. indenting the first line
6. a famous painter
7. my grandparents
8. the planet, Pluto
9. pencils
10. Martin Luther King, Jr.
11. a camera
12. my first day in school
13. how he got his first singing job
14. the pictures are very interesting
15. he or she remembers all the words on a page

Review and Extend, page 132 (TE), 124 (SE)

5. A **seismograph** records the intensity and duration of earthquakes.
6. A **geographer** studies the physical features of the earth.
7. **Graphology** is the study of handwriting, especially as a clue to personality.
8. A **graphologist** studies handwriting.

222

LESSON 18

Review and Extend, page 148 (TE), 140 (SE)

Bonus: Blood travels from the heart through arteries and to the heart through veins.

LESSON 20

Review and Extend, page 162 (TE), 154 (SE)

Bonus: Someone who tries and tries again is persistent. This person shows self-discipline, because he makes himself keep trying, even when things look bleak.

LESSON 23

Review and Extend, page 185 (TE), 177 (SE)

1. A **gourmet** chef might send his **resumé** to a new restaurant to get a job cooking at a better place.
2. It would be a **faux pas** to wear **pajamas** to a fancy party because **pajamas** are indoor clothes for sleeping.
3. You might shout "**Eureka**!" when you find the solution to a difficult **algebra** problem.
4. You would turn the lights on the **patio** out after the **finale** because the concert is over.
5. When he hears about the **typhoon**, the **admiral** might order the fleet not to go out on the sea.

LESSON 24

Use Words in Context, page 190 (TE), 181 (SE)

1. You shouldn't write a news story without a **kernel** of truth because it is important to be accurate when you report the news.
2. You shouldn't talk back to a **colonel** because an important military officer commands respect.
3. You wouldn't try to become a **baron** in the United States because the United States doesn't have noblemen.
4. You shouldn't try to grow plants on **barren** land because the land is not fertile.
5. You shouldn't play a **chord** of music too loudly when others are trying to sleep because you will keep them awake.
6. You shouldn't use a thin **cord** because the cord will break too easily.
7. You shouldn't wear an undergarment made of **coarse** fabric because it will not be comfortable.
8. You shouldn't look for a race **course**, because since there are no people, one would not have been built.
9. You shouldn't **aid** someone if you don't know how to help because you can make the situation worse.
10. You shouldn't be rude to your **aide** because you should always be polite, especially to people who help you.

Put Words Into Action, page 191 (TE), 182 (SE)

1. We should take the most direct **course** past the Moon.
2. A **colonel** or other military person should lead the voyage.
3. We should bring water, food, tools, and **cord**.
4. We can strum a **chord** or two on a guitar to entertain ourselves on the six-month flight.
5. Mars has a **barren** landscape.
6. The soil is **coarse**, rough, and rocky.
7. You can't plant any crops, not even a **kernel** of corn!
8. I can give you a lot of **aid** as you plan your trip.
9. You will need an **aide** on board to help with the things that need to be done if the mission is to be successful.
10. Choose a scientist, not a **baron**.

LESSON 25

Review and Extend, page 199 (TE), 189 (SE)

1. If you **lend** a book to someone, you expect that person to return it.
2. A **bizarre** creature you read about in a story might be Bigfoot.
3. You might need a **carton** to carry groceries home from the supermarket.
4. You might **canvass** the neighborhood to find out how many people support a new bill.
5. If you particularly liked a movie, you might **persuade** a friend to go see it.
6. At a **bazaar** you might buy unusual clothing.
7. You might give your **assent** to a friend's plan if you agree with it.
8. You might **borrow** someone's umbrella when it is raining.

LESSON 26

Use Words in Context, page 204 (TE), 193 (SE)

1. You need a burst of energy to keep on going when you are tired.
2. You would want the fact that you should be in the show to be **as plain as the nose on your face**.
3. You **get the upper hand** by working hard and being prepared.
4. You might **catch forty winks** after playing soccer or jumping hurdles.
5. You can politely ask that person to stop.
6. When you **bark up the wrong tree**, you don't find the answer you need.
7. An **eager beaver** might volunteer to help with props, costumes, sets, and even sell tickets.
8. You are sad because it means you won't win.
9. You will have a hard time accomplishing your goals.
10. You are likely to lose.

Powerful Vocabulary for Reading Success   **Transparency 1**

Word	My Thinking	Meaning

Author's Big Idea or Subject is _____

_____ is connected to the idea of _____ because _____

_____ is connected to the idea of _____ because _____

_____ is connected to the idea of _____ because _____

_____ is connected to the idea of _____ because _____

_____ is connected to the idea of _____ because _____

Powerful Vocabulary for Reading Success   **Transparency 3**

Word Attribute Chart

Words	What's Special About This Word?	How I Will Remember It	Meaning

Graphic Organizers

Umbrella Chart

Idea Web

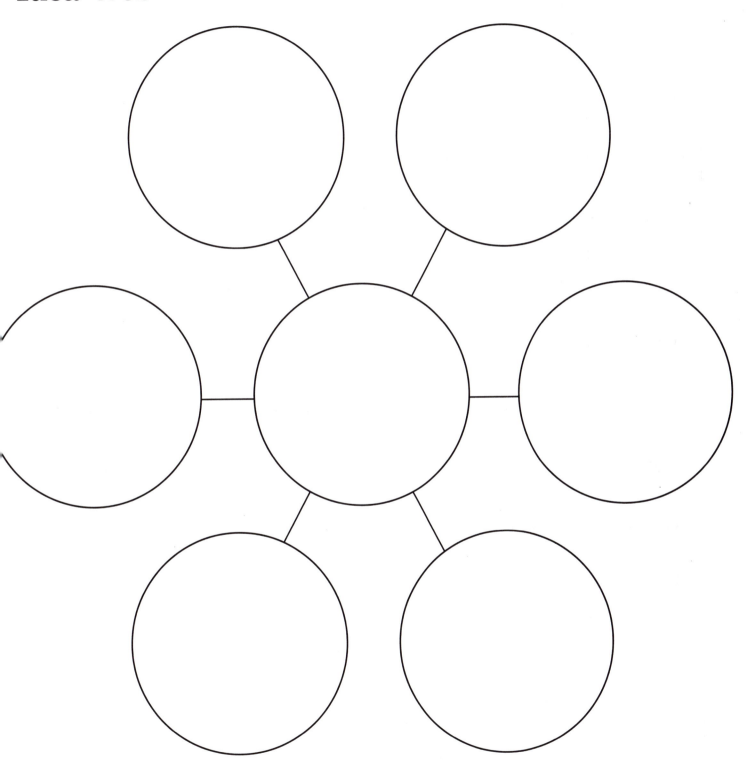

Graphic Organizers

Graphic Organizers

5 Ws and H Chart

Who?	
What?	
When?	
Where?	
Why?	
How?	

Problem/Solution Chart

Problem

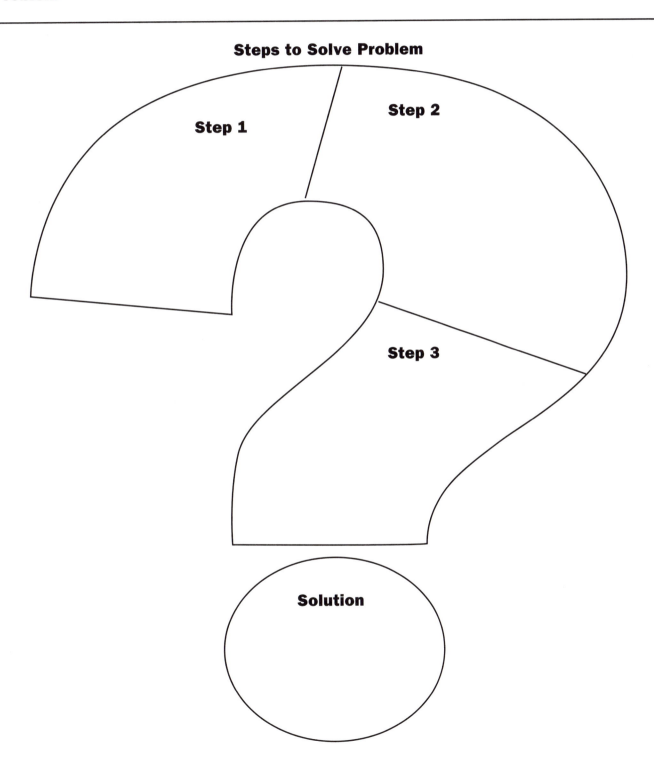

Graphic Organizers

Word Map

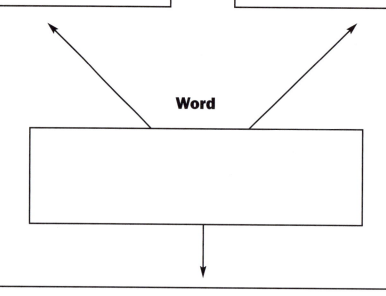

Meaning

1. _____
2. _____

Part of Speech

3. _____
4. _____

Word

How do you use this word in a sentence?

5. Use first meaning : _____

_____

6. Use second meaning: _____

_____

Lesson 1 **advantage** (ad-**van**-tij)	Lesson 1 **agent** (**ay**-juhnt)	Lesson 1 **challenge** (**chal**-uhnj)
Lesson 1 **foundation** (foun-**day**-shuhn)	Lesson 1 **genius** (**jee**-nee-uhss or **jeen**-yuhss)	Lesson 1 **mainland** (**main**-luhnd)
Lesson 1 **mechanic** (muh-**kan**-ik)	Lesson 1 **nuisance** (**noo**-suhnss)	Lesson 1 **obstacle** (**ob**-stuh-kuhl)
Lesson 1 **precaution** (pri-**kaw**-shuhn)	Lesson 1 **pursuit** (pur-**soot**)	Lesson 1 **rival** (**rye**-vuhl)
Lesson 1 **scheme** (**skeem**)	Lesson 1 **target** (**tar**-git)	Lesson 1 **vehicle** (**vee**-uh-kuhl)
Lesson 2 **apologize** (uh-**pol**-uh-jize)	Lesson 2 **assemble** (uh-s**em**-buhl)	Lesson 2 **boost** (**boost**)
Lesson 2 **coax** (**kohks**)	Lesson 2 **concentrate** (**kon**-suhn-trate)	Lesson 2 **consult** (kuhn-**suhlt**)
Lesson 2 **devote** (di-**voht**)	Lesson 2 **irritate** (**ihr**-uh-tate)	Lesson 2 **manage** (**man**-ij)
Lesson 2 **refer** (ri-**fur**)	Lesson 2 **reject** (ri-**jekt**)	Lesson 2 **reveal** (ri-**veel**)
Lesson 2 **topple** (**top**-uhl)	Lesson 2 **transport** (transs-**port**)	Lesson 2 **weaken** (**week**-in)

noun: something difficult that requires extra effort or work	*noun*: 1. a person who arranges things for other people; 2. a person who represents other people	*noun*: something that helps you or is useful to you or gives you a better chance
noun: the largest mass of land of a country or continent	*noun*: an unusually smart or intelligent person	*noun*: 1. base; 2. the basis on which something stands
noun: barrier	*noun*: a bother or annoyance	*noun*: person skilled at repairing machinery
noun: someone or something that is an opponent or competitor	*noun*: the act or instance of chasing someone or something	*noun*: action taken ahead of time to prevent something dangerous from happening
noun: something used to carry people or objects over land or sea or through the air	*noun*: 1. a goal; 2. something that is aimed at	*noun*: a plan or plot to do something
verb: 1. to lift; 2. to increase	*verb*: 1. to put together; 2. to gather in groups	*verb*: to say you are sorry about something
verb: to go to another person or resource for information and advice	*verb*: to focus on something	*verb*: 1. to persuade someone by asking in a pleasant and easy way; 2. to urge
verb: to control or direct	*verb*: to annoy or bother	*verb*: to give time and effort to some purpose
verb: 1. to show or make known; 2. to uncover	*verb*: to refuse to accept something	*verb*: to tell someone to go to a certain person or place for help or information
verb: to lose strength	*verb*: to move someone or something from one place to another	*verb*: 1. to fall over; 2. to make something fall over

Lesson 3 **approve** (uh-**proov**)	Lesson 3 **associate** (uh-**soh**-see-ayte)	Lesson 3 **attempt** (uh-**tempt**)
Lesson 3 **broadcast** (**brawd**-*kast*)	Lesson 3 **conquer** (**kong**-kur)	Lesson 3 **dedicate** (**ded**-uh-kate)
Lesson 3 **emerge** (i-**murj**)	Lesson 3 **flourish** (**flur**-ish)	Lesson 3 **organize** (**or**-guh-nize)
Lesson 3 **overwhelm** (*oh*-vur-**welm**)	Lesson 3 **pursue** (pur-**soo**)	Lesson 3 **resemble** (ri-**zem**-buhl)
Lesson 3 **restore** (ri-s**tor**)	Lesson 3 **surrender** (suh-**ren**-dur)	Lesson 3 **withdraw** (wiTH-**draw** *or* with-**draw**)
Lesson 4 **adventurous** (ad-**ven**-chur-uhss)	Lesson 4 **assorted** (uh-**sort**-ed)	Lesson 4 **beloved** (bi-**luhv**-id)
Lesson 4 **confident** (**kon**-fuh-duhnt)	Lesson 4 **distinguished** (diss-**ting**-gwishd)	Lesson 4 **easygoing** (**ee**-zee-goh-ing)
Lesson 4 **fragile** (**fraj**-il)	Lesson 4 **fragrant** (**fray**-gruhnt)	Lesson 4 **heroic** (hi-**roh**-ik)
Lesson 4 **massive** (**mass**-iv)	Lesson 4 **mature** (muh-**chur** *or* muh-**tyur**)	Lesson 4 **mischievous** (**miss**-chuh-vuhss)
Lesson 4 **outstanding** (*out*-**stand**-ing)	Lesson 4 **peculiar** (pi-**kyoo**-lyur)	Lesson 4 **shrewd** (**shrood**)

verb: to try to do something	*verb*: to connect with something	*verb*: to check over something and give a good rating
verb: to devote a lot of time and energy to something	*verb*: to defeat and take control	*verb*: 1. to send out a program over radio or television; 2. to announce widely
verb: to put in a certain order	*verb*: to grow and do well	*verb*: to come out into the open
verb: to be or look like someone or something	*verb*: to chase after	*verb*: to overpower or overcome completely
verb: 1. to drop out; 2. to remove or take away something	*verb*: 1. to give up; 2. to give something or yourself to someone else	*verb*: to bring back to its original condition
adjective: adored; loved deeply	*adjective*: various kinds of	*adjective*: 1. liking excitement and adventure; 2. daring
adjective: calm and relaxed	*adjective*: 1. known for important things; 2. dignified	*adjective*: self-assured and secure
adjective: very brave or daring	*adjective*: sweet-smelling	*adjective*: 1. delicate; 2. easily broken
adjective: tends to get into trouble	*adjective*: grown-up	*adjective*: very large
adjective: clever; sharp	*adjective*: strange or odd	*adjective*: extremely good

Lesson 5 **annual** (**an**-yoo-uhl)	Lesson 5 **billowy** (**bil**-oh-wee)	Lesson 5 **breathtaking** (**breth**-*tay*-king)
Lesson 5 **convenient** (kuhn-**vee**-ny-uhnu)	Lesson 5 **dense** (**denss**)	Lesson 5 **distant** (**diss**-tuhnt)
Lesson 5 **ebony** (**eb**-uh-nee)	Lesson 5 **genuine** (bjen-**yoo**-uhn)	Lesson 5 **luminous** (**loo**-muh-nuhss)
Lesson 5 **perilous** (**per**-uhl-uhss)	Lesson 5 **sincere** (sin-**sihr**)	Lesson 5 **spectacular** (spek-**tak**-yuh-lur)
Lesson 5 **spotless** (**spot**-liss)	Lesson 5 **unique** (yoo-**neek**)	Lesson 5 **wondrous** (**wuhn**-druhss)
Lesson 6 **clearly** (**klihr**-lee)	Lesson 6 **earlier** (**ur**-lee-ur)	Lesson 6 **eventually** (i-**ven**-choo-uh-lee)
Lesson 6 **everywhere** (**ev**-ree-wair)	Lesson 6 **firmly** (**furm**-lee)	Lesson 6 **frequently** (**free**-kwent)
Lesson 6 **immediately** (i-**mee**-dee-it-lee)	Lesson 6 **largely** (**larj**-lee)	Lesson 6 **mostly** (**mohst**-lee)
Lesson 6 **naturally** (**nach**-ur-uhl-ee)	Lesson 6 **outside** (*out*-**side**)	Lesson 6 **practically** (**prak**-tik-lee)
Lesson 6 **precisely** (pri-**sisse**-lee)	Lesson 6 **rapidly** (**rap**-id-lee)	Lesson 6 **widely** (**wide**-lee)

adjective: exciting; thrilling; very beautiful; takes your breath away	*adjective*: swelling, as in waves	*adjective*: yearly
adjective: far away; removed	*adjective*: thick; crowded	*adjective*: 1. easy to reach or use; 2. useful
adjective: 1. shining; 2. glowing in the dark	*adjective*: 1. real, not fake; 2. honest	*adjective*: deep black; made of a hard black wood
adjective: 1. remarkable; 2. dramatic; exciting	*adjective*: 1. honest; truthful; 2. heart-felt	*adjective*: dangerous
adjective: marvelous; fills you with wonder and amazement	*adjective*: one of a kind	*adjective*: perfectly clean
adverb: 1. at some time after a series of events; 2. at last	*adjective*: 1. before the expected or arranged time; 2. before the present time	*adverb*: in a way that is easy to understand or picture
adverb: very often	*adverb*: 1, not moving; 2. not bending; 3. not giving way easily under pressure; 4. solidly	*adverb*: in all places
adverb: almost entirely; largely	*adverb*: mainly; mostly	*adverb*: 1. without delay; 2. at once
adverb: 1. very nearly but not quite; 2. in a practical manner	*adverb*: in the open air; not inside	*adverb*: 1. as might be expected; 2. without a doubt
adverb: 1. by a large number of people; 2. over a great distance	*adverb*: moving very quickly	*adverb*: exactly

Lesson 7 **bridge** (brij)	Lesson 7 **bureau** (**byur**-oh)	Lesson 7 **cabinet** (**kab**-in-it)
Lesson 7 **contract** (**kon**-trakt)	Lesson 7 **harbor** (**har**-bur)	Lesson 7 **mold** (mohld)
Lesson 7 **peer** (pihr)	Lesson 7 **pelt** (pelt)	Lesson 7 **range** (raynj)
Lesson 7 **refrain** (ri-**frayn**)	Lesson 7 **rest** (rest)	Lesson 7 **rung** (ruhng)
Lesson 7 **steer** (stihr)	Lesson 7 **temper** (**tem**-pur)	Lesson 7 **vent** (vent)
Lesson 8 **approval** (uh-**proov**-uhl)	Lesson 8 **bustle** (**buh**-suhl)	Lesson 8 **civil** (**siv**-il)
Lesson 8 **commotion** (kuh-**moh**-shuhn)	Lesson 8 **consent** (kuhn-**sent**)	Lesson 8 **corridor** (**kor**-uh-dur)
Lesson 8 **drenched** (**dren**-chud)	Lesson 8 **fumble** (**fuhm**-buhl)	Lesson 8 **glory** (**glor**-ee)
Lesson 8 **gnarled** (narld)	Lesson 8 **gravity** (**grav**-uh-tee)	Lesson 8 **hallway** (**hawl**-way)
Lesson 8 **honor** (**on**-ur)	Lesson 8 **knotty** (**not**-ee)	Lesson 8 **mishandle** (miss-**han**-duhl)

noun: 1. a piece of furniture with shelves and drawers; a cupboard; 2. a group of advisors for the head of government	*noun*: 1. a chest of drawers; 2. an office that provides information or another service	*noun*: 1. a structure built over a river or other body of water so that people can cross it; 2. a card game for four players; *verb*: 3. to connect
noun: 1. a furry fungus that grows in damp places or on old food; *verb*: 2. to model or shape something	*noun*: 1. a place where ships settle or unload their cargo; *verb*: 2. to hide someone or to take care of someone	(**kuhn**-trakt) *noun*: 1. a legal agreement; (kuhn-**trakt**) *verb*: 2. to get
noun: 1. an area of open land used for a special purpose; 2. a cooking stove	*noun*: 1. an animal skin with fur or hair still on it; *verb*: 2. to strike or beat	*noun*: 1. a person of equal standing; *verb*: 2. to take a careful look at something
noun: 1. one of the horizontal steps on a ladder; *verb*: 2. to make a clear sound; past participle of ring	*noun*: 1. the others or the remaining part of something; *verb*: 2. to relax or sleep	*noun*: 1. repeated words in a song or poem; *verb*: 2. to stop yourself from doing something
noun: 1. an opening through which smoke or air can pass; *verb*: 2. to show or let out emotion	*noun*: 1. a tendency to get angry; *verb*: 2. to make things less harsh or difficult	*noun*: 1. male cattle; *verb*: 2. to move a vehicle in a certain direction
adjective: courteous; well behaved; polite	*verb*: a lot of noisy activity; commotion	*noun*: acceptance of a plan or idea; consent
noun: a passageway; hallway	*noun*: agreement; approval	*noun*: rush; lots of activity; bustle
noun: great fame; honor	*verb*: to drop or handle poorly; mishandle	*adjective*: completely wet; soaked
noun: a long passageway; corridor	*noun*: importance; seriousness	*adjective*: twisted and lumpy with age; knotty
verb: to deal with poorly; to fumble	*adjective*: having many hard spots of lumps; gnarled	*noun*: respect and a good reputation; glory

Lesson 8 **pesky** (**pess**-kee)	Lesson 8 **polite** (puh-**lite**)	Lesson 8 **seriousness** (**sirh**-ee-uhss-ness)
Lesson 8 **soaked** (**soh**-kuhd)	Lesson 8 **troublesome** (**truh**-buhl-suhm)	Lesson 9 **allowed** (uh-**loud**)
Lesson 9 **dismiss** (diss-**miss**)	Lesson 9 **distracted** (diss-**trak**-ted)	Lesson 9 **dull** (**duhl**)
Lesson 9 **focused** (**foh**-kuhssd)	Lesson 9 **forbidden** (fur-**bid**-uhn)	Lesson 9 **frail** (**frayl**)
Lesson 9 **glistening** (**gliss**-uhn-ing)	Lesson 9 **hardy** (**har**-dee)	Lesson 9 **high-priced** (**hye**-*prissed*)
Lesson 9 **hire** (**hire**)	Lesson 9 **inexpensive** (in-ik-**spen**-siv)	Lesson 9 **inferior** (in-**fihr**-ee-ur)
Lesson 9 **meaningful** (**mee**-ning-fuhl)	Lesson 9 **misery** (mi-**zuhr**-ee)	Lesson 9 **optimist** (**op**-tuh-mist)
Lesson 9 **pessimist** (pess-uh-**miss**-tik)	Lesson 9 **pleasure** (**plezh**-ur)	Lesson 9 **senseless** (**senss**-liss)
Lesson 9 **superior** (suh-**pihr**-ee-ur *or* soo-**pihr**-ee-ur)	Lesson 10 **casually** (**kazh**-oo-uhl-lee)	Lesson 10 **dignity** (**dig**-nuh-tee)
Lesson 10 **gigantic** (jye-**gan**-tik)	Lesson 10 **impressive** (im-**press**-ive)	Lesson 10 **patience** (**pay**-shuhnss)

noun: importance; gravity	*adjective*: having good manners; civil	*adjective*: annoying; troublesome
adjective: 1. given permission to do something; 2. permitted	*adjective*: difficult; pesky	*adjective*: completely wet or left in water; drenched
adjective: 1. colorless, very little or no color; 2. boring	*adjective*: 1. having your thoughts and attention on something else; 2. not concentrating	*verb*: to allow to leave or to let someone go
adjective: weak, delicate, light	*adjective*: not allowed or approved	*adjective*: 1. showing great attention; 2. concentrating on a single thing
adjective: expensive; costing a lot of money	*adjective*: courageous and daring	*adjective*: shining in a sparkling way
adjective: lower in quality or value	*adjective*: not costing a lot; cheap	*verb*: to employ somebody to work for you, or pay somebody to do a job for you
noun: someone who believes that things will turn out for the best	*noun*: 1. something that causes great unhappiness; 2. a condition of great unhappiness	*adjective*: 1. having meaning and purpose; 2. significant
adjective: 1. foolish; 2. without purpose or meaning	*noun*: a feeling of enjoyment or satisfaction	*noun*: somebody who always expects the worst to happen in every situation
noun: a quality that makes someone worthy of honor and respect	*adverb*: in a way that is not planned or not formal	*adjective*: 1. higher in rank; 2. above average in quality
noun: the ability to remain calm and not be hasty	*adjective*: having a strong or striking effect	*adjective*: huge; very large; enormous

Lesson 10 **perish** (**per**-ish)	Lesson 10 **reassure** (ree-uh-**shur**)	Lesson 10 **suitable** (**soo**-tuh-buhl)
Lesson 10 **thrive** (**thrive**)	Lesson 10 **vividly** (**viv**-id-lee)	Lesson 11 **biannual** (bye-**an**-yoo-uhl)
Lesson 11 **biceps** (**bye**-seps)	Lesson 11 **bifocals** (**bye**-*foh*-kuhlz)	Lesson 11 **binoculars** (buh-**nok**-yuh-lurz)
Lesson 11 **biweekly** (**bye**-week-lee)	Lesson 11 **multicolored** (**muhl**-ti-kuhl-urd)	Lesson 11 **multimillionaire** (**muhl**-ti-mil-yuhn-*air*)
Lesson 11 **multitude** (**muhl**-ti-tood)	Lesson 11 **octagonal** (ok-**tag**-uh-nuhl)	Lesson 11 **octopus** (**ok**-tuh-puhss)
Lesson 11 **triangular** (trye-**ang**-guh-lur)	Lesson 11 **triathlon** (trye-**ath**-lon)	Lesson 11 **tricycle** (**trye**-suh-kuhl *or* **trye**-sik-uhl)
Lesson 11 **tripod** (**trye**-*pod*)	Lesson 11 **tristate** (**trye**-*state*)	Lesson 12 **African** (**af**-ruh-kuhn)
Lesson 12 **announcer** (uh-**noun**-sur)	Lesson 12 **artisan** (**ar**-tuh-zuhn)	Lesson 12 **aviator** (**ay**-vee-ay-tor)
Lesson 12 **civilian** (si-**vil**-yuhn)	Lesson 12 **employee** (em-**ploi**-ee *or* em-**ploi**-**ee**)	Lesson 12 **janitor** (**jan**-uh-tur)
Lesson 12 **jurist** (**jur**-ist)	Lesson 12 **laborer** (**lay**-bur-ur)	Lesson 12 **mathematician** (*math*-uh-muh-**tish**-uhn)

adjective: right for a particular purpose or occasion	*verb*: 1. to calm; 2. to give confidence or courage	*verb*: 1. to spoil; 2. to be destroyed before its time
adjective: 1. happening twice a year; 2. occurring every two years	*adverb*: clearly or distinctly	*verb*: 1. to do well; 2. to flourish or prosper
noun, plural: a device used with both eyes to see things that are very far away	*noun, plural*: eyeglasses with two different sections of each lens, one for seeing things up close and one for seeing things farther away	*noun, plural*: the large set of muscles in the front of your upper arm between you shoulder and inner elbow
noun: a person with many millions of dollars	*adjective*: having many colors	*adjective*: 1. happening twice a week; 2. happening once every two weeks
noun: a sea animal with eight long tentacles or arms	*adjective*: having eight sides or angles	*noun*: a great many things or people
noun: a vehicle with pedals that has three wheels, one in the front and two in the back	*noun*: a long distance race that is made up of three events	*adjective*: having three sides or angles
noun: 1. a person from Africa; *adjective*: 2. having to do with Africa	*adjective*: involving or touching three states	*noun*: a three-legged stand or stool
noun: a person who flies a plane; a pilot	*noun*: a person who makes crafts	*noun*: a person who reports or announces information
noun: a person who looks after and cleans buildings	*noun*: a person who is employed by or works for another person	*noun*: a person not in the military
noun: someone who studies or practices mathematics	*noun*: a person who labors or does physical work, usually an unskilled worker	*noun*: 1. a person who works in the law; 2. a lawyer or judge

Lesson 12 **naturalist** (**nach**-u-ral-*ist*)	Lesson 12 **nominee** (nom-uh-**nee**)	Lesson 12 **pedestrian** (puh-**dess**-tree-uhn)
Lesson 12 **spectator** (**spek**-tay-tur)	Lesson 12 **veterinarian** (*vet*-ur-uh-**ner**-ee-uhn)	Lesson 13 **curriculum** (kuh-**rik**-yuh-luhm)
Lesson 13 **cursive** (**kur**-sive)	Lesson 13 **excursion** (ek-**skur**-zhuhn)	Lesson 13 **immortal** (i-**mor**-tuhl)
Lesson 13 **immortality** (i-**mor**-*tal*-uh-tee)	Lesson 13 **kaleidoscope** (kuh-**lye**-duh-*skope*)	Lesson 13 **microscopic** (mye-kruh-**skop**-ik)
Lesson 13 **microwave** (**mye**-kroh-*wave*)	Lesson 13 **mortal** (**mor**-tuhl)	Lesson 13 **mortality** (**mor**-*tal*-uh-tee)
Lesson 13 **occurrence** (uh-**kur**-ence)	Lesson 13 **periscope** (**per**-uh-*skope*)	Lesson 13 **recurring** (ri-**kur**-ing)
Lesson 13 **stethoscope** (**steth**-uh-*skope*)	Lesson 13 **telescopic** (*tel*-uh-skop-ik)	Lesson 14 **brainstorm** (**brayn**-*storm*)
Lesson 14 **brainteaser** (**brayn**-teez-uhr)	Lesson 14 **brainwash** (**brayn**-*washsh*)	Lesson 14 **downhearted** (**doun**-har-ted)
Lesson 14 **footbridge** (**fut**-*brij*)	Lesson 14 **foothill** (**fut**-*hil*)	Lesson 14 **footnote** (**fut**-*noht*)
Lesson 14 **headdress** (**hed**-*dress*)	Lesson 14 **headline** (**hed**-*line*)	Lesson 14 **headlong** (**hed**-*lawng*)

noun: someone who travels on foot	*noun*: a person named to run for office; a candidate	*noun*: a person who studies nature
noun: a group of courses of study that are connected	*noun*: a doctor who takes care of animals	*noun*: someone who watches an event
adjective: 1. not subject to death; 2. living or lasting forever; *noun*: 3. one who lives forever	*noun*: 1. a trip away from home; 2. a short journey in which you might do a lot of running around or back and forth	*noun*: 1. a form of handwriting in which each letter runs into or is joined to the next letter; script; 2. *adjective*: written in this style
adjective: 1. too small to be seen by the eye alone; 2. very small	*noun*: 1. a tube in which glass and mirrors create patterns of color and light; 2. a constantly changing set of colors	*noun*: unending life or fame
noun: the condition of being a creature that can die	*adjective*: 1. capable of causing death; 2. not living or lasting forever; *noun* 3. one who is subject to death	*noun*: an electromagnetic wave that can pass through solid objects; an oven that cooks very quickly by using this type of wave
adjective: happening over and over	*noun*: an instrument in the shape of a tube with prisms and mirrors that allows you to see someone or something that is far above you	*noun*: an event; something that takes place
noun: 1. a sudden powerful idea; *verb*: 2. to think of new ideas	*adjective*: 1. able to see at great distances; 2. relating to a telescope—an instrument that allows you to see objects that are very far away	*noun*: a medical instrument used to listen to sounds from the heart, lungs, and other areas of the body
adjective: filled with sadness	*verb*: to make someone accept or believe something by saying it over and over again	*noun*: a mentally challenging puzzle or problem
noun: information at the bottom of the page that explains something in the content on that page	*noun*: a low hill at the base of a mountain or mountain range	*noun*: a bridge for walking across a river or other body of water on foot
adverb: without hesitation or thinking	*noun*: the title of a newspaper article, which is usually set in large type	*noun*: a decorative covering for the head

Lesson 14 **headstrong** (**hed**-strong)	Lesson 14 **headwaters** (**hed**-waw-turs)	Lesson 14 **heartbroken** (**hart**-broh-kuhn)
Lesson 14 **heartland** (**hart**-land)	Lesson 14 **heartwarming** (**hart**-worm-ing)	Lesson 15 **acronym** (**ak**-ruh-nim)
Lesson 15 **anonymous** (uh-**non**-uh-muhss)	Lesson 15 **antonym** (**an**-toh-nim)	Lesson 15 **denominator** (di-**nom**-uh-nay-tur)
Lesson 15 **nameless** (**naym**-less)	Lesson 15 **namely** (**naym**-lee)	Lesson 15 **namesake** (**naym**-sayk)
Lesson 15 **nametag** (**naym**-tag)	Lesson 15 **nominal** (**nom**-i-nuhl)	Lesson 15 **nominate** (**nom**-uh-nate)
Lesson 15 **nomination** (nom-uh-**na**-shuhn)	Lesson 15 **nominator** (**nom**-uh-na-tur)	Lesson 15 **pseudonym** (**sood**-uh-nim)
Lesson 15 **rename** (ri-**naym**)	Lesson 15 **synonym** (**sin**-uh-nim)	Lesson 16 **autobiographical** (aw-toh-bye-oh-**graf**-i-kuhl)
Lesson 16 **autobiography** (aw-toh-bye-**og**-ruh-fee)	Lesson 16 **autograph** (**aw**-tuh-graf)	Lesson 16 **biographical** (bye-oh-**graf**-i-kuhl)
Lesson 16 **biography** (bye-**og**-ruh-fee)	Lesson 16 **graphic** (**graf**-ik)	Lesson 16 **graphics** (**graf**-iks)
Lesson 16 **graphite** (**graf**-ite)	Lesson 16 **monograph** (**mon**-uh-graf)	Lesson 16 **oceanography** (oh-shuh-**nog**-ruh-fee)

adjective: very sad or filled with sadness	*noun*, plural: the waters from which a river rises	*adjective*: stubborn or determined to have your own way
noun: a word formed from the first or first few letters of the words in a phrase	*adjective*: causing happiness and pleasure	*noun*: an area or territory at the center of a country
noun: 1. a trait that two or more people have; 2. the number that is below the line in a fraction that names how many equal parts the whole number can be divided into	*noun*: a word that means the opposite of another word	*adjective*: written or done by a person whose name is not known or made public
noun: a person named after another person	*adverb*: 1. that is to say; 2. specifically	*adjective*: 1. lacking a name; 2. not able to be described or named
verb: to name someone as the right person to do a job, hold an office, or receive an honor	*adjective*: 1. in name only; 2. very small or slight	*noun*: a badge telling the name of the person wearing it
noun: a false or made-up name, especially a pen name	*noun*: a person who names another person to run for office, do a job, or win a prize	*noun*: the act or instance of naming or appointing a person to office
adjective: having to do with your own life story	*noun*: a word that means the same or nearly the same as another word	*verb*: to give a new name to someone or something
adjective: having to do with someone else's life	*noun*: 1. a person's own signature; *verb*: 2. to write your name or signature on something	*noun*: the life story of a person written by that person
noun, *plural*: images such as drawings, maps, and graphs, especially those made using technological devices such as computers	*adjective*: 1. having to do with art and design or handwriting; 2. very realistic	*noun*: the life story of a person written by someone other than that person
noun: the science that deals with the oceans and the plants and animals that live in them	*noun*: a short book or long article on a single, limited subject	*noun*: a soft, black mineral used as lead in pencils and also used in paints and coatings

Lesson 16 **paragraph** (**pa**-ruh-*graf*)	Lesson 16 **phonograph** (**foh**-nuh-*graf*)	Lesson 16 **photograph** (**foh**-tuh-*graf*)
Lesson 16 **photographic** (foh-tuh-**graf**-ik)	Lesson 16 **photography** (foh-**tog**-ruh-fee)	Lesson 17 **approximate** (uh-**prok**-si-muht)
Lesson 17 **calculate** (**kal**-kyuh-late)	Lesson 17 **certain** (**sur**-tuhn)	Lesson 17 **estimation** (**ess**-ti-ma-shuhn)
Lesson 17 **probability** (**prob**-uh-bil-i-tee)	Lesson 18 **aorta** (ay-**or**-tuh)	Lesson 18 **artery** (**ar**-tuh-ree)
Lesson 18 **atrium** (**ay**-tree-uhm)	Lesson 18 **capillary** (**kap**-uh-ler-ee)	Lesson 18 **vein** (**vayn**)
Lesson 19 **condensation** (*kon*-den-**say**-shuhn)	Lesson 19 **droplet** (**drop**-lit)	Lesson 19 **evaporation** (i-**vap**-uh-ra-shuhn)
Lesson 19 **precipitation** (*pri*-sip-i-**tay**-shuhn)	Lesson 19 **water vapor** (**waw**-tur-*vay*-pur)	Lesson 20 **compassion** (kuhm-**pash**-uhn)
Lesson 20 **cooperation** (koh-**op**-uh-ra-shuhn)	Lesson 20 **persistence** (pur-**sist**-enss)	Lesson 20 **self-discipline** (**self**-*diss*-uh-plin)
Lesson 20 **trustworthy** (**truhst**-*wur*-THee)	Lesson 21 **bibliography** (*bib*-lee-**og**-ruh-fee)	Lesson 21 **citation** (**si**-tay-shuhn)
Lesson 21 **data** (**day**-tuh)	Lesson 21 **paraphrase** (**pa**-ruh-*fraze*)	Lesson 21 **valid** (**val**-id)

noun: a picture made by the action of light upon a surface; a picture taken by a camera	*noun*: a machine that plays disk-shaped records on which sounds have been recorded in grooves	*noun*: a series of sentences that develop one main idea; it begins on a new line and is usually indented
adjective: 1. more or less correct or exact; *verb*: 2. to come up with an answer that is more or less correct	*noun*: the making of pictures by exposing film in a camera to light	*adjective*: 1. having to do with recalling from memory the exact order in which a long list of names was read; 2. having to do with photography
noun: 1. an answer that you believe is close to the exact answer; 2. the act of coming up with an answer that is close to the exact answer	*adjective*: 1. will definitely happen; 2. sure	*verb*: to find the answer by using mathematics
noun: a blood vessel that carries blood away from the heart, but not the main tube	*noun*: the main blood vessel in the heart; the main tube that transports blood to all of the arteries	*noun*: how likely something is to happen
noun: a blood vessel that carries blood to the heart	*noun*: one of the tiny tubes that carries blood between the arteries and the veins	*noun*: either of the two upper chambers on both sides of the heart
noun: the process by which a liquid becomes a gas	*noun*: a tiny drop or quantity of liquid	*noun*: the process by which water vapor becomes a liquid
noun: kindness and mercy	*noun*: water in its gaseous form, formed by condensation	*noun*: the falling of water from the sky in the form of rain, sleet, or snow
noun: self-control	*noun*: the quality of refusing to give up	*noun*: 1. teamwork; 2. the quality of working well with others
noun: a note that gives credit to a source	*noun*: 1. a list of books and other writings about a specific subject; 2. the list of sources used to write a research paper	*adjective*: reliable; able to be depended on
adjective: trustworthy; reliable; well grounded	*verb*: to restate a text or passage in your own words	*noun*: information or facts

Lesson 22 **classify** (**klass**-uh-fye)	Lesson 22 **elaborate** (i-**lab**-uh-rate)	Lesson 22 **evidence** (**ev**-uh-duhnss)
Lesson 22 **judgment** (**juhj**-muhnt)	Lesson 22 **revise** (ri-**vize**)	Lesson 23 **admiral** (**ad**-muh-ruhl)
Lesson 23 **butte** (**byoot**)	Lesson 23 **cashmere** (**kash**-mihr)	Lesson 23 **eureka** (u-*ree*-kuh)
Lesson 23 **gourmet** (gor-**may**)	Lesson 23 **kangaroo** (*kang*-guh-**roo**)	Lesson 23 **menu** (**men**-yoo)
Lesson 23 **mesa** (**may**-suh)	Lesson 23 **moustache** (**muhss**-*tash*)	Lesson 23 **pajamas** (puh-**jahm**-uhz)
Lesson 23 **parka** (**par**-kuh)	Lesson 23 **patio** (**pat**-ee-oh)	Lesson 23 **safari** (suh-**fah**-ree)
Lesson 23 **sherbet** (**shur**-buht)	Lesson 23 **tortilla** (tor-**tee**-yuh)	Lesson 24 **aid** (**ayd**)
Lesson 24 **aide** (**ayd**)	Lesson 24 **baron** (**ba**-ruhn)	Lesson 24 **barren** (**ba**-ruhn)
Lesson 24 **chord** (**kord**)	Lesson 24 **coarse** (**korss**)	Lesson 24 **colonel** (**kur**-nuhl)
Lesson 24 **cord** (**kord**)	Lesson 24 **course** (**korss**)	Lesson 24 **kernel** (**kur**-nuhl)

ails, facts, and ... you prove ... others	*verb*: to add details to make fuller or more complete	*verb*: to put things into groups according to their characteristics or traits
...er in the Navy	*verb*: to change and correct something to improve it	*noun*: an informed opinion, evaluation, or decision
noun: an exclamation meaning "I have found it!"	*noun*: a soft wool	*noun*: a large mountain with steep sides and a flat top that stands by itself
noun: a detailed list of food in a restaurant	*noun*: an Australian animal with short front legs and long, powerful hind legs	*noun*: 1. a person who knows and appreciates fine foods; *adjective*: 2. a word describing a food store or restaurant that provides fine food
noun, plural: clothes worn for sleeping	*noun*: the hair that grows above the upper lip	*noun*: a small high plateau or tableland with steep sides
noun: a trip to see animals, especially in eastern Africa	*noun*: a paved area next to the house used for dining or relaxing; a courtyard	*noun*: any hooded coat or jacket
verb: to assist or help	*noun*: a flat Spanish bread	*noun*: frozen fruit dessert
adjective: not fertile; empty	*noun*: a nobleman	*noun*: an assistant; a shortened form of the word *aide-de-camp*, which is a word from French that means "military officer acting as a secretary or helper"
noun: an officer in the U.S. Military	*adjective*: not smooth; rough	*noun*: three or more tones that create a pleasant sound or harmony
noun: 1. a grain or seed; 2. the most important part of something	*noun*: 1. path; 2. a series of lessons that helps you learn a subject	*noun*: string

Lesson 25 **accent** (**ak**-sent)	Lesson 25 **ascent** (uh-**sent**)	Lesson 25 **assent** (uh-**sent**)
Lesson 25 **bazaar** (buh-**zar**)	Lesson 25 **bizarre** (bi-**zar**)	Lesson 25 **carton** (**kar**-tuhn)
Lesson 25 **cartoon** (kar-**toon**)	Lesson 25 **canvas** (**kan**-vuhss)	Lesson 25 **canvass** (**kan**-vuhss)
Lesson 25 **convince** (kuhn-**vinss**)	Lesson 25 **persuade** (pur-**swade**)	Lesson 26 **a fly in the ointment**
Lesson 26 **a leg to stand on**	Lesson 26 **as plain as the nose on your face**	Lesson 26 **badger someone**
Lesson 26 **bark up the wrong tree**	Lesson 26 **be an eager beaver**	Lesson 26 **catch forty winks**
Lesson 26 **get a second wind**	Lesson 26 **get the upper hand**	Lesson 26 **not by a long shot**

| omething; prove | noun: 1. an upward slope or rise; 2. moving or rising up | noun: 1. the way that you pronounce things; verb: 2. to stress or emphasize |

container usually ...dboard or plastic | adjective: strange, odd, fantastic | noun: a market, especially one held outdoors

verb: 1. to gather support; 2. to ask people for their opinions and votes; 3. to examine carefully | noun: a strong coarse cloth | noun: a drawing or animated comic strip

something or someone that upsets a situation or causes a problem | verb: to succeed in making someone do something | verb: to make someone see the truth or believe what you have to say

pester or bother someone | easy to see | a supportable position

take a short nap | have a lot of enthusiasm; be too enthusiastic | search for clues or answers in the wrong place

not at all; definitely not | get in a position that makes you superior to someone else; get the advantage | get enough energy to become active again